Of Elephants
and Toothaches

Of Elephants and Toothaches

Ethics, Politics, and Religion in Krzysztof Kieślowski's *Decalogue*

Eva Badowska and Francesca Parmeggiani

Editors

FORDHAM UNIVERSITY PRESS

New York 2016

Copyright © 2016 Fordham University Press

All rights reserved. No part of this publication may be reproduced, stored in a retrieval system, or transmitted in any form or by any means—electronic, mechanical, photocopy, recording, or any other—except for brief quotations in printed reviews, without the prior permission of the publisher.

Fordham University Press has no responsibility for the persistence or accuracy of URLs for external or third-party Internet websites referred to in this publication and does not guarantee that any content on such websites is, or will remain, accurate or appropriate.

Fordham University Press also publishes its books in a variety of electronic formats. Some content that appears in print may not be available in electronic books.

Visit us online at www.fordhampress.com.

Library of Congress Cataloging-in-Publication Data

Of elephants and toothaches : ethics, politics, and religion in Krzysztof Kieślowski's Decalogue / edited by Eva Badowska and Francesca Parmeggiani. — First edition.
  pages cm
Includes bibliographical references and index.
ISBN 978-0-8232-6710-1 (cloth : alk. paper) —
ISBN 978-0-8232-6927-3 (pbk. : alk. paper)
 1. Dekalog (Television program) 2. Kieślowski, Krzysztof, 1941–1996—Criticism and interpretation. 3. Television programs—Poland—Moral and ethical aspects. 4. Religion on television. I. Badowska, Eva, editor. II. Parmeggiani, Francesca, editor.
PN1992.77.D44043 2016
791.45′72—dc23
2015017365

Printed in the United States of America

18 17 16   5 4 3 2 1

First edition

CONTENTS

Introduction: "Within unrest, there is always a question"
EVA BADOWSKA AND FRANCESCA PARMEGGIANI — 1

1. Rules and Virtues: The Moral Insight of *The Decalogue*
WILLIAM JAWORSKI — 15

2. Tablets of Stone, Tablets of Flesh: Synesthetic Appeal in *The Decalogue*
JOSEPH G. KICKASOLA — 30

3. *Decalogue One*: Witnessing a Responsible Ethics of Response from a Jewish Perspective
MOSHE GOLD — 51

4. Visual Reverberations: *Decalogue Two* and *Decalogue Eight*
EVA M. STADLER — 80

5. Remember the Sabbath Day, to Keep It Holy: *Decalogue Three*
JOSEPH W. KOTERSKI, S.J. — 95

6. *Decalogue Four*: The Mother up in Smoke, or "Honor Thy Father and Thy Mother"
GABRIELLA RIPA DI MEANA — 108

7. *Decalogue Five*: A Short Film about Killing, Sin, and Community
MICHAEL BAUR — 122

8. States of Exception: Politics and Poetics in *Decalogue Six*
EVA BADOWSKA — 140

9. *Decalogue Seven*: A Tale of Love, Failing Words, and Moving Images
FRANCESCA PARMEGGIANI — 165

10. *Decalogue Eight*: Childhood, Emotion, and the Shoah
EMMA WILSON — 181

11. Divine Possession: Metaphysical Covetousness in
    Decalogue Nine
     PHILIP SICKER   197
12. Laughter Makes Good Neighbors: Sociability and the
    Comic in *Decalogue Ten*
     REGINA SMALL   216

Acknowledgments   231
List of Contributors   233
Index   237

Of Elephants
and Toothaches

Introduction: "Within unrest, there is always a question"

Eva Badowska and Francesca Parmeggiani

Krzysztof Kieślowski's *Dekalog* (*The Decalogue*, 1989), which the film critic Robert Fulford has called "the best dramatic work ever done specifically for television,"[1] had arguably humble beginnings. The director recalls a chance meeting in the streets of Warsaw in the early 1980s with an attorney friend, Krzysztof Piesiewicz: "I bumped into him. It was cold. It was raining. I'd lost one of my gloves. 'Someone should make a film about the Ten Commandments,' Piesiewicz said to me. 'You should do it.'"[2] In a later documentary, the director adds, "I thought [Piesiewicz] had gone mad."[3] The idea continued to percolate, gradually developing into a project consisting of "ten propositions, ten one-hour films," a solution conceptually closest to the "ten words" of the Commandments (*KK*, 143). But Kieślowski was not yet thinking about directing *The Decalogue* himself, reasoning that it would make a great debut project for ten up-and-coming young directors: "For a long time in Poland television has become the natural home for directorial débuts." In fact, the project seemed, at the time, tailor-made for television production, since the state television network "wasn't interested in one-off films. It wanted serials and, if pushed, agreed to cycles." As the project developed, Kieślowski became invested in it, and, in the end, "realized rather selfishly" that he wanted to direct it himself (*KK*, 144). The notion of representing ten different perspectives survived in the finished work only in that "each of the ten films was made by a different lighting cameraman" (*KK*, 156).[4]

The form that *The Decalogue* eventually took is variously described as a serial, a series, or a cycle, but Kieślowski preferred to think of it as a cycle, emphasizing the discontinuity among the episodes. Unlike in a typical television series, characters do not regularly reappear, and there is no progression of narrative from week to week.[5] Like a literary, musical, or pictorial cycle (the Arthurian cycle, for instance, or Richard Wagner's four-opera *Ring Cycle*, or Giotto's frescoes in the Scrovegni Chapel in Padua, Italy), *The Decalogue* is composed of ten freestanding but interrelated parts that focus on a central concept. The cycle raises, in a unique visual language, the enduring questions of ethics and the law, questions that are instantiated but not resolved by the Ten Commandments. While individual episodes do, in fact, respond closely to specific ethical imperatives, the overall relationship between *The Decalogue* and the Ten Commandments is a "tentative one."[6] Correspondences between commandments and episodes are uncertain and provisional and surely never one-to-one: For instance, both *Six* and *Nine* deal with adultery; *Five* does not have the monopoly on the question of "killing," as related questions come up in *One*, *Two*, and *Eight*. Conversely, too, all episodes could be said to comment on the first (or second, depending on the religious tradition) commandment, as characters struggle to articulate meaning in the apparent absence of any certainty that there are "no other gods" (Exod. 20:3 RSV). Or, if we are reminded of the love precept in the New Testament, "This I command you, to love one another" (John 15:17 RSV), the series transcends the Ten Commandments altogether, for all characters experience love or its absence.[7] The episodes of *The Decalogue* are thoroughly interconnected, as are the Ten Commandments (and the New Testament addition) to which they refer.

Earlier critics of the film series paid great attention to identifying specific correspondences between individual episodes and applicable commandments. Those who, like Joseph G. Kickasola, acknowledge the Polish Catholic context out of which the films emerged discern compelling connections between the layout of the episodes and the traditional Catholic catechetical formula of the Ten Commandments.[8] On the other end of the spectrum, Slavoj Žižek, writes in a typically contrarian fashion that the "majority of interpreters take refuge in the alleged ambiguity of this relationship. . . . Against this easy way out, one should emphasize the *strict* correlation between the episodes and the Commandments: each installment refers to only one Commandment, but with a 'shift of gear': *Decalogue* 1 refers to the second Commandment, etc., until, finally, *Decalogue* 10 brings us back to the first Commandment."⁹

The present collection, however, is based on the assumption that the series loosely follows the traditional catechetical formula (see Joseph W. Koterski's essay in this volume), and that the dominant design of the cycle is rooted in this pedagogical simplification of the biblical text. This does not preclude other fruitful connections between the films and the Ten Commandments, as long as any desire for an all-encompassing "strict" theory à la Žižek is laid to rest. For instance, *The Decalogue*, when read alongside a rabbinical interpretation of the biblical text, reveals meanings that the catechetical formula may be said to eclipse (see Moshe Gold's essay in this volume).

Even more striking is the fact that the Ten Commandments were chosen as an inspiration for a film made in Poland in the 1980s by one of cinema's most outspokenly agnostic directors. To audiences familiar with Cecil B. DeMille's 1923 *The Ten Commandments* (or its 1956 remake), Kieślowski's variation on the same theme may rightly appear to have very little to do with the story of Moses or even with its twentieth-century rendition, such as in the second half of the 1923 silent film. Kieślowski has no use for either the epic story or its modern didactic application. The Polish 1980s—after the imposition of martial law on December 13, 1981, and before the Round Table agreements that effectively brought the communist era to an end in April 1989—were dark and chaotic: "Tension, a feeling of hopelessness, and a fear of yet worse to come were obvious" (*KK*, 143). It is against this background that Kieślowski and Piesiewicz present a series of ten films about nothing less epic than "individuals in difficult situations" (*KK*, 145). Aiming to pose "essential, fundamental, human and humanistic questions" (*KK*, 144), not the kind bound to politics and place, each episode of *The Decalogue* portrays a different protagonist trapped in the midst of a complex ethical dilemma that also encompasses the larger sphere of the family and the community. These individuals, who are "caught in a struggle" and "[go] round and round in circles" (*KK*, 145), cannot be lifted out of their impasses by any moralistic application of the Commandments. When a naïve young journalist once caught Kieślowski in the midst of filming *Two* and asked if *The Decalogue* would be a "treatise about the moral code," the director responded bluntly: "You use awfully serious language. I don't think it will be a treatise about any moral code. I don't know if such a thing really exists, if it can function. These films are simply about life."¹⁰ Though in *Kieślowski on Kieślowski* the director alludes to "think[ing] that an absolute point of reference does exist," it is not at all clear that God or religion embody such an absolute (*KK*, 149). Just a page later, the director suggests that this point of reference may well be internal, since we are all "in a position to set our own, inner compass" (*KK*, 150). Faith and religion are constantly invoked and endlessly queried in *The Decalogue*, but rarely do they seem to offer a solution that the protagonists can accept as final or viewers can take repose in. The interrogation of the ethical impasse does not let up at the end of each episode. The protagonists come up against the Commandments, usually failing to measure up. Pining for answers, they appear to sink deeper into conflict, irresolution, or stasis. Above all else, they are fallen, and their sins, if such they be, cannot be easily expiated; there is no apparent escape from the ethical morass. If *The Decalogue* at all belongs under the rubric of religious art, it is only insofar as there is "a spiritual dimension embedded in [Kieślowski's] sensual textures."[11] The moments of transcendence are fleeting and reside in the simplest of human gestures (a touch, a hug); within memories about the dead loved ones; or within musical backgrounds and haunting photography.

The ethical anxiety inherent in Kieślowski's cinema exceeds the confines of both religious and cinematic conventions. The Polish genre of "cinema of moral anxiety" (*kino moralnego niepokoju*) popular in the late 1970s often portrayed young characters who stand up against compromised social systems in order to defend basic moral values. But Kieślowski did not wish to see himself reflected in the moniker, and he did not accept it as an accurate historical description of the cinema of the late 1970s, either. With the usual delight in demolishing the assumptions of pompous interviewers, he once quipped: "I don't feel any moral anxiety . . . this phrase only pigeonholes, which infuriates me."[12] Even though artists are notoriously reluctant to recognize themselves in established historical or critical categories, Kieślowski is correct that this particular label fails to elucidate the ethical complexities he studies in his films. In Kieślowski, there is nothing quite as simple as a confrontation between a righteous individual and a corrupt social group. If anything, both are compromised and shot through with opposite forces. While the "cinema of moral anxiety" fails to capture Kieślowski's art, the feelings of anxiety, disquiet, or restlessness—and the aspiration, against all odds, to an elusive tranquility (*spokój*)—are fundamental to his ethos: "It is unrest [*niepokój*] that makes me get up in the morning, and not love, hope, or whatever else you mentioned. Within unrest, there is always a question."[13]

Kieślowski maintained, "You can't change anything through film," but he believed in filmmaking that fostered dialogue: "I make films to converse about some subject that I feel is important."[14] The *Decalogue* cycle certainly fulfilled his wish to communicate with his audiences about questions he deemed essential, even universal. In an interview with Alberto Crespi, the director emphasized that he "would like [*The Decalogue*] to be a dialogue with the viewer on life, as sincere as possible."[15] Stanley Kubrick, the director's great admirer, explains that Kieślowski and Piesiewicz achieve this effect of dialogue by "allowing the audience to *discover* what's really going on rather than being told. . . . You never see the ideas coming and don't realize until much later how profoundly they have reached your heart."[16]

This collection of essays extends this concept of dialogue to critical readings of the films as well. The relative paucity of English-language sources on the film cycle remains somewhat shocking: Of the ten book-length publications on the series, only one, by Christopher Garbowski (1996), is available in English.[17] Garbowski's short book remains a valuable resource, as it was one of the first systematic attempts at an interpretation of the film series and of the early critical reactions in Polish, English, and French. Written in the middle of the most active decade in Kieślowski scholarship, which immediately followed the director's success with Western audiences in the early 1990s, it did not yet enjoy the benefit of a longer historical view or of subsequent critical appraisals. The remaining monographs in French, German, Italian, and Polish have not been translated into English. Not only does the present collection fill this gap in English-language criticism on *The Decalogue*, but it also offers an approach that is unique among all the existing sources on the series: It represents a broadly multidisciplinary and interdisciplinary array of critical voices that comprise a collaborative conversation by North American and European scholars from such diverse areas of research as comparative literature, English, film studies, French, Italian, philosophy, psychoanalysis, and rabbinical studies. Indeed, *The Decalogue*, in its intertextual interplay with the Ten Commandments and with multifarious other literary, philosophical, and filmic works, positively demands both a multidisciplinary approach and an interdisciplinary methodology. The breadth and complexity of its motifs call for a medley of critical voices from varied disciplines: theology, philosophy, literature, film studies, psychoanalytic studies, and even the law. No other study of comparable diversity exists in North America or Europe.

The contribution of this collection of essays is not limited to its methodological diversity and intertextual scope. Our aim is to reorient the dominant approach to *The Decalogue* by placing its aesthetic and formal concerns—which have dominated critical work thus far—into dialogue with ethical, political, and religious discourses, that is, the "elephants" and "toothaches" Kieślowski is preoccupied with. The ensuing dialogue has a dual effect: It returns the film cycle to its diverse historical and existential contexts while demythologizing—situating and concretizing—its meanings. Instead of undercutting the cycle's open-ended structure, this approach demonstrates again and again how the films query and exceed their discursive frameworks. The cyclical nature of the work also makes— and insists that viewers and critics make—connections outside of the diegesis.

For example, the near-universality of the films, which the director achieves by referencing the Ten Commandments and by depoliticizing and aestheticizing his narratives, itself becomes readable in this approach both as a legitimate artistic purpose and a historical or ideological effect. Kieślowski began to aspire to artistic universality early on. In *Kieślowski on Kieślowski*, he admitted to hoping that *The Decalogue* could be marketed abroad (145). Such aspirations were not easy to voice at the time; the dissidents would deem them unpatriotic, and the censors disloyal. Kieślowski's international ambitions aside, humanity's "toothaches" are indeed his enduring concern: "Both the deep believer and the habitual skeptic experience toothaches in exactly the same way. I always try to speak about toothaches—always. If I am successful in talking about toothaches, I think everyone will understand me."[18]

His great theme involves questions with a near-universal scope, such as individual responsibility; the place of God and religion in modernity; the deep psychological and legal implications of familial relationships and biological bonds; love, desire, and material greed. *Of Elephants and Toothaches* presents Kieślowski as relentlessly soliciting an ethical response to these philosophical queries—in the form of both an inner disquiet and an interpersonal dialogue—from the viewer and the critic. To see oneself as filming toothaches is to portray one's themes not as abstract but as shared, physical, and immediate. Kieślowski's vivid image of the toothache also acknowledges that the effect of universality is achieved at the level of embodied experience. The collection tackles these complicated problems accordingly by examining concretes, such as the masterful use of multifaceted visual tropes and techniques: liquids and containers, mirrors and lenses, angles and lighting, silences and sounds, and the blending of abstract images with documentary techniques. The volume draws attention as well to the intricate connections among sensual, emotional and intellectual experiences of individuals, building bridges from bodily pain to theological insight.

Of Elephants and Toothaches also aims to elucidate an aspect of Kieślowski's approach to cinematic practice that is best summed up by his image of the elephant, which recurs in the director's autobiographical narratives, from *Krzysztof Kieślowski: I'm So-So . . .* (1995) to *Kieślowski on Kieślowski*.[19] In the latter, Kieślowski confesses to a tendency to appropriate other people's memories as his own: "I steal them and then start to believe that they happened to me" (6). But the story of the elephant in the street that follows is more nuanced:

> I was going to infant school and clearly remember walking with my mum. An elephant appeared. It passed us by and walked on. Mum claimed she'd never been with me when an elephant walked by. There's no reason why, in 1946, after the war, an elephant should appear in Poland, when it was hard even to get potatoes. Nevertheless, I can remember the scene perfectly well and I clearly remember the expression on the elephant's face. (*KK*, 6)[20]

It is hard to accept that the elephant represents a memory, even borrowed from another person, at all. It is much more likely that the story constitutes a false memory that belongs to "dreams of such power that they materialized into what I thought were actual incidents" (*KK*, 6). One may read this image as an instance of Kieślowski's mastery at showing the unseen, the invisible. Here, we wish to portray the elephant as an image of the filmic effect, an image of art and the artistic impulse, as it stands for the highly improbable but artistically imperative and vividly present imaginative reality. This imaginative reality is to the artist, and consequently to his viewers, as compelling as a remembered past. If the toothache signifies the shared, commonly understood reality (even though pain can only be privately experienced), the elephant is a materialization of one person's imaginative figment, which can only become communally shared by means of art. The elephant's gigantic stature and excessive visibility contrast further with the miniature (private, invisible) world of the toothache, but what the images share is as important as what separates them: Both insist on physical and/or aesthetic concretization in lieu of philosophical abstraction. In this way, the elephant and the toothache appropriately bookend Kieślowski's filmic project.

The order of the essays that follow generally mirrors the sequence of the films in *The Decalogue*, with two exceptions, William Jaworski's "Rules and Virtues: The Moral Insight of *The Decalogue*" and Joseph Kickasola's "Tablets of Stone, Tablets of Flesh: Synesthetic Appeal in *The Decalogue*."

These essays open the volume because they offer a reading of the series as a whole. Jaworski examines how *The Decalogue* suggests an alternative interpretation of the Ten Commandments, as descriptions of attitudes and patterns of behaviors and their effects, rather than rules, along the line of virtue-based ethical theories. Kickasola reflects upon Kieślowski's ability throughout the series to represent human experience as multisensory cognition, pushing the boundaries between sensing and understanding. The ethical concerns Kieślowski addresses affect the body and the mind (or the spirit) of his characters and the viewer alike, and are the cognitive object of sensual perception and intellectual reasoning both at the diegetic and extradiegetic levels. Each critic relies on a distinctive methodology to discuss Kieślowski's work and artistry; in fact, both approaches—one engaging primarily ethical questions and matters of content, the other addressing questions of representation and reception—are always in dialogue throughout the collection. For this reason, we also chose a simple sequencing of the remaining essays over a rigid overarching and organizing structure that we feared would induce a reading of the volume as a collection of two or more competing scholarly perspectives rather than a plurality of constantly intersecting and mutually enriching critical voices.

The order of the essays reflects the thematic continuity from one critical contribution to the next, but it does not suggest an exclusive progression from ethical and religious concerns, which could be perceived as dominant in the discussions of *One* through *Five*, to aesthetic and poetic issues seemingly more central in the analyses of *Six* through *Ten*. A shift in emphasis in the critical attention to each and all of the films is only apparent. As a whole, this collection may acknowledge and perhaps even reproduce, albeit unintentionally, the way the Ten Commandments themselves are traditionally viewed as falling into two natural groups—the first five regulating the relationship between God and humans, the others addressing relationships among humans. In fact, it encourages other interpretive paths while valuing and highlighting the uniqueness of each critical voice and disciplinary affiliation independently of our ordering principle. For example, Moshe Gold's essay, "*Decalogue One*: Witnessing a Responsible Ethics of Response from a Jewish Perspective," addresses the fundamental question of the affective and intellectual responses that define the actions of Kieślowski's characters and that the filmmaker demands of his viewer. This essay sets the stage particularly for the analyses of *Five*, *Six*, *Seven*, and *Eight*. In "Visual Reverberations: *Decalogue Two* and *Decalogue Eight*," Eva Stadler explores Kieślowski's cinematic artistry in the two *Decalogue* episodes that are explicitly linked from a thematic viewpoint, the "abstract visual style" of *Two* and the "almost documentary quality" of *Eight*. The filmmaker's stylistic signature, characterized by an obsessive attention to interior ambiance and outdoor settings, lighting and sounds, camera movements and angles, and, most of all, editing, emerges as a focal critical point also in the essays on *One, Four, Six, Seven, Eight,* and *Nine*. Kieślowski, who once defined films as "fairy tales about people," underscores the importance of the director's work in the cutting room: "There's [a] level to editing and it's the most interesting one. That is the level of constructing a film. *It's a game with the audience, a way of directing attention, distributing tension.* . . . The elusive spirit of a film, so difficult to describe, is born only there, in the cutting-room" (*KK*, 202, emphasis added).[21]

In "*Decalogue Four*: The Mother up in Smoke, or 'Honor Thy Father and Thy Mother,'" psychoanalyst Gabriella Ripa di Meana plays with Kieślowski's ability "to direct attention" and "distribute tension" and the arbitrary relation that exists between the commandment and the film's content. In *Four*, Kieślowski explores the emergence of the subject of the unconscious as the subject of ethics par excellence, and challenges received notions of honor and dishonor by representing the story of love and desire between a daughter, her father, and her unknown, dead mother. At the center of Ripa di Meana's original interpretation is the letter as an object and a trope. The letter is the mother's letter within the father's letter of the filmic narrative; it is thus the signifying core of the father-mother-daughter triangle, and of the daughter's identity formation as a daughter and a woman. The letter is also the literal meaning of the commandment in relation to the film; the commandment triggers the disclosure and working of meaning in this and every other film of *The Decalogue*.

The theme of love, of the experience or absence of various forms of love—whether pure and selfless, or possessive, selfish and greedy, idealized or sensual; like the love binding a mother to her child, or a father to his daughter, or a brother to his kin, or two friends, or a citizen to his or her fellow, or the love drawing individuals to material things, and so on—recurs consistently in the readings here collected. In "Remember the Sabbath Day, to Keep It Holy: *Decalogue Three*," Joseph Koterski discusses the connection Kieślowski establishes between what it means "to keep something holy" and our mindfulness of the love commitments and call of charity to others in our lives. For Koterski, Kieślowski expands on what the third commandment mandates. What constitutes a lawful and compassionate community—but still a community of "sinners" (*SP*, 67)—and what obligations humans have to one another to affirm their dignity but also transcend their individuality are at the core of Michael Baur's reading of *Five* in "*Decalogue Five*: A Short Film about Killing, Sin, and Community."

In Eva Badowska's "States of Exception: Politics and Poetics in *Decalogue Six*," the personal and the social are still deeply intertwined. Badowska discusses Kieślowski's transition from documentary to fiction film as representing the profound alienation of the individual in the public and private spheres in Poland in the 1980s—especially in the form of systematic intrusion in and devaluation of intimacy and privacy. Philip Sicker's analysis of *Nine* in "Divine Possession: Metaphysical Covetousness in *Decalogue Nine*"—a meditation on the entwined concepts of omniscience and possession inherent in the ninth commandment—similarly begins with a consideration of Kieślowski's exposure and critique of pervasive surveillance systems. Sicker demonstrates that in *Nine*, covetous jealousy takes the form of a desire for metaphysical possession, a complete penetration of another's interior life that seeks to imitate God's surveillance of thought and feeling. Both Badowska and Sicker draw attention to Kieślowski's intense awareness of cinema's ability to infiltrate and possibly violate private lives, and his relentless effort to create a visual language that is both inquisitive and self-critical.

In "*Decalogue Seven*: A Tale of Love, Failing Words, and Moving Images," Francesca Parmeggiani also addresses the question of the difficult linguistic and thematic balance that Kieślowski sought in his cinema. In the case of *Seven*, a little girl's disarticulated cry in the film's beginning and her silent gaze at the end not only frame a story of found (and yet, lost again) love, and the director's investigation into the various forms love may take or the ways in which familial and intergenerational relationships develop, but also demand of viewers a suspension of their indifference. In "*Decalogue Eight*: Childhood, Emotion, and the Shoah," Emma Wilson still focuses on a child's perspective, but she looks at the question of the gaze, the face, the gestures, of the "missing" child, and the demand of the child "who returns." Personal memories and collective history are interwoven in the narrative structure of the film. By examining the ways in which (audio)visual media and art forms summon an ethical response through appeal to the emotions, touch and embodied memory, Wilson also explores the excessive (ethical) context the Shoah proves in thinking about child suffering, and the intense, emotive, mnemonic investment in the child in representation.

Familial bonds and the ideas of community and sociability return to center stage in Regina Small's essay, "Laughter Makes Good Neighbors: Sociability and the Comic in *Decalogue Ten*," which aptly ends the volume. Drawing on Henri Bergson's "Laughter" (1901) to analyze the "comic mechanization" of the main characters' obsession with their father's stamp collection in the final episode of *The Decalogue*, Small argues that laughter functions as a moral corrective for both the characters and the viewer. Kieślowski thus concludes the series with an image that underscores the importance, and perhaps even the moral imperative, of human interconnectedness.

There is no end to the elephants and toothaches of art and life, as there is no end to ethical and theological investigations, moral unrest, political engagement, aesthetic experience, and critical conversations. As each essay originates from and responds to the "human and humanistic questions" raised in Kieślowski's films, in the other essays of the collection, and by theologians, philosophers, and cultural, literary and film scholars from both sides of the Atlantic, they ultimately embody and carry on the dialogue that Kieślowski believed to be the driving force and objective of his artistic project.

NOTES

1. Robert Fulford, "Kieslowski's Magnificent *Decalogue*," *The National Post*, May 14, 2002, http://www.robertfulford.com/Decalogue.html (accessed November 18, 2012). The series was produced in 1988. It first aired from December 10, 1989, to June 29, 1990, although *Ten* was shown earlier (in June 1989). Prior to its airing, the series was presented at international film festivals in Italy, Spain, and Brazil and was shown in a movie theater in Warsaw on October 20–24, 1989; see Matilda Mroz, *Temporality and Film Analysis* (Edinburgh: Edinburgh University Press, 2012), 137. *The Decalogue*, though originally made for TV, occupies a prominent place in the core curriculum of twentieth-century cinema. It ranks highly on the top-hundred lists of film critics, trade publications, and national magazines, not just among the greatest foreign films (*Movieline Magazine*) but also on "The A List," the National Society Film Critics' ranking of "100 Essential Films," and on *Time*'s "All-Time 100 Movies." *The Decalogue* is also a winner of nine national and international awards, including the FIPRESCI Prize at the Venice Film Festival (1989), the Critics' Award at the São Paulo International Film Festival (1989), Best Foreign Language Film from the Chicago Film Critics Association (1997), and the Bodil Award for the Best European Film (1991). See *The A List: The National Society of Film Critics' 100 Essential Films*, ed. Jay Carr (New York: Da Capo Press, 2002); "100 Greatest Foreign Films," *Movieline Magazine*, http://www.filmsite.org/foreign100.html (accessed November 13, 2012); Richard Corliss, "All-Time 100 Movies" *Time*, February 5, 2012, http://entertainment.time.com/2005/02/12/all-time-100-movies

(accessed November 13, 2012). See also "100 Best Films of the 1990s," *Slant Magazine*, November 5, 2012, http://www.slantmagazine.com/film/feature/the-100-best-films-of-the-1990s/334/page_9 (accessed November 12, 2012). However, *Slant* is wrong to place the film series in the 1990s. As mentioned, it was made and first shown in the late 1980s, even as it only became influential outside of Poland in the 1990s.

2. Krzysztof Kieślowski, *Kieślowski on Kieślowski*, ed. Danusia Stok (London: Faber and Faber, 1993), 143. Further references will be cited in the text using the abbreviation *KK*.

3. "Conversations with Kieślowski (1991) 1/6" (video), http://www.youtube.com/watch?v=5wr12J7DvAg (accessed November 12, 2012). Trans. Eva Badowska.

4. There were actually nine (not ten) cinematographers involved in the project. *Three* and *Nine* were both photographed by Piotr Sobociński. The other directors of photography were Wiesław Zdort (*One*), Edward Kłosiński (*Two*), Krzysztof Pakulski (*Four*), Sławomir Idziak (*Five*), Witold Adamek (*Six*), Dariusz Kuc (*Seven*), Andrzej Jaroszewicz (*Eight*), and Jacek Bławut (*Ten*).

5. In an interview for Polish television, Kieślowski remarked, "For myself, I think of it as a cycle" ("Krzysztof Kieślowski Pegaz cz.1" [video], http://www.youtube.com/watch?v=LpyDDmOIohs [accessed November 4, 2012]. Trans. Eva Badowska).

6. Krzysztof Kieślowski and Krzysztof Piesiewicz, *Decalogue: The Ten Commandments*, trans. Phil Cavendish and Susannah Bluh (London: Faber and Faber, 1991), xiv. Further references will be cited in the text using the abbreviation *D*.

7. Tadeusz Sobolewski suggests that "[è] un Decalogo che parla di un amore che non c'è!" ("it is a Decalogue that speaks of a nonexisting love," trans. Francesca Parmeggiani). Tadeusz Sobolewski, "La solidarietà dei peccatori," in *Kieślowski*, ed. Małgorzata Furdal and Roberto Turigliatto (Turin: Museo Nazionale del Cinema, 1989), 66. Further references to Sobolewski's article will be cited in the text using the abbreviation *SP*.

8. This set of correlations is neatly tabulated by Kickasola in his *The Films of Krzysztof Kieślowski: The Liminal Image* (New York: Continuum, 2004), 164.

9. Slavoj Žižek, *The Fright of Real Tears: Krzysztof Kieślowski between Theory and Post-Theory* (London: British Film Institute, 2001), 111.

10. "Krzysztof Kieślowski Pegaz cz.1" (video), http://www.youtube.com/watch?v=LpyDDmOIohs (accessed November 4, 2012). Trans. Eva Badowska. An English dubbed version of this 1988 video segment is also available,

with the title "On the Set of *The Decalogue*," in *The Decalogue*, DVD, directed by Krzysztof Kieślowski (Chicago: Facets Video, 2003), disc 3.

11. Annette Insdorf in Ulrika Brand, "Conversation on Kieslowski with Annette Insdorf," *Columbia University Record* 25, no. 8 (November 12, 1999), http://www.columbia.edu/cu/record/archives/vol25/08/2508_Insdorf _Kieslowski.html (accessed November 20, 2012).

12. "Krzysztof Kieślowski Pegaz cz. 2" (video), http://www.youtube .com/watch?v=Ig3Wswp41Vc (accessed November 13, 2012). Trans. Eva Badowska.

13. Hanna Krall, interview with Krzysztof Kieślowski, "Zrobiłem i mam," in *Kino Krzysztofa Kieślowskiego*, ed. Tadeusz Lubelski (Krakow: Universitas, 1997), 272. Trans. Eva Badowska.

14. "Kieslowski Meets the Press" (1988), in *The Decalogue*, DVD.

15. Alberto Crespi, interview with Krzysztof Kieślowski and Krzysztof Piesiewicz, "La mia Bibbia senza certezze" (1989), in Furdal and Turigliatto, *Kieślowski*, 183. Trans. Francesca Parmeggiani.

16. Stanley Kubrick, "Foreword," in *D*, vii.

17. We were able to locate ten volumes—two edited collections and eight monographs—entirely dedicated to the series: Emanuela Imparato, *Krzysztof Kieślowski: Il Decalogo—Per una lettura critica* (Rome: AIACE, 1990); *Il decalogo di Kieślowski: Ricreazione narrativa*, ed. Gina Lagorio (Casale Monferrato: Piemme, 1992); *Das Gewicht der Gebote und die Möglichkeiten der Kunst: Krzysztof Kieslowskis "Dekalog"—Filme als etische Modelle*, ed. Walter Lesch and Matthias Loretan (Freiburg: Universitätsverlag und Herder, 1993); Véronique Campan, *Dix brèves histoires d'image: Le Décalogue de Krzysztof Kieślowski* (Paris: Presses de la Sorbonne Nouvelle, 1993); Christopher Garbowski, *Krzysztof Kieślowski's* Decalogue *Series: The Problem of the Protagonists and Their Self-Transcendence* (Boulder, Colo.: East European Monographs; New York: Columbia University Press, 1996); Gabriella Ripa di Meana, *La morale dell'altro. Scritti sull'inconscio dal* Decalogo *di Kieślowski* (Florence: Liberal Libri, 1998); Chiara Simonigh, *La danza dei miseri destini: Il* Decalogo *di Krzysztof Kieślowski* (Turin: Testo & Immagine, 2000); Marek Lis, *Figury Chrystusa w* Dekalogu *Kieślowskiego* (Opole: Redakcja Wydawnicza Wydziału Teologicznego Uniwersytetu Opolskiego, 2007); Jan Ulrich Hasecke, *Die Warheit des Sehens: Der "Dekalog" von Krzysztof Kieślowski* (Qindie and CreateSpace Independent Publishing Platform, 2013); and Yves Vaillancourt, *Jeux interdits. Essai sur le "Décalogue" de Kieślowski* (Québec City: Presses de l'Université Laval, 2014). The following English-language books contain substantial chapters on *The Decalogue*: *Lucid Dreams: The Films of Krzysztof Kieślowski*, ed. Paul Coates (Trowbridge, UK: Flicks Books, 1998); Annette

Insdorf, *Double Lives, Second Chances: The Cinema of Krzysztof Kieślowski* (New York: Miramax Books, 1999); Marek Haltof, *The Cinema of Krzysztof Kieślowski: Variations on Destiny and Chance* (New York: Wallflower Press, 2004); Slavoj Žižek, *The Fright of Real Tears: Krzysztof Kieślowski between Theory and Post-Theory* (London: British Film Institute, 2001); *After Kieślowski: The Legacy of Krzysztof Kieślowski*, ed. Steven Woodward (Detroit: Wayne State University Press, 2009); and the aforementioned books by Joseph G. Kickasola, *The Films of Krzysztof Kieślowski: The Liminal Image*, and Matilda Mroz, *Temporality and Film Analysis*.

18. "Conversation with Kieślowski (1991) 1/6."

19. *Krzysztof Kieslowski: I'm So-So* . . . , directed by Krzysztof Wierzbicki, Kulturmøde Film (1995).

20. It is important not to misread the image of the elephant as "elephant in the room" (in this case, elephant in the street). The idiom is not present in Polish; in fact, the idiomatic association with elephants in Polish is along the lines of the English expression "bull in a china shop" (where in Polish one says "elephant in a china shop"). Neither idiomatic meaning is relevant to this story.

21. Tadeusz Sobolewski, "Ultimate Concerns," in Coates, *Lucid Dreams*, 19. Trans. Paul Coates.

CHAPTER I

Rules and Virtues: The Moral Insight of *The Decalogue*

William Jaworski

The Ten Commandments are often taken to represent a prototypical rule-based approach to ethics. What the Commandments are supposed to provide, on this interpretation, is a set of rules for evaluating the status of actions as right or wrong. They are thus taken to be similar in their goals to modern moral theories such as Kantian ethics or utilitarianism. I will call this the "moralizing interpretation" of the Commandments, which goes hand in hand with a single-discipline conception of moral inquiry. According to this conception, serious moral inquiry is the task of philosophy alone. Other disciplines may be able to feed information into the philosopher's calculations, but the task of rendering that information morally relevant in the form of precise, universally applicable moral principles is the philosopher's special charge.

There are nevertheless philosophical reasons for rejecting the moralizing interpretation of the Commandments in favor of a more holistic alternative. That alternative is illustrated by the films of Krzysztof Kieślowski's *Decalogue*. The ten episodes display how the Commandments are best understood not as rules along the lines of those proposed by modern moral theories, but as descriptions of patterns of thought, feeling, and action that can influence human well-being for better or for worse. The focus of the Commandments, on this interpretation, is not on discrete actions that ought or ought not to be done, but on human life as a whole, and how various patterns of thinking, feeling, and acting can enable us to live well or prevent us from doing so.

The philosophical reasons that motivate the holistic interpretation of the Commandments also motivate a multidisciplinary conception of moral inquiry, for if the Commandments concern not abstract rules, as the moralizing interpretation would have it, but the rich tapestry of human life as a whole, then nonphilosophical disciplines do more than simply feed information into the philosopher's moral calculus; their input becomes essential to the very process of creating moral understanding. In line with this conception of moral inquiry, the films of *The Decalogue* show us vividly how the Commandments are woven into the tapestry of human life in ways that often escape our notice. Given their focus on attitudes and patterns of behavior—as opposed to discrete actions extracted and isolated from the lives in which they can only exist as parts—attempts to identify concrete, datable occurrences that either violate or conform to a rule often fail. By contrast, abandoning those attempts in favor of the holistic alternative often leaves us wondering whether the various strands of human life could consist of anything but the Commandments.

Perhaps above all the films movingly highlight two aspects of human life. First, they highlight the pervasive character of human failure and frailty, the way we can all strive for love, freedom, security, fulfillment, esteem, and yet fail in our best attempts to achieve them. Second, the films highlight the enduring character of human hope—hope in the possibility that our ultimate fate will not be determined by our past failures, hope that we might rediscover love and freedom even in the midst of tragedy and loss.

Rule-Based Ethics and the Moralizing Interpretation of the Commandments

Modern ethical theories are typically concerned with articulating a principle or principles for evaluating the moral status of actions. The job of ethics, as they conceive of it, is to formulate abstract principles, rules, or guidelines that can be applied to the concrete actions of concrete individuals in order to determine whether those actions are good or bad, right or wrong. The application of these principles typically takes the form of a calculus or decision procedure. Kantian ethics and utilitarianism are the most popular representatives of rule-based ethical thinking.[1]

Utilitarians take the rightness or wrongness of an action to be determined by its consequences, whereas Kantians take it to be determined by the principle on which the agent acts. Even though they differ on what constitutes the rightness or wrongness of an action, utilitarians and Kantians share a commitment to three ideas. First, they both claim that ethical theorizing aims at articulating rules or principles that can be applied to particular actions (or in some cases principles) in order to determine their rightness or wrongness. Second, they both take moral evaluation to consist in an abstract cognitive procedure: trying to conceive the universal application of the agent's principle in the Kantian case, and calculating the net gain or loss of pleasure that results from an action in the utilitarian case. Finally, both take the ultimate focus of ethical theorizing to be discrete actions—even forms of rule utilitarianism, which look to evaluate moral principles, take the latter to be right or wrong in proportion to their tendency to result in right or wrong actions.

The moralizing interpretation takes the Commandments to be in the same business as modern moral theories. It claims that the Commandments represent a premodern attempt to do more or less the same thing that Kantians and utilitarians are doing. The Commandments articulate principles to which discrete actions must conform if they are to count as morally permissible, and moral evaluation consists in determining whether particular actions violate any of the principles.

Understood in this way, however, the Commandments are problematic for well-rehearsed philosophical reasons. I will mention just three.

1. *The problem of generality versus specificity*: Rule-based ethical theories must articulate moral principles that balance the demand for generality (the demand that they apply to all people in all circumstances) with the demand for specificity (the demand that they be applicable to specific agents in specific circumstances). Many attempts to formulate universal ethical principles fail to satisfy one requirement or the other. The Commandments, in particular, fail to satisfy the specificity requirement, for they are so general that they do not tell us what to do (or to think or feel), but only what not to do. As a result, they lack content specific enough to tell us how to live.

2. *The problem of justification*: Every rule-based ethical theory must provide some justification or grounds for why its particular set of principles is the set according to which we should live. Why, for instance, must we

avoid killing? Why should we not covet our neighbor's goods? Why not steal? Answering these questions can often be very difficult without invoking contentious metaethical and metaphysical theses.

3. *The problem of accounting for rule-following or rule-breaking*: Rule-based ethical theories must provide a general account of the costs and benefits for human life of following or breaking the rules they endorse. Suppose, for instance, that someone is unable to follow the principles—the way an alcoholic might be incapable of following the principle "Do not drink to excess." A rule-based ethical theory must give an account of the significance of this type of case. Moreover, what in general are the implications for human life of following or breaking a moral rule? The fifth commandment says, "Thou Shalt Not Kill." But what if I do? We are all aware that killing might have legal or social implications, ones that could be dodged with sufficient ingenuity. But are there any implications for my life that cannot be dodged? Perhaps I will become an immoral person, one that constantly breaks moral rules. But why should I care about that? If being moral amounts simply to obeying certain principles, why should I care about being moral? Why should I think that being moral is a good thing? Any rule-based ethical theory has to be able to answer questions of this sort. It must situate its principles within a broader account of rule-following and rule-breaking and their significance for human life. Again, this is a difficult task to accomplish without invoking contentious metaethical and metaphysical assumptions.

Human Striving for the Good Life and the Antimoralist Challenge

The third of the aforementioned problems with rule-based ethical theories is especially important for our discussion. It raises the question of whether human behavior is capable of conforming to abstract principles and what implications this might have for human well-being. Concrete human life is gritty and imperfect, unpredictable and indeterminate. It does not lend itself easily to the imposition of strict principles. One reason for this is that human nature is inherently limited in so many ways. Even if I judge that following a certain moral principle is for the best, I might still be unable to follow that principle in practice. The spirit is willing, but the flesh is inevitably weak. A more important reason to doubt the possibility of human life conforming to abstract principles derives from an account of human striving.

Human life is fundamentally driven by desire. Part of being human is precisely the desire for certain goods: for life, love, pleasure, joy, freedom, security, power, health, wealth, status, and esteem. We are constantly striving to live well, to get as much out of life as we can. Our day-to-day existence is an exercise in trying to achieve such goods—strategizing about how to secure them and negotiating obstacles to their realization. Seen against the backdrop of human striving, the Commandments can look like a system of principles that inhibit our natural inclination to achieve these goods. They can appear as a force of alienation, something that arises not from human nature but rather against it as an impediment to human fulfillment. The upshot is that a life based on the Commandments or an analogous set of principles could only be one that ends up crushing rather than liberating the human spirit. An antimoralist view of this sort has often motivated various diagnoses of traditional moral theories in terms of class struggle, or power, or some other form of social control. Since the imposition of abstract principles on human striving could only inhibit human well-being, antimoralists argue, traditional morality could only be an instrument used by some to dominate and oppress others.

The founding assumption of this type of antimoralist view is that abstract ethical rules are at best orthogonal to human flourishing and are at worst impediments to it. There are at least three ways of responding to this worry. Naïve antimoralists jettison traditional morality without exploring the possibility of alternative ways of understanding its content. Naïve moralists, on the other hand, endorse the content of traditional morality without attempting to respond to the charges of antimoralists. A third option is to articulate an understanding of traditional morality that clarifies how its content fits into a more general account of human flourishing. This option endorses the content of traditional morality while yet responding to the charges of antimoralists. This is the view, I want to suggest, that is represented by Kieślowski's *Decalogue*. Its depiction of people and the circumstances in which they find themselves shares the antimoralist's skepticism that human life can conform to abstract principles, and yet it also shares the moralist's conviction that traditional morality is deeply important to human well-being. In what follows, I will develop this idea by appealing to an ethical theory based not on rules but on the creative exercise of human abilities.

Virtue Ethics

The films of *The Decalogue* generally resist attempts to identify concrete datable occurrences as violations of a rule. They instead situate the actions of the characters within a broader fabric of thoughts, feelings, attitudes, dispositions, and personality and character traits. Consequently, the films suggest an interpretation of the Commandments different from the moralizing one. In what follows I will propose an interpretative strategy based on an ethics of virtue or virtue ethics.

The original philosophical architects of virtue ethics were Plato and Aristotle, but other representatives include Augustine and Aquinas, and more recently Elizabeth Anscombe, Alasdair MacIntyre, and, I would suggest, Krzysztof Kieślowski.[2] *The Decalogue* provides moral theorists with resources to develop a virtue-ethical interpretation of the Commandments, an interpretation it expresses in flesh-and-blood terms using the medium of film. From the standpoint of virtue ethics, meditating on the films of *The Decalogue* proves more useful for developing one's moral understanding than attempting to formulate abstract principles of the sort that characterize the endeavor of modern moral philosophy.

An ethics of virtue takes its starting point from unremarkable observations about human life. We are animals who have evolved in response to a range of environmental pressures largely beyond our control. As a result, we have physiological, social, and spiritual needs, which we are constantly trying to satisfy. In general, we strive to live well, to achieve lives filled with as many good things as we can: love and security, pleasure and joy, health and freedom, wealth, power, status, and esteem. The central idea of virtue ethics is that we cannot achieve human goods, especially those distinctive of human life at its best, by following abstract rules, but only by carefully cultivating certain patterns of thought, feeling, and action. Living well involves the practiced balancing of a range of desires and demands that constitute the raw material of human life. It involves learning how to weave the various strands of human existence together into a well-proportioned whole. Those strands include making decisions about what to do and how to feel and act; managing hardship; dealing with other people; managing sensual pleasures; estimating and evaluating people's abilities and knowledge; managing self-exertion, one's attitudes and behavior toward truth; the relationship between time and tasks; anger, sadness, and other emotional states; humor, one's physical appearance; managing conversation; managing trust placed in others and in oneself, one's intellectual skills; managing failures and mistakes; managing sexuality and one's weaknesses and vulnerabilities.

According to an ethics of virtue, there are better and worse ways of managing these aspects of human life. What makes the better ways better is that they enable us to flourish. They enable us to achieve the goods that we desire—the physiological, social, and spiritual needs we demand—in a way that does not disfigure life as a whole with imbalance and disproportion. Traditionally, these better patterns of thought, feeling, and action have been called "virtues." Virtues are character traits or dispositions—patterns of thought, feeling, and action—that enable us to live well. Vices, on the other hand, are patterns of thought, feeling, and action that if cultivated will inevitably damage and disfigure human life. Consider some simple examples.

Eleanor wants to learn to play the piano. In order to achieve that end and its associated goods, she is going to have to work hard; she will have to practice. Practice involves hardship, and hence it requires the ability to exert oneself and channel one's energies to accomplish the task despite hardship. If Eleanor manages hardship well, if she has discipline and fortitude, then she will be able to achieve the goal of playing the piano and thus secure the goods associated with it. If, on the other hand, she does not have fortitude—if, for instance, she is disposed to quit in the face of hardship and is unable to channel her energies in the face of it—then she will not be able to achieve what she wants. Musicianship and the goods associated with it will remain beyond her grasp. This is true not just of musicianship, but of many other things as well: dancing, mathematics, writing, speaking, and athletics, as well as the management of friendship, marriage, health, wealth, and countless other things. All of them involve dealing with hardship in one way or another. The fortitude that enables Eleanor to succeed in one area will enable her to succeed in others. Possessing the ability to channel her energies and stick to a difficult task despite its difficulty will help her achieve the goods associated with a range of activities. Conversely, lacking that ability will hinder her achievement in a range of activities.

Consider another example. Eleanor's efforts will be greatly assisted if she is able to benefit from the advice and constructive criticism of others such as her piano teacher and fellow students. If Eleanor is able to take constructive criticism for what it is worth, if she has the humility to do so, she will be much better off than if she lacks it. If she is arrogant and dismisses the evaluations of others, or if she lacks self-esteem to the point of being crushed by constructive criticism, then, as in the case of fortitude, it is not just Eleanor's piano-playing that will suffer, but many other aspects of her life as well: her friendships, her relationships with coworkers, her marriage, and so on.

Given their widespread impact on the potential for human well-being, character traits such as fortitude and humility count as virtues; and conversely, arrogance, laziness, and weakness of will count as vices. A human life that incorporates the virtues will end up being better than a life that incorporates the vices. The virtues enable their possessors to achieve the goods that characterize human life at its best; they are precisely the patterns of thought, feeling, and action that enable us to live lives with love, freedom, security, and joy. Vices, on the other hand, have the opposite effect; they diminish our capacity to achieve these goods; they are the patterns of thought, feeling, and action that prevent us from being loving, free, secure, and joyful.

What is important to recognize about the virtues is that they are not rules but abilities. Each has two components: (1) the ability to make accurate judgments about what contributes to living well under the circumstances, and (2) the ability to think, feel, and act in accordance with those judgments. Temperance, for instance, involves the ability to judge accurately how to indulge in sensual pleasures in a way that contributes on the whole to living well, combined with the ability to indulge in sensual pleasures in just that way. The person who is temperate with regard to drinking, for instance, knows what to drink, how much to drink, when to drink, and with whom to drink, and he or she drinks in accordance with those judgments. The temperate person's abilities to make accurate judgments about drinking and to think, feel, and act accordingly cannot be codified in an abstract set of principles any more than, say, Michael Jordan's ability to play basketball could be codified in an abstract set of principles. Both involve concrete abilities acquired by concrete individuals in response to concrete circumstances—abilities that continue to be concretely exercised in concrete situations. Life presents us with complexities, and we determine who we are in coping with them, in trying to navigate through them, in trying to resolve the tensions among the competing demands that arise in trying to live well. In these kinds of concrete circumstances, character is both formed and expressed; in them we manifest concretely our potential for good or evil, as Zofia (Maria Kościałkowska), the professor of ethics, says in *Eight*. Attempts to formulate abstract principles to express what the exercise of those abilities amounts to could provide approximations at best, and distortions at worst, of what the virtues are.

Because the virtues have this concrete, ability-driven character, and because they have a direct bearing on our ability to live well—they are character traits that enable us to live well—it turns out that, on a virtue-ethical theory, being moral is less like following an abstract algorithm and more like producing a work of art, or engaging in musical or athletic performance. There might be constraints that mark the bounds of intelligibility, or aesthetic appreciation, or what counts as a legal move in a game, but on the whole engaging in these activities is a creative and dynamic process that involves the exercise of concrete skills that were learned and that are now exercised in concrete situations.

A Virtue-Ethical Interpretation of the Commandments

What do the Ten Commandments mean in the context of a virtue theory? To someone who endorses the moralizing interpretation of the Commandments, it is unclear whether the Commandments are compatible with virtue theory at all. Virtue ethics is based on motivation and empowerment, the acquisition and exercise of concrete abilities. The Commandments, on the other hand, constitute a list of abstract principles. What could one possibility have to do with the other? The genius of Kieślowski's *Decalogue* is that it fleshes out an answer to this question. It shows us what the Commandments mean in terms of the day-to-day rhythms of human life, our day-to-day strivings to live well. From this perspective, the Commandments appear not as abstract principles governing various categories of action—principles to which actions must conform on pain of qualifying as "wrong"; they appear rather as descriptions of broad patterns of behavior: thought and feeling, as well as action. The films show us what happens to human lives that incorporate various patterns of thinking, feeling, and acting. They thereby provide a basis for an account of traditional morality capable of responding to the antimoralist challenge.

Consider, for instance, the fifth commandment: "You shall not kill" (Exod. 20:13 RSV). Exponents of the moralizing interpretation often take this to be the paradigmatic moral rule. Taken strictly, this understanding of the commandment is problematic. Does it prohibit killing in self-defense, for instance? Conversely, does it permit hideous acts of violence that fall short of actually killing someone? Affirmative answers to these questions strike many people as absurd. That is why exponents of the moralizing interpretation typically gloss the fifth commandment in a way that prohibits violence and permits killing in self-defense. But why do these answers seem absurd? According to a virtue-ethical interpretation of the commandment, the reason is that we can recognize that an act of wanton killing represents a broader pattern of behavior—one that can have destructive implications for human well-being. The cultivation of that pattern is what the commandment warns against. It effectively says: Do not cultivate the habits of thought and feeling that would enable you to murder lest you alienate yourself from the goods you most deeply desire. That pattern of behavior comprises not just murder, however, but other forms of violence as well: The habits of mind that enable murder are the same as those enabling

Figure 1-1. Jacek in *Decalogue Five*.

hideous acts of violence. The commandment can thus be extended to the latter as well. On the other hand, since the attitudes that motivate killing in self-defense are not of the same sort, their cultivation need not alienate one from the goods associated with living well. The commandment, then, need not be taken to proscribe killing in self-defense.

An understanding of the fifth commandment along these lines is illustrated in *Five*. The film gives us a glimpse into the character of a young man, Jacek Lazar (Mirosław Baka). Jacek coolly walks the other way as he sees two men brutally assault a third in the street; he callously chases away the pigeons being fed by an elderly woman; and he drops a rock from a highway overpass to break the windshield of an oncoming car. He assaults a man in a public restroom for no apparent reason, and he ultimately lures a cabdriver, Waldemar (Jan Tesarz), to a remote location to murder him. Jacek has incorporated patterns of thinking, feeling, and acting that have devastating consequences for the achievement of human fulfillment. He lives a life of profound social isolation—something expressed even in the sickly hues and penumbral shadows in which he is filmed (Figure 1-1).[3] That isolation crystallizes as he is caught, tried, convicted, and ultimately executed for his crime.

The film displays in a matter-of-fact way what it would mean to cultivate the pattern of behavior prohibited by the commandment, and it extends the scope of that pattern by drawing a parallel between Jacek and Waldemar, whom we see engaged in similarly callous acts. Joseph G. Kickasola describes the parallel in the following terms:

> Jacek deliberately scares away an old woman's pigeons. He pushes a man into a latrine. He drops the rock on a busy highway. In the same

callous manner, Waldemar leaves Dorota [a pregnant woman] and her husband, sexually harasses Beata (the vegetable market worker), and cruelly honks to scare a passing man and his dogs. This point/counterpoint of cruelties leaves the viewer with the impression that the two men (who have not met) are actually engaged in a game of bitter one-upsmanship. Their solidarity in contempt is a poisonous kinship, and one wonders whether Waldemar might have just as likely killed Jacek as the other way around. (205)

One way of interpreting the parallel between Jacek and Waldemar is to say that each has cultivated patterns of behavior that result in a social and spiritual death long before undergoing the biological deaths we witness in the film.

Moreover, *The Decalogue* sets up a further parallel with Polish society as a whole. Kickasola remarks, "There is a certain deadness that permeates the entire *Decalogue*" (174), and he notes that *Five* suggests that "Polish society may not be so different from the lonely halls of the penal institution" (202). The judge who tries Jacek's case describes the verdict as "inevitable." We watch the executioner (Zbigniew Zapasiewicz) making the arrangements for Jacek's hanging with a cool, clinical familiarity that bespeaks experience and above all routine: "Custom hath made it in him a property of easiness," as Horatio remarked to Hamlet.[4] On the other hand, when Jacek's defense attorney, Piotr (Krzysztof Globisz), struggles with the question of whether he could have intervened in Jacek's life to avert the crime, the judge dismisses the sentiment: "You are too sensitive for this profession," he replies. Is a society that makes killing a property of easiness also spiritually dead? Is it a society that is capable of contributing to human flourishing? Or is it instead a society that has lost the ability to help its members cultivate the patterns of thought, feeling, and action every human needs to live well?

All the films of *The Decalogue* illustrate how patterns of thought, feeling, and action influence our ability to secure the goods we most deeply desire in life. *One*, for instance, illustrates how worshipping false gods does not amount to burning pigeons before stone idols, but placing our trust in things that are ultimately incapable of providing us with what we most deeply want in life. *Two* and *Eight* show us that lying is not a straightforward matter of saying what is untrue; utterances that betray the life and love we most deeply desire are lies whether those utterances be true or not. *Four* shows us how the constancy of love and care, not biology, is what matters most in defining our relationships to those we call mother and father.

Six illustrates the dangers of cultivating an attitude that trivializes human sexuality and divorces it from its connection to human intimacy. *Seven* shows us that stealing encompasses a broad range of attitudes, feelings, and circumstances that bear only a family resemblance to the paradigm case of absconding with someone else's goods. We see how various forms of theft can influence human life and alienate us from the ones we love and the ones we ought to love. *Nine* shows us that it is possible not just to covet our neighbors' spouses, but our own spouses as well, and that human fulfillment is threatened by an attitude that treats people as possessions.

Frailty and Hope

There are two aspects of human life that the films illustrate in an especially powerful way: the enduring character of human frailty and the equally enduring character of human hope. They mark what is perhaps *The Decalogue*'s deepest insight into the human condition.

Failure is as real a part of human life as anything else. We all pursue the good life, and yet we invariably make choices and cultivate patterns of behavior that hinder us in our pursuit. One of the most insightful features of *The Decalogue* is the way it reveals the myriad ways we are capable of failing, the myriad ways we fall short of realizing what is best for us and for others. Like any other aspect of human life, however, there are better and worse ways of managing failure. The better ways correspond to virtues. Among them is hope.

Hope, one might say, is the ability to believe that failure is not the end of the human story. Importantly, however, hope is not the same as optimism. Optimism concerns what we can reasonably expect given antecedent conditions. Based on what I know about someone's abilities, history, and current circumstances, I might be rationally justified in supposing that he or she will succeed at a certain kind of task. Hope does not have this aspect of making a rational projection about what future states of affairs are likely to result given past and present conditions. In fact, hope is perfectly compatible with pessimism about the human condition. The data on human life gathered hitherto do not lend themselves easily to optimism, to the reasonable expectation that the future of humankind will be any better than its past. On the contrary, the history of humanity gives us every reason to suppose there will continue to be injustice, corruption, greed, falsehood, violence, oppression, ideology, theft, war, and indifference. We have every reason, in other words, to believe the cliché that history will repeat itself, that the future of humankind will resemble its scarred past.

Hope, however, reaches beyond this reasonable expectation. It is the ability to believe that, despite humanity's dismal penchant for repeating again and again the same mistakes, failure is nevertheless not the whole of the human story.

The films of *The Decalogue* are hopeful but not optimistic. The events they depict do not give us reason to suppose that the characters' futures will be any better than their wounded pasts. They do not have the determinacy of Hollywood-style happy endings. They are instead characterized by the indeterminacy of real hope. They leave open the possibility that the future will not be defined by the past; that failure is not the whole story; that the inertia of human failure will not outpace the meaningfulness of future human striving. But neither do they ignore that inertia, nor is it the case that the future appears completely unproblematic, completely untouched by past entanglements. Consider, for instance, the husband and wife, Andrzej (Olgierd Łukaszewicz) and Dorota (Krystyna Janda), in *Two*. The final scene shows Andrzej joyfully telling the doctor (Aleksander Bardini) that he and Dorota are expecting a child. What he does not know—what she and the doctor have both concealed from him—is that the child has been fathered by another man. Likewise, Zofia and Elżbieta (Teresa Marczewska), the women in *Eight*, are reconciled with each other, but we are reminded in the final scene that not everyone has been reconciled to the past, including the tailor (Tadeusz Łomnicki) once falsely accused of collaborating with the Gestapo. In *Four* we look forward as Michał (Janusz Gajos) and Anka (Adrianna Biedrzyńska), a father and daughter, try to reevaluate their relationship after the discovery that she may not in fact be his biological daughter. But the letter, which had seemed throughout the film to hold the key to that reevaluation, is burned beyond readability (Figure 1–2). Human life is filled with sorrow and loss. *The Decalogue* gives us so many images of human frailty, and yet despite that the films all end with an image of hope.

Ten communicates this idea perhaps most clearly of all. Two brothers, Jerzy (Jerzy Stuhr) and Artur (Zbigniew Zamachowski), discover that they have inherited a stamp collection worth millions. Although they initially claim to be indifferent to material possessions, they grow increasingly jealous of the collection, enticed by its countless promises of future gain and well-being. When the collection is stolen through their own folly, the brothers turn on each other: Each tells the police investigator in secret that he suspects the other of having stolen it. Although they ultimately discover who is really responsible for the theft, they have no way of proving it, and hence no way of retrieving the collection. They come to terms with their

Figure 1–2. The letter burns beyond readability in *Decalogue Four*.

loss, and each comes to terms with his betrayal of the other. In the final scene, they confess their betrayals and exchange forgiveness. They also discover that they have both acquired an interest in stamp collecting and have independently purchased the same (common and inexpensive) series of stamps. We see them with foreheads pressed one to the other, laughing through their tears at the absurdity of their situation and in newfound appreciation of brotherly love in the midst of loss. As Kickasola describes it:

> The two men have coveted, desired, been selfish, possessive, and suspicious of others. Yet in the end, they share their new material interests, combining the stamps to make a series. . . . Giving oneself away to a loved one marks the beginnings of morality and its teleology. The final, uncanny "chance" occurrence [the discovery that they have both purchased the same stamps] precipitates the miracle of reconciliation. (241)

Our situation is like that of the brothers. Human life seems to hold out to each of us the promise of unlimited gain. But the reality of living reveals that promise to be illusory; it reveals the true character of human limitation and ultimately loss. And yet there is still the possibility of rediscovering love, freedom, and joy in the midst of that loss and in full recognition of human frailty and limitation. Witnessing their plight and the plights of the other characters in *The Decalogue* inspires us with a desire that this possibility should be realized, that all should be well for the characters and for ourselves despite all we have done to make it unwell. Ultimately, then, *The Decalogue* suggests the image of a forgiving universe—a universe in which despite our folly we are not ultimately crushed by the weight of our past failures; we instead discover that the most worthwhile aspects of human life, the most cherished of human connections, are forged in the experience of failure and shared vulnerability.

NOTES

1. See Immanuel Kant, *Grounding for the Metaphysics of Morals*, trans. James W. Ellington (Indianapolis: Hackett, 1993), 30–31; and John Stuart Mill, *Utilitarianism* (Indianapolis: Hackett, 2001).

2. The *locus classicus* for the virtue-ethical tradition is Aristotle's *Nicomachean Ethics*. See the edition translated by Terence Irwin (Indianapolis: Hackett, 1999). The contemporary revival of that tradition is due principally to Alasdair MacIntyre's *After Virtue: A Study in Moral Theory* (Notre Dame, Ind.: University of Notre Dame Press, 1984). For an introduction to G. E. M. Anscombe, see *Ethics, Religion and Politics*, vol. 3, *Collected Philosophical Papers* (Minneapolis: University of Minnesota Press, 1981).

3. Joseph Kickasola tells us, "For this episode of the series, Kieślowski returned to one of his most trusted cinematographers, Sławomir Idziak . . . [who] ordered over 600 custom-made, green filters of the 'crueller, duller, emptier' look of the film. . . . Apart from the skewing of color, another effect of the filter is the amplification of contrast, plunging the world into stark divisions between inky blackness and points and slashes of light. Even the light of day appears impotent in the face of this darkness." Joseph G. Kickasola, *The Films of Krzysztof Kieślowski: The Liminal Image* (New York: Continuum, 2004), 202. Further references will be cited in the text.

4. William Shakespeare, *Hamlet*, in *William Shakespeare: The Complete Works*, ed. Peter Alexander (London: Collins, 1988), 1065 (V.1.63).

CHAPTER 2

Tablets of Stone, Tablets of Flesh: Synesthetic Appeal in *The Decalogue*

Joseph G. Kickasola

> It very quickly became clear that these would be films about feelings and passions, because we knew that love, or the fear of death, or the pain caused by a needle-prick, are common to all people, irrespective of their political views, the colour of their skin or their standard of living.... We decided to place the action of *Decalogue* in a large housing estate, with thousands of similar windows framed within the establishing shot. Behind each of these windows, we said to ourselves, is a living being, whose mind, whose heart and, even better, whose stomach is worthy of investigation.
>
> —KRZYSZTOF KIEŚLOWSKI

In the films *The Double Life of Veronique* (1991) and *The Three Colors Trilogy* (1992–94), Krzysztof Kieślowski left behind most of the aesthetic trappings of his early documentaries and moved into more sensuous and formalistic territory.[1] Much of the power of Kieślowski's later cinema hinges on the aesthetics of immediacy—that is, the perceived directness of affect-as-meaning it produces.[2] I argue that in the series of films before *Veronique*—the monumental *Decalogue* series (1989)—we see hints of this stylistic shift as he searched for new ways of expressing the spiritual and moral themes that interested him.[3] If we draw upon a crude dualistic analogy—that is, the factual ideations of the documentary as corresponding to mind and the sensuous nature of form as appealing to body—we might say that *The Decalogue* demonstrates a dialectic between the mind and body, stylistically and thematically.

It is not clear that Kieślowski would have wanted his career to be seen in this stark way, as if his documentaries were coldly intellectual and his later features were lacking ideas. If anything, Kieślowski saw himself on a singular trajectory in pursuit of reality, and his later features simply strain into those areas of metaphysical reality that resist reportage or easy figuration.[4]

In *The Decalogue*, Kieślowski is reacting to (and working within) a cultural and historical construct, that of the Ten Commandments. Here, a particularly interesting dynamic evolves as a tension between the ideal, rational, abstract, disembodied Word (the Commandments as an abstract ideal) and the body that comprehends, struggles with, and lives through it.

As I will discuss, in recent years a wide variety of otherwise disparate thinkers have argued for a notion of embodied meaning. In other words, in contrast to the strict alignment of meaning with its linguistic manifestations, they argue for meaning and knowledge that is bodily, prelogical, and epistemologically heavy. These thinkers—ranging from cultural theorists to philosophers to neuroscientists—often disagree about a great many things, but they may be united under the moniker of embodied epistemology, in that they see a fundamental symbiosis between sense perception, emotion, and knowledge.

In this essay I will use this general triangulation and this literature of embodiment to explore a particular dimension of Kieślowskian immediacy in *The Decalogue*. Kieślowski was not interested in the exposition of the Ten Commandments but rather in their sensual and dynamic force in our contemporary lives. Throughout the films, he treats sensual evocation to be part and parcel of real knowledge. His sensual strategy in effect does not tell us what the Commandments propositionally mean, but how they mean, even as we appropriate their meanings through the films. In this vein, I would like to trace one particular sensory path in *The Decalogue*, that of tactile synesthetic appeal. This path will serve as an example of the sort of lived meaning for which, I believe, Kieślowski aimed.

I will begin with a general discussion of synesthesia, so that we might define and clarify our terms. In the process, I will survey a number of interrelated epistemological concepts that reveal a paradoxical power in Kieślowski's images—a strength he intuitively understood as crucial—that even when certain sensual experiences like touch are amputated from the physical contact that gives them life, their cinematic evocation can still resonate with a certain immediacy of meaning. This will be followed by a discussion of specific examples of synesthetic appeal in the films of *The Decalogue*, and some reflection on the impact of synesthetic immediacy on the overall theological tone of the series.

Understanding Synesthetic Appeal

Synesthesia is a general term that encompasses all experiences in which stimulus from one sensory mode evokes or literally triggers another. The range between evoking and triggering can be wide, from everyday synesthesia (e.g., commonplace matching of shape between touch and vision) to the clinical variety of synesthesia (a very literal engagement of secondary sense through a unique sensual pathway, which likely arises from hard neurological wiring in clinical cases). My emphasis here will be on the universal, everyday variety.[5]

When I say "everyday" synesthesia I am essentially talking about cinematic phenomena that appeal transmodally. Transmodal processing—that is, the confluence of modes of perception (such as sight and touch, for instance)—is a very large part of everyday perception, but we are only just beginning to understand the complexities of its mechanics. We often use multiple senses to comprehend something, and some senses (such as touch) regularly evoke an image (feel and identify your car keys in your pocket or purse, for instance) even if you are not seeing that image with your eyes. Transmodal appeals are considered a form of synesthetic appeal for this very reason; one sense triggers a memory from another sense experience. Films, of course, hinge on this experience as well, and the phenomenon is ubiquitous, but some films highlight and function through transmodal qualities more than others, and in Kieślowski's case, this is critical to his approach to the subject matter.

Phenomenologist Maurice Merleau-Ponty once wrote, "The senses translate each other without any need of an interpreter and are mutually comprehensible without the intervention of any idea."[6] More recently, neuroscientists Barry E. Stein and M. Alex Meredith noted that some stimulus features, such as intensity, form, number, and duration are believed to be amodal—that is, not the function of one particular modality—and are, in fact, transferred readily across modalities, and are thus transmodal.[7] The ramifications of this theory for our study of Kieślowski are that much of what we consider to be everyday synesthetic experiences are these properties of stimuli—like time, intensity, form, number, and duration—that directly transfer through various modalities. These elements function as a type of vocabulary for Kieślowski's nonverbal eloquence regarding the lived experience of *The Decalogue*.

In order to incarnate and animate the abstract ideals of the Commandments, everyday synesthetic experience must be epistemologically heavy even as it is immediate (i.e., bypassing linguistic mediation). For centuries in Western philosophy there has been a division between so-called higher mental operations and lower ones, with historically varying degrees of emphasis placed on the former, but rarely equal epistemological status granted to the latter. The former operations (e.g., language, intellect, reason, rationality, reflection, and so on) have been privileged over sensation, emotion, feeling, intuition, and even perception itself. By contrast, the literature of embodiment largely reinforces two assertions made by the phenomenologist Edmund Husserl over a hundred years ago: the epistemological heaviness of intuition and imagination, and the fundamental idea of intentionality (that we reach out or intend toward meaning in all perception).[8]

The film critic Vivian Sobchack draws upon a later phenomenologist, Merleau-Ponty, who avoided some of the transcendental idealist traps into which Husserl fell and managed to detail how any evaluation of cinematic perception must always account for the body of the subject.[9] In her essay "What My Fingers Knew," she articulates a bodily, precognitive, nonlogical, immediate tactile knowledge, synesthetically evoked by seeing Jane Campion's film *The Piano* (1993). The opening shot of the film is an abstract image, revealed only in the second shot to be a woman's fingers underwater with sunlight shining between them. Clearly, Sobchack's reaction to the shot is fundamentally contingent on memory recall, but her account makes it clear that this is not mere semiosis of the linguistic variety:

> Despite my "almost blindness," the "unrecognizable blur," and resistance of the image to my eyes, *my fingers knew what I was looking at*—and this *before* the objective reverse shot that followed to put those fingers in their proper place. . . . From the first (although I didn't consciously know it until the second shot), my fingers *comprehended* that image, *grasped* it with a nearly imperceptible tingle of attention and anticipation and, offscreen, "felt themselves" as a potentiality in the subjective and fleshy situation figured onscreen. And this *before* I refigured my carnal comprehension into the conscious thought, "Ah, those are fingers I am looking at." . . . Those fingers were first known sensually and sensibly as "these" fingers and were located ambiguously both offscreen and on—subjectively "here" as well as objectively "there," "mine" as well as the image's. . . . We do not experience any movie only through our eyes. We see and comprehend and feel films with our entire bodily being, informed by the full history and carnal knowledge of our acculturated sensorium. (*Carnal Thoughts*, 63)

Here is the rub: The essence of the experience and what makes it knowledge is the content of that memory, but content is only valuable to the extent that it is reified and experienced. Her fingers "know," and she knows that she knows through experience. Likewise, the synesthetic migration of abstract visual forms into the haptic domain says something about the transmodal properties of such images. I have argued elsewhere that abstraction (including editing strategies that highlight abstraction, similar to those Sobchack describes) is fundamental to Kieślowski's style.[10]

Along these same lines, Laura U. Marks argues for the weightiness of non-verbal knowledge as it is cinematically transmitted. She contends "that many new works in film and video call upon memories of the senses . . ." and the title of her book, *The Skin of the Film*, "suggests the way vision itself can be tactile, as though one were touching a film with one's eyes."[11] She calls this "haptic visuality," an emphasis on the synesthetic relation between sight and touch, and argues that Gilles Deleuze's "Time-Image" cinema offers her a model and terminology with which to discuss these "new languages" which are not verbal, as Deleuze draws on the philosopher Henri Bergson, who always embodied memory in the senses. Marks writes:

> I have found it necessary to understand how meaning occurs in the body, and not only at the level of signs. The elements of an embodied response to cinema, the response in terms of touch, smell, rhythm, and other bodily perceptions, have until recently been considered "excessive" and not amenable to analysis. I will argue that they can indeed be analyzed—or, more properly, met halfway. Ultimately I argue that our experience of cinema is mimetic, or an experience of bodily similarity to the audiovisual images we take in. Cinema is not merely a transmitter of signs; it bears witness to an object and transfers the presence of that object to viewers. (xvii)

Sobchack and Marks find an unusual complement in an important aesthetician from the analytical school of philosophy, Jenefer Robinson, whose book *Deeper than Reason* (2005) argues that emotion should not be the Cinderella of the epistemological family, and reason should not be the wicked stepmother. Her question of what emotion is leads her to believe it is an exceptionally efficient (however general) appraisal of a given situation. If it is an appraisal (and Robinson makes a very comprehensive case), it is a type of evaluation that yields a type of nonverbal knowledge. Some emotions are, in fact, "quick and dirty non-cognitive affective appraisals."[12]

If we were to summarize what this immediate knowledge is, we might say that it is epistemologically heavy and direct knowledge, which precedes verbal language and includes bodily experience (including synesthetic, transmodal evocation) and emotion, both of which convey knowledge without the mediation of verbal categories. These are the feelings at the gut—or "stomach"—to which Kieślowski alluded in the quote opening this essay.

Part of the reason philosophers and film theorists are returning to these notions of bodily experience and direct knowledge is that the hard sciences are too. Many neurologists are leaning away from the old dichotomy of sensing vs. understanding, precisely because there does not seem to be a direct, linear process from the low to the high stages in perception; the model is more like parallel processing than linear flow.[13] Likewise, a lot of very fundamental perceptual work happens in the low areas, such that it is hard to imagine thinking without them. If that is so, perhaps even these low stages have a claim to knowledge. The psychologist Rudolf Arnheim argued for years that both intellect and intuition are essential for what it means to be human, and one should not be preferred over the other. In one of his many essays on the matter, he writes:

> As far as the differences between verbal and nonverbal language are concerned, I will cite only the obvious example that many verbal languages treat things and actions as separate entities, whereas the directly perceptual media, especially the ones presenting movement such as pantomime or film, display them as aspects of an inseparable experience. . . . Both means, the resources of direct experience and the instruments of concepts, are needed, whether by a scientist or an artist or indeed by any person curious about the world where he or she is living.[14]

Arnheim's idea of the projection of meaning is nearly identical to Husserl's intentionality. It is worth noting that most neuroscientists support this notion of active perception today.[15] Likewise, philosopher and cognitive theorist Mark Johnson has recently developed an entire theory of aesthetics based on intentionality, the primacy of emotion, and the deep, visceral foundations of knowledge.[16] Thus, scientists have affirmed the Husserlian hunch on intentionality and epistemological weight. This forms a foundation for our exploration of everyday synesthesia, what scientists consider a type of multisensory process.

The everyday synesthetic experience is what I would call a diluted or semi-sensation. It is not exactly a memory, though memory drives it: It is a physiological, sensual response that evokes a cascade of other physiological and sensory responses, forming an epistemologically heavy dynamic of immediate meaning in the perceiver. This is quite different from semantically mediated knowledge.

The next section will analyze some instances where cinema is synesthetically evocative, and I hope to show that this is not merely association or memory, or that our visceral reactions are merely crude impulses. Rather, both of those elements are inextricably bound together to form experiential knowledge, something close to Sobchack's "what my fingers knew" in her articulation of an embodied existential phenomenology.

The Synesthetic Immediate in The Decalogue

The preceding section formed a philosophical and neurophysiological case for sensuous knowledge. It is precisely this type of knowing that enables Kieślowski's lived theological reflection to function. Our examples from *The Decalogue*, to be explored here, will merely serve as that: examples, occasions for experiential knowledge. Kieślowski draws on common memories, and neurophysiological sympathies, to convey the lived experiences of his characters, as they navigate the arenas of morality demarcated by the Commandments.

One might argue that this cinematic resonance is not unique to Kieślowski or even *The Decalogue*. However, one might also reflect on the theological substrate undergirding the series, to which I alluded earlier in this essay. By tackling some of the most foundational sets of ideas in Western culture, Kieślowski attempts to inject the Commandments with life, animating them as zones of experience in which we struggle to connect the ideal with the lived body.

One way he does this is through haptic synesthetic appeal, which takes on several stylistic manifestations. For instance, close-up shots of objects appeal to the haptic sense through a magnification of texture. Particularly intense, abstract visuals have a function all their own in Kieślowski's cinema, but their synesthetic qualities lie in their emphasis on primary sensory qualities (some of which—such as intensity and form—hold transmodal appeal).[17] Shots of the tactile organs (hands, skin, and tongue) are also common, and they evoke a strong mimetic response. Images of hands induce strong synesthetic reactions, and powerful images of hands about to cut or being cut can be found in episodes *Two* and *Three*. Finally, haptic associations include images of things that have some natural or indexical relationship with the sense of touch (e.g., a shot of a flame evokes the memory of the feeling of heat, or pain, or both).[18]

We might say that Kieślowski's films appeal to the universal triangulation of sense experience, emotion, and morality. This is most evident in *One*, where Paweł's metaphysical questions—"who is God?"—are answered by a hug from his aunt Irena:

AUNT: What do you feel now?

PAWEŁ: I love you.

AUNT: Exactly. That's where he is.

In our perception of the conversation, we are given a standard, back-and-forth edited conversation. Paweł and his aunt do not appear in the same frame throughout their verbal, intellectual conversation. The end of this Socratic dialogue, however, culminates not in a linguistic answer, but a sensual one, as the two characters draw close into one frame. We see this proximity, but we also, transmodally, sense the smell of the aunt's coat, the texture of her clothing, and the haptic intimacy of the diminished space between the characters. Kieślowski seems to be indicating here that the *Decalogue* series will present the possibility of God through the context of human relationships and sensual experience (the aunt and her nephew, and the intimate contact between them). In this way, Kieślowski presents the Commandments as abstract ideals that purport to order human life. Yet, their real impact is found in the nonverbal, emotional and sensual dynamic they create. They must be animated within a human sensual arena to have any real force, effect, or—as we have discussed—complete meaning.

Indeed, we might initially consider the first episode as something of a template for how Kieślowski utilizes such appeals. It is worth noting that *One*, like so many of the episodes, begins with almost no dialogue. Here we see Kieślowski employing a stream of sensual appeals as well as looks and glances that index emotions. One image is the mangy frozen hair of the dead dog touched by Paweł, with which we might contrast Paweł's later petting of the guinea pig, a cuddly little animal strikingly noted for its sharp teeth. From a semiotic perspective, the guinea pig is not a sign for soft sentiment. Rather, through synesthetic evocation of contrasting sensations, Kieślowski problematizes a simplistic logical equation. Through sensation, the animal is at once felt to be lovable and threatening.

This sort of paradoxical duality is common in the synesthetic appeals Kieślowski makes throughout *The Decalogue*, and it functions as a phenomenological analogue to the intellectual paradoxes that are inherent in most theologies. To cite an example Kieślowski himself often pursued, how can one propositionally believe in fate or predestined future and still preserve some notion of free will? Theologians have wrestled with this paradox for

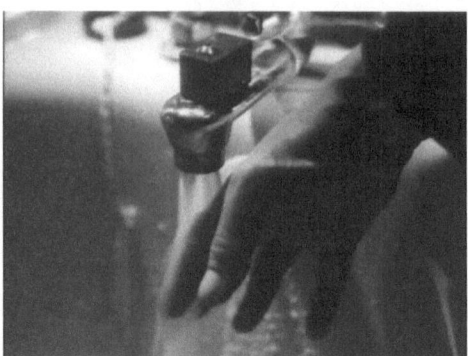

Figure 2-1. Haptic appeal in *Decalogue One*.

centuries, and many have labeled it a divine mystery beyond verbal or intellectual reach. However, we often experience things that embody the paradoxes, and so we know them bodily, but not intellectually. In this case, the dialectic of the cuddly creature and its menacing sharp teeth manifests a concrete, sensual binary rather than a propositional one. This, and many other examples like it, suggests that we live through the paradox rather than intellectually resolve it.

The synesthetic appeals also inform our understanding of the characters and do something to advance the plot. For instance, Paweł shows his aunt a device to turn on the water in his apartment. His aunt, being a sensual person who touches and engages the world more than she talks, sticks her hand in the stream. It is interesting that Kieślowski, fighting against the limiting time of 50 minutes for this episode, chooses to spend the extra time watching the aunt putting her hand in the water, for no other reason than to experience the water rushing over her skin. We might naturally see this in semiotic terms: She is a woman who is connected to water, moving water, as it stands as a symbol of life (and where frozen, still water will become a symbol of death) (Figure 2-1).

However, this interpretation can work only retroactively, since it is not part of the original experience of perceiving the image. What is primary is the synesthetic response: We sympathetically (Marks would say "mimetically") remember something of the feeling of wetness on fingers, and that memory works more in the mode of feeling than abstract fact. Likewise, it is a key sensation for us to feel water (as well as the coldness of the dog fur and the milk bottle Paweł touches), because it will become central to what Paweł tragically feels at the end of the film. Cold water also elicits pity in *Three*, when the cruel jailor hoses down the naked drunk, as well as humor

Tablets of Stone, Tablets of Flesh   39

in the opening to *Four*, as father and daughter playfully douse each other with water. These are not merely symbols or propositions, but sensory engagements with the things that universally matter: life, death, joy, pain, love, and fulfillment.

Later, Paweł's touch of the blade of the skate represents childhood wonder, but synesthetically it evokes an instantaneous danger or pain reaction that provides the story, even as it expresses another ironic binary, with childhood wonder and pain rolled into one image. Fire is a similar binary, which can be warm and comforting as well as painful. In addition to the campfire of the young man in *One*, images of flames (and flames near hands) can be found in *One*, *Two*, *Three*, and *Four*.

The father's walk on the frozen ice plays out a particularly interesting transmodal theme in Kieślowski's *Decalogue*: the experience of tension and testing of limits. Kieślowski lingers on the image of the father walking on the ice, giving us time to anticipate whether the ice will break or not, and giving us synesthetic markers of its solidity. We might call this haptic testing, and it is a common theme throughout *The Decalogue*, a sensual analogue to the ideas of the Commandments as conceptual, intellectual limits. Characters often pensively nudge and push things, as if testing their material boundaries. These small challenges often happen at high emotional moments for the characters, and may serve as a search for reality in a surreal moment, or as tests of the physical laws of the universe, performed in the hope that there may be some escape from them. The central point is not that there are such material limits, but that we know those limits bodily and we often wish to negotiate or transcend them. For instance, in *Two*, Dorota slowly pushes a mug of tea to the edge of the table, until it finally falls. In *Four*, a father, after hearing his daughter had an abortion, aimlessly pushes around some cordials on a table. In *Five*, ominously, Jacek nudges a rock closer and closer to the edge of the bridge rail, until it falls onto traffic below, causing an accident (Figure 2–2).

Throughout the rest of *The Decalogue*, we see numerous other examples of these sorts of synesthetic engagements. For the sake of brevity, I will not itemize them all here, but only draw attention to a few more examples that might expand our understanding of how Kieślowski utilizes the synesthetic immediate to express what he called "essential, fundamental, human and humanistic questions."[19] We might develop some themes here, within which these synesthetic engagements can be contextualized: synesthetic evocations of life, struggle, and death.

We might include in the category "life" synesthetic moments of haptic intimacy (for example, when Paweł hugs his father after the chess match

Figure 2–2. Haptically testing limits in *Decalogue Two*.

in *One*) and sexual tension (as in most of *Three*, the story of an affair in the making, or in *Four*, when Anka's drama coach tells her to "get closer" to her fellow actor). We remember in *Seven* that little Ania will not let go of her father's finger, while her mother Majka asks in vain for kisses and tender hugs.

In *Six*, the relationship between synesthetic appeal and voyeurism is made plain, and the bodies of the characters become Kieślowski's script. We may wish to touch Magda, even as her lover touches her. This intimacy provokes the jealous Tomek to report a fictitious gas leak, after which, in a sort of mad joy, he wildly punches the wall out of an embodied surplus of emotion. When Magda spills her milk, she plays in it with her finger. Later, Tomek's hands on Magda's thighs send him over the edge. Before long, he cuts his wrists. In each case, Kieślowski synesthetically appeals through lingering, carefully constructed, wordless images.

In a sense, all the episodes are about struggle on some level, but *Two* manifests this theme the most synesthetically. For instance, after Dorota coolly picks the leaves off her houseplant and mangles the stem, Kieślowski's camera hangs on a close-up of the slowly rising remains of the plant. The stem rises, bit by ugly bit, refusing to die. In Andrzej's hospital room, the dripping of water on the bed frame, peeling paint, and the drowning bee all exude a tension of time and duration that excruciatingly appeals to our sense of touch, and the embodied, sympathetic struggle for movement and life.

In *Five*, the most visceral of all the episodes, we are given this same struggle unto inexorable death. The agonizing detail of each of Jacek's blows, and Waldemar's desperate bodily surges and twitches in death, are matched only by the unbearable synesthetic tensions mercilessly present at Jacek's hanging. The Russian Formalist Viktor Shklovsky famously said that the purpose of art was to "make the stone feel stony."[20] In Jacek's hands the heavy, unrelenting stone feels so to mortal effect. Indeed, the entire episode is steeped in synesthetic evocation, from Jacek's menacing twisting of the rope around his hands to his slovenly consumption of the pastry in the café.[21]

Finally, we might see *Eight* as one of the most direct instances of the mind/body dialectic. The film begins with a moving camera, a child's hand clasping an adult's hand in the frame. The child's finger moves delicately, trustingly, setting the synesthetic and emotional stakes high enough that we wince when we learn of her betrayal later. The old professor Zofia says nothing throughout the opening sequence of the film but, instead, exercises, exerts, and comes to rest on the rough, wooden rail. The crooked picture frame symbolizes something of the outside forces which philosophy never seems quite to conquer, even as it disrupts our transmodal sense of balance. This episode—which has more dialogue than most others and deals far more with abstract ideals, language, and rationality—is constantly being balanced by human touch and forces beyond control or articulation. The acrobatic rubber man in the park—who transmodally strains and pulls through our sense of our own bodily limitations—synesthetically embodies the balance between ideals and embodied knowledge: "It's just a matter of exercise," he says to Zofia. Even though the man declares that it may be "too late" for Zofia to learn the embodied practice of flexibility, Kieślowski suggests otherwise.[22] Elżbieta, in the end, begins to pray again (one of the few overtly religious images in the series), and Zofia and Elżbieta have several tender moments of contact. The film ends with a silent image of reconciled touch between them—where God is, according to Aunt Irenka in *One*—thoughtfully observed from a distance by the weary, jaded tailor.

Kieślowski's *Decalogue* presents the ideals of the Commandments as they meet the embodied, living person. He does not pretend that this meeting is always happy, easy, or even fully comprehensible, but our bodies know something of these Commandments and the reality to which they speak. Kieślowski's embodied appeals remind us of their relevance, and—literally—engage us in their meanings. Their meanings, and the ideals they embody, are directly connected to theological assertions, which Kieślowski treats more like metaphysical themes. To conclude this essay, the relationship between these themes, their theological substrate, and the synesthetic immediate dynamic warrants some reflection.

Theology and Synesthetic Appeal

In *Carnal Thoughts*, Sobchack has sketched out an existential, phenomenological, descriptive account of *One* that is articulate, insightful, and similar to my account, at least in some of its phenomenological concepts. What I have called "evocative" and "transmodal" phenomena, she refers to as "mimetic ana-logic" (89), and what I have called "nonrational knowledge" she refers to as "emotional turbulence" that has "equal weight" with "logical contingence" in Kieślowski's cinema (90). In effect, she sees Kieślowski as demarcating the boundaries at which our "irrational" senses, desires, fears and dreams confront the brutal, limiting, material realities (87). I would not, generally, use the term irrational, but there is an overall sympathy between our arguments.

Sobchack ignores any kind of theological underpinning or context to the films, and sees everything phenomenologically in terms of material existential experience and secular conjectures beyond that experience, such as contemporary chaos theory, which attempts to track patterns of randomness and orderliness in the universe quite apart from any first cause (90 n. 7). Her descriptions about how the "lived body" makes "sense" of the experience is inflected—she readily admits—by her own philosophical presuppositions which are radically material and leave little room for anything beyond what she calls a "concrete metaphysics," which contemplates the interface of material body and material world (1–2, 87). She comes close to a theological concept when discussing the inexplicable and ominous "I am ready" of the computer screen in *One*, but couches it in standard cultural studies language (i.e., "an emotional signature of otherness that doesn't deign to ingratiate itself" [92]).[23] She conceives of Kieślowski as a pessimist-yet-humanist, "tormented by transcendence" despite the "harsh dialectics" of his films, which undermine stable religious metaphysical systems (86, 107–108).

For sure, one ought to be cautious when applying theological concepts to Kieślowski, given his dubious theological commitments and well known suspicion of organized religion. However, I would like to open up the materialist bracket here and allow for some theological reflection. We are, surely, free to assume that theological ideas are not out of bounds in a film built on the structure of the Ten Commandments, and there is evidence to suggest that Kieślowski himself was concerned with more than material reality.[24] Rather than pursue a particular theology, however, it seems wiser to pursue some more general—rather than dogmatic—philosophical theology here. What I mean by this is not to insist upon a particular religious portrait of God or the particular creeds of a given church, but to see the Commandments as a type of zone, within which one can engage the questions of ultimate reality, morality, and purpose. There is evidence to suggest that Kieślowski felt this way about the films. His friend, the filmmaker Agnieszka Holland, once remarked:

> I think that Krzysztof is somebody who had an incredibly deep need to believe in something transcendental. He did believe, but at the same time he wasn't really the member of any church, and his relationships toward the religious were less theological than ethical and metaphysical.[25]

Within a broad theological context, one finds some parallels that Kieślowski himself might have found attractive. Kieślowski's need for "something transcendental" may very well grow from the same ground as the anti-materialist, anti-positivistic concerns of Poland's most famous religious son, Karol Wojtyła, Pope John Paul II (whose photo appears, and whose person is discussed, in the very first *Decalogue* installment, and comically in *Nine*). Wojtyła was known as a serious philosopher, theologian, and even a poet, but his most significant achievement, in the eyes of most Poles, was simply as a native son, unafraid to speak out about the oppression in his own country. At the time *Decalogue* was made, few figures—religious or otherwise—were more important to the ordinary Pole than he was.[26]

Remarkably, Wojtyła's theological approach to the body is contrary to much of religious history, where sensual experience and Western religious ideas have not been good bedfellows. Note how sensory experience is also akin to synesthetic experience in this quote, from renowned art historian David Freedberg:

> From Clement of Alexandria (with all his antipathy to images) to Bernard Berenson (with all his love of them), *the eyes are the channel to the other senses. These are what are dangerous, or enlivening, or both—touch above all.* Once our eyes are arrested by an image, so the argument more or less runs from Plato onward, we can no longer resist the engagement of emotion and feeling.... We may be moved; we strive to touch the unloving object before us. Whether inevitable processes or merely inclinations, these are what detract from the purity of mental operations *tout court*. That higher side of our beings that sets us apart from animals, the realm of intellect and spirit, is brought down and sullied. (Emphasis added)[27]

Wojtyła's approach, however, is to argue that a proper theology of the body begins with the notion of the material world as a divine gift (including our material bodies, and all their sensual modes of understanding). He fights against a Cartesian—or neo-Manichaean—division between matter and spirit, and argues forcefully that human beings should never be reduced to "mere matter."[28] He sees official strictures on sensual life not as a Manichean tendency, but rather as its opposite: a safeguard for assuring the "dignity of the body" (309). As for the human person, he admits an aspectual dualism of body and spirit, but does not admit a dualism of person: "We cannot consider the body as an objective reality outside of man's personal subjectivity" (364–365). Thus, whereas Wojtyła might applaud Sobchack for the importance she has placed upon the body in perception and the generation of meaning, he would likely be concerned that the philosophical basis for her approach—her "concrete metaphysics"—still contains the danger that the body (and hence the other) will be reduced to "mere matter," and thus abused as an "object" (94–96).

Kieślowski, no doubt, differed from the pope on many things, but they did share essential concerns for sensory experience, a bodily experience of the world, and that life and truth not be measured solely in scientific, material, or rationalistic terms. This is the essence of the quote that opened this essay, the Kieślowskian tripartite "mind," "heart," and "stomach." It is also at the heart of Kieślowski's assertion—after hours of study of religious commentaries and philosophies surrounding the "meaning" of *The Decalogue*—that he and cowriter Krzysztof Piesiewicz felt no compunction to articulate an authoritative interpretation of the Commandments. Rather, "we wished to say: 'We know no more than you. But maybe it is worth investigating the unknown, if only because the very feeling of not knowing is a painful one'" (*KK*, xiv). The "pain" of "not knowing" is, it seems, indexical of the Commandments' significance for this generation.

Wojtyła's theology of the body aims at the celebration of personhood—persons as unity of body and spirit—as a remedy to those who would treat the body as an object. Such a notion is also at the heart of Martin Buber's I-Thou binary.[29] Buber's conception of treating something as an "it" is to treat reality (be it a person or a tree) as an object for use or mastery. Rather, he encourages us to consider all of reality as a "Thou," not objectified, but giving and receiving in reciprocal relation to us. The Commandments, in summary, can be seen as a set of principles for avoiding the temptation to mastery.[30] Kieślowski's synesthetic appeals may be seen as simulations of that very struggle, even as it also presents sensory alternatives to an arrogant neo-Manichaeism. Mastery is, after all, a temptation that is both intellectual and sensual.

Kieślowski critiques the former, neo-Manichaean temptation in the very first episode. "Eliot said poetry is what's untranslatable," Paweł's father remarks in his lecture, and this is another clue to Kieślowski's pursuit of the Commandments (all that meaning attached to and suggested by those words, but which cannot be circumscribed by the words themselves). He goes on, in his materialistic fashion, to describe a godlike computer ("Try to imagine an interpreter capable of accumulating all knowledge of words and language with an unlimited memory that can be used at any time"), and as he speaks we ironically see that precise thing that the computer cannot truly have: feeling-as-meaning, indexed by a close-up on his hands. Significantly, this view belongs to his curious and affectionate young son, who has recently been told by his aunt that God dwells in the touch between persons. As Sobchack's example has shown, hands are often the gateway for synesthetic experience, not simply conceptual symbolism of such experience.

The sensual temptation to mastery is found at the intersection of desire, body, action, and morality, and so it is natural that Kieślowski's synesthetic appeals would function so effectively here as well. For example, the cruel hosing of the drunk by the anti-Semitic orderly in *Three* provokes a double-synesthetic response: that of mastery and power over another, and a painful, haptic sympathy of cold. Likewise, our abstract, rational knowledge of anti-Semitism informs our emotional and moral response. The balance here should not be lost. The temptation to hate the body must be countered by sensual knowledge, as it is through that appeal that so much of our sense of meaning, purpose, and ethics are foundationalized. At the same time, the senses are often inclined toward mastery and must be tempered by principle and compassion.

In Kieślowski's case, not only does he rely upon transmodal evocation, but he also uses it as a means of amplifying the sensual interface of the body with a given ideal. Essentially, this animation is through struggle, through experiential knowledge and the sense of pressure and limit, and the emotion within the thematic space the command demarcates.[31] No episode is like a sermon or a lesson, but rather, as Kieślowski says, "the films . . . [are] influenced by the individual Commandments to the same degree that the Commandments influence our daily lives" ("Introduction," xiv).

Kieślowski surely struggled over spiritual issues and nothing approaching a religious conversion or certainty has been documented, but struggle, to the religious mind, is an essential part of the faith experience. The prominent "harsh dialectics" in Kieślowski's films, as Sobchack describes them (*Carnal Thoughts*, 106–108), are also complemented by numerous, mysterious occasions of grace, salvation, redemption, and joy. We should note that the family contact that defined God and opened *The Decalogue* (Paweł and his aunt embracing) returns in one of the final images of *Ten*. We see two reconciling brothers, who not only forgive each other but press their foreheads together: a symbolic and haptic union of mind and body, to heal the Manichaean rift and to close this monumental film series.

It is in these hopeful moments that the religious hope for the body makes its presence known in Kieślowski's cinema. The theologian T. J. Gorringe argues that God has purposed sensual life as a mode of his own self-expression, and within this embodied experience we might find hope.[32] It is a hope of human touch and sensual delight which facilitates healing, as suggested in episode *Eight*, through Zofia and Elżbieta's reconciled embrace. Intellectual and moral questions remain, but healing begins nonetheless. As Gorringe writes, "Through the exercise of our senses, God moves towards the creation of a new world, a world of the celebration and affirmation of bodies, and therefore of the creator who imagined them and gave us them materially, as the consummate sign of the grace of God's essential nature" (27).

Unlike Gorringe, Kieślowski was not setting out to find a theology of the body, but even so his *Decalogue* exhibits the same embodied drama of human brokenness and redemption. Kieślowski picked the Ten Commandments as his structure because, in his own words, he looked around Warsaw and had the impression that he was "watching people who didn't really know why they were living" (*KK*, 143). He simply wanted to see if these abstract ideas mattered, and if that mattering is measured by lived experience.

As Rudolf Otto wrote in his meditation on *The Idea of the Holy*, the rational and nonrational are the warp and woof of the spiritual fabric.[33] One cannot have authentic religious experience without both, and Kieślowski's films address each of these perceptive arenas. His work is about the dance between the intuitive, intentional, emotional, and rational self and the raw forces of the world. Meaning is the essential dynamic, and in Kieślowski's hands the Ten Commandments are less a set of decrees for him to interpret and more a description of the dance (and the dance floor), as well as the zones of sense, movement, and morality. One may assume that the Commandments are simply expressions of norms or ideas, but the consummate achievement of Kieślowski's films is that he demonstrates how these ideas still matter, that they form occasions for living encounters with the spiritual, however broadly one wishes to define it. In this light, it becomes clear that synesthetic appeal is a chosen vehicle to accomplish what has historically been a primary goal of religious experience—that is, in Cytowic's words, "to describe that which transcends language" (*The Man Who Tasted Shapes*, 319).[34]

This essay has only begun to chart Kieślowski's embodied approach to meaning. Kieślowski's affirmation of the body as the ground of knowledge acts as a corrective to overly idealist approaches to the Commandments. In other words, Kieślowski stitches the abstract ideal back into the body, where it matters, even as he ruminates on the instance of its mattering. We are not simply minds, pursuing the Divine, shirking off the body. Neither are we just brains, biomaterially processing input. The cinematic incarnation of the Decalogue reminds us who we are, and it asks us who we wish (and ought) to be, body and soul.

NOTES

1. For the epigraph, see Krzysztof Kieślowski, "Introduction," in Krzysztof Kieślowski and Krzysztof Piesiewicz, *Decalogue: The Ten Commandments*, trans. Phil Cavendish and Susannah Bluh (London: Faber and Faber, 1991), xiii. Further references will be cited in the text.

2. On immediacy in Kieślowski, see Joseph G. Kickasola, *The Films of Krzysztof Kieślowski: The Liminal Image* (New York: Continuum, 2004), 41–89.

3. For more on this transition, see ibid., 15–26.

4. See a more extended argument on this point in ibid., 41–89.

5. It may be—if neuroscientist Richard Cytowic is correct—that the two types are physiologically related. If so, this promises further support for theories of embodied knowledge. Cytowic puts forth numerous amplified clinical examples in his groundbreaking studies *Synesthesia: A Union of the Senses* (Cambridge, Mass.: MIT Press, 2002) and *The Man Who Tasted Shapes* (Cambridge, Mass.: MIT Press, 2003). Further references to these works will be cited in the text. Cytowic's principal clinical example centers on his friend Michael, who really feels a geometrical, tactile shape in his fingertips when he tastes certain foods (*The Man Who Tasted Shapes*, 4).

6. Maurice Merleau-Ponty, *The Phenomenology of Perception*, trans. Colin Smith (London: Routledge & Kegan Paul, 1962), 235.

7. Barry E. Stein and M. Alex Meredith, *The Merging of the Senses* (Cambridge, Mass.: MIT Press, 1993).

8. Husserl's theories are most exhaustively explained in *Logical Investigations*, trans. J. N. Findlay (London: Routledge & Kegan Paul, 1970), and in *Ideas: General Introduction to Pure Phenomenology*, trans. W. R. Boyce Gibson (New York: Collier Books, 1962).

9. Sobchack lays out her phenomenological approach in *The Address of the Eye* (Princeton: Princeton University Press, 1992) and gives more extended examples of application to individual films in *Carnal Thoughts: Embodiment and Moving Image Culture* (Berkeley: University of California Press, 2004). Further references to these works will be cited in the text using the abbreviated titles, respectively, *Address* and *Carnal Thoughts*.

10. See Kickasola, *The Films of Krzysztof Kieślowski*, 65–89.

11. Laura U. Marks, *The Skin of the Film: Intercultural Cinema, Embodiment, and the Senses* (Durham, N.C.: Duke University Press, 2000), xi. Further references will be cited in the text. Giuliana Bruno has also generated a conception of the haptic in cinema, which she utilizes in her exploration of space and touch in *Atlas of Emotion: Journeys in Art, Architecture, and Film* (London: Verso, 2002), 6–7.

12. Jenefer Robinson, *Deeper than Reason: Emotion and Its Role in Literature, Music, and Art* (Oxford: Oxford University Press, 2005), 55–56. It is important to note, however, that emotion and feeling are not always the same thing, but we instinctively know them to be related, as with the common phrase "you hurt my feelings." This may be because emotions can be an appraisal of oneself. Such is Jesse J. Prinz's central argument in his book *Gut Reactions: A Perceptual Theory of Emotion* (New York: Oxford University Press, 2004), 230.

13. Semir Zeki, *Inner Vision: An Exploration of Art and the Brain* (Oxford: Oxford University Press, 1999), 68.

14. Rudolf Arnheim, *The Split and the Structure: Twenty-Eight Essays* (Berkeley: University of California Press, 1996), 22–23.

15. This group would include Antonio D'Amasio, who has convincingly argued for the confluence of emotion and reason, confounding the distinction that he labels "Descartes' Error." His neurological research shows how fundamental emotion and sensation are to so-called cool rationality. See also Zeki, *Inner Vision*.

16. Mark Johnson, *The Meaning of the Body: Aesthetics of Human Understanding* (Chicago: University of Chicago Press, 2007), 1–15.

17. In *The Films of Krzysztof Kieślowski*, I detail how Kieślowski's use of abstract imagery is particularly aimed at liminal experience, between immanent and transcendent realities (41–89).

18. Though Marks does not itemize these areas as I have, this is essentially the same stylistic territory that she describes in *The Skin of the Film*. Her chosen directors utilize these appeals to find communication where a

language has been lost to diaspora. Similarly, Kieślowski sought to transcend his particular culture in this series, and this concern grew even greater in his later features. It is no accident that his synesthetic appeals really begin here, and become much more prominent in his features after *The Decalogue*.

19. In the same interview, he gives us an idea of what these questions are: "What is the true meaning of life? Why get up in the morning? Politics don't answer that." Krzysztof Kieślowski, *Kieślowski on Kieślowski*, ed. Danusia Stok (London: Faber and Faber, 1993), 144. Further references to this work will be cited in the text using the abbreviation *KK*.

20. Viktor Shklovsky, "Art as Technique," in *Russian Formalist Criticism: Four Essays*, ed. and trans. Lee T. Lemon and Marion J. Reis (Lincoln: University of Nebraska Press, 1965), 11–12.

21. One might also consider the evocations of the sense of taste throughout the films of *The Decalogue*, a discussion beyond the scope of this essay, but synesthetically powerful all the same. Some examples include the importance of drinks like tea, milk, and vodka in episodes *One*, *Two*, *Three*, *Six*, *Eight*, *Nine*, and *Ten*.

22. As I have discussed in *The Films of Krzysztof Kieślowski*, the contortionist is the embodiment of some key themes, not as they are questions answered logically, but as perennial questions that must be simply lived through in hope (229).

23. The quotation here actually comes from Peter Schjeldahl's discussion of folk art, which Sobchack applies to this scene. Peter Schjeldahl, "Folks," *New Yorker*, January 14, 2002, 88.

24. Most interviews with Kieślowski show evidence of this, but a particularly compelling one, in which he spends a lot of time discussing the nature of human spiritual mysteries, may be found in *Lucid Dreams: The Films of Krzysztof Kieślowski*, ed. Paul Coates (Trowbridge, UK: Flicks Books, 1999), 160–174.

25. Interview with Milos Stehlik, http://www.facets.org/decalogue/holland.html (accessed October 10, 2003).

26. Likewise, Wojtyła was a Polish hero because he became the head of a universal church out of an oppressive, atheistic government. He not only symbolized the potential and hope for the resistance to Communism, but he returned to communist Poland and subversively preached for the dignity of human beings in the midst of that oppression. A moving account of Wojtyła's 1983 return is found in Timothy Garton Ash, *The Uses of Adversity: Essays on the Fate of Central Europe* (New York: Vintage, 1990), 47–60. This occurred just a few years before the filming of *The Decalogue*.

27. David Freedberg, *The Power of Images: Studies in the History and Theory of Response* (Chicago: University of Chicago Press, 1989), 358.

28. John Paul II, *Man and Woman He Created Them: A Theology of the Body*, trans. Michael Waldstein (Boston: Pauline Books, 2006), 95, 303–307. Further references to this work will be cited in the text. This collection of reflections has been interpreted as a thoughtful defense of traditional Catholic teaching on marriage, and it largely is. However, for our purposes here, it can also be viewed as a larger theological approach to the problem of Cartesian dualism, which has historically led to the denigration of the body.

29. Martin Buber, *I-Thou*, trans. Walter Kaufmann (New York: Scribner's Sons, 1970). Further references will be cited in the text.

30. There is a long tradition in cultural studies of considering vision as a dissecting, objectifying sense, and so it would seem that Kieślowski's images may appeal to mastery, even if the Commandments resist it. However, I believe that vision is more complicated than that, and, in short, Kieślowski's images often place us in a state of suspense and awe—even submission—in the presence of the Other. For more on Kieślowski's visual strategies for confounding our sense of mastery, see Kickasola, *The Films of Krzysztof Kieślowski*, 41–89.

31. For instance, in *One*, the command "You shall have no other gods before me" (Exod. 20:3 RSV), takes on no overt didactic presence, but rather creates the theme within which the characters try to live. In general, I view Kieślowski's approach to the Commandments as flowing from the Catholic ordering, and in terms of a flexible overlap between different commands (see Kickasola, *The Films of Krzysztof Kieślowski*, 162–164).

32. T. J. Gorringe, *The Education of Desire: Towards a Theology of the Senses* (Harrisburg, Pa.: Trinity Press International, 2001), 4. Gorringe highlights many of these occasions for embodied theology. He points out that, in the Christian scriptures, "God chooses embodiment, and not just in Christ. God chooses materiality in the first place, according to Genesis" (9). Likewise, the Scriptures are full of synesthetic metaphors that suggest something more than abstract intellect (e.g., "Taste and see that the Lord is good" [Ps. 34:8, Job 20:18], and Jesus is said to have "tasted death for all" [Hebrews 2:9]). Further references will be cited in the text.

33. Rudolph Otto, *The Idea of the Holy*, trans. John W. Harvey (New York: Oxford University Press, 1958), 2–3.

34. Cytowic notes how synesthetic and religious experiences are similar in many respects. He writes: "In *The Varieties of Religious Experience* William James spoke of . . . [the] four qualities [of religious ecstasy] of ineffability, passivity, noesis, and transience. We should note that these are also qualities of synesthesia" (*Synesthesia*, 319). His case that religious experience and synesthesia emerge from a common fount (the limbic system) is inferential at best, but it does show a certain parallelism between the two, which, at least, suggests a common objective between aesthetic and religious experiences.

CHAPTER 3

Decalogue One: Witnessing a Responsible Ethics of Response from a Jewish Perspective

Moshe Gold

> When a minister, rabbi, or priest attempts to solve the ancient question of Job's suffering through a sermon or lecture, he does not promote religious ends but, on the contrary, does them a disservice. The beauty of religion, with its grandiose vistas, reveals itself to man not in solutions but in problems, not in harmony but in the constant conflict of diversified forces and trends.
>
> —RABBI JOSEPH B. SOLOVEITCHIK

> PAWEŁ (THE YOUNG SON): "For the peace of her soul." You didn't mention a soul.
>
> KRZYSZTOF (THE FATHER): It's a form of words of farewell: there is no soul.
>
> PAWEŁ: Auntie says there is [a soul].
>
> KRZYSZTOF: Some find it easier to live thinking that.
>
> PAWEŁ: And you?
>
> KRZYSZTOF: Me? Frankly, I don't know.
>
> —KRZYSZTOF KIEŚLOWSKI, *Decalogue One*

Creating a Tentative Relationship between Verse and Film

Viewers and critics commonly question the relationship between Krzysztof Kieślowski's ten films entitled *The Decalogue* and the biblical Decalogue. Although the films and the screenplays receive diverse theoretical, theological, and emotional responses, few studies have considered Kieślowski's work from the perspective of Hebrew scripture, even more precisely, from the perspective of specific rabbinic and halakhic traditions of responses to those verses.[1] Given that Kieślowski is portraying Poland, a Catholic country, most critics have privileged readings of the films from a Christian perspective. Yet in neglecting interpretations that offer rabbinic perspectives, we have failed to understand adequately the complex relationship—one might even call it a hermeneutic encounter, both biblical and philosophical—between film and commandments, a relationship that Kieślowski himself claims informed his research. The director notes that although he and fellow screenwriter Krzysztof Piesiewicz read widely from "both Old and New Testaments . . . we decided fairly quickly to dispense with all of this. . . . We didn't want to adopt the tone of those who praise or condemn. . . . Rather, we wished to say: 'We know no more than you. But maybe it is worth investigating the unknown, if only because the very feeling of not knowing is a painful one.'"[2] Instead of creating a specific and direct correlation among the Ten Commandments and the film series, they "found it easier to solve the problem of the relationship between the films and the individual Commandments: a tentative one. The films should be influenced by the individual Commandments to the same degree that the Commandments influence our daily lives" (xiii–xiv).

By on the one hand seeking a direct correlation among the films and the Ten Commandments and on the other hand ignoring the origins of the verses—words first uttered in Hebrew scripture to the Jewish people—past criticism has failed to explore the presence of Jewish interpretations of the Ten Commandments that, as I will show, lie dormant in the films. Indeed, if we understand that Kieślowski's reference to "our lives" can refer to more than the two screenwriters, then our analysis of the religious dimensions of the film ought to include Jewish responses as well. Becoming more aware of the ample Jewish exegetical traditions can help elucidate the nuances of Kieślowski's film and the particulars of the Decalogue. At the same time, Kieślowski's work presents critical challenges to Jewish readers of the Decalogue who do not stay attuned to complicated ways that these principles influence their "daily lives." If the response to the biblical Decalogue remains routine and rationalized to such an extent that one disregards the verses' intricacies and dilemmas, then the experiential and living significance of the yoke of these principles can become antiquated and irrelevant.

The commentaries I will adduce address existential and ethical significations from within the language and ethos of the biblical text. Moreover, we can better understand much of Kieślowski's work once we experience it alongside the work of Rabbi Joseph B. Soloveitchik (1903–1993), one of the twentieth century's preeminent scholars of Halakha and rabbinic hermeneutics, philosophy, ethics, and intertextual traditions.[3] Though these two asymptotically related lines of thought never actually touch, the reverberations that resound as the lines get closer address those perennial questions that beset—and, in part, define—human existence.

I argue that the insights on traditional Jewish material suggested in many of the lectures and texts of R. Soloveitchik demonstrate that Kieślowski's *Decalogue* might best be witnessed as enactments of a responsible ethics of response.[4] By writing almost exclusively about the first two verses of Exodus 20—literally just sixteen words in the Hebrew text: "And God spoke all these words, saying: I am the Lord, your God, Who took you out of the land Egypt, from the house of slaves"—I explicitly work against the tendency in Kieślowski criticism to omit altogether the opening of Exodus 20 from discussion. In addition, I demonstrate that although the words of the Decalogue in Exodus are indeed addressed to the Jewish people at Mount Sinai, R. Soloveitchik's exegetical works on these two terse verses portray many insights that Kieślowski's film dramatizes, from a non-Jewish perspective and without clear resolutions, yet with utmost importance for those who continue to ask questions that challenge people of all faiths. Both Jewish and non-Jewish viewers can leave the film with stark situations and dilemmas that demand responsible responses. Here, I use the word "responses" to include characters' responses in the film (such as Paweł's [Wojciech Klata] father's response to his son's death or to the mysterious stranger or to the notion of a soul), the Jewish people's responses to God in Exodus (as depicted in biblical verses and classic rabbinic commentaries), the divine response to humans (unique and ambiguous moments in the film such as the wax tears on the Madonna's face, and God's response to the Jewish people's suffering in the house of bondage), and Kieślowski's viewers' responses to his work (such as those demanded by the camera).

I argue that with just this infinitesimally small portion of rabbinic interpretation that I cannot fully represent in these pages, viewers of *Decalogue One* will begin to notice the array of responses in the film building in intensity, creating a demand for responsible responses by anyone confronting Kieślowski's film. While Kieślowski is less interested in specific answers, he is precise in presenting the daily ethical dilemmas and limitations his characters encounter with each other, which he channels via a mysterious sense of transcendence that haunts much of his film. Focusing nearly exclusively on framing scenes in *One* that have not been adequately addressed by film critics, I claim that lingering, haunting images and sequences of human responses and facial expressions actually *demand* that human beings who watch and listen to the film acknowledge the fullness of possibility in the cinematic event by responding to the ethical obligation Kieślowski announces. The exact nature of each participant's response will vary, as I will discuss with R. Soloveitchik's interpretation of an ancient conflict of interpretations—but a response is, dare I say, commanded.

Moreover, a complex rabbinic and halakhic perspective on the Decalogue is a necessary addition to any critical notion of how the commandments "influence our daily lives" in the empirical world as we experience it: "All the frames of reference constructed by the philosophers and psychologists of religion for explaining the varieties of religious experience cannot accommodate halakhic man as far as his reaction to empirical reality is concerned."[5] By presenting a minute portion of a detailed rabbinic perspective on the prefatory words of the Decalogue, I wish to refute the following kind of critical claim: "[*One*] is a meditation on what for Kieślowski would be the first of the Ten Commandments: 'Thou shalt not worship false gods.'"[6] Not only does this falsely overemphasize the "first" part of the biblical Decalogue (it summarily dismisses the very two verses that my entire essay, and, I claim, *One*, address), but it also suggests a far too exclusive "meditation" on "false gods."

And God [Elokim] spoke all these words, saying . . . (Exod. 20:1)[7]

The narrative of *One* begins not with a causal, Aristotelian sequence, but rather with a powerful sense of empirical reality: ice, water, a lake, and the banks of a lake. As viewers can attest, the first few moments of the film, while focused on empirical nature, present a luminescent and haunting musical and imagistic (though not static) preface to the narrative proper. Why? Let us go back to Exodus for a moment. Though not in many lists of the Decalogue, the first verse of chapter twenty in Exodus, according to traditional rabbinic exegesis, signifies an abundance of information with each of its seven words.

Let us first examine the rabbinic understanding of the word "Elokim," which is too often simply translated as "God." Indeed, this issue of translation stays attuned to Kieślowski's film, for much of the father's (Henryk Baranowski) academic lecture and work concern the problems inherent in translating what many consider to be untranslatable (he mentions, for instance, Eliot's comments on poetry). Rashi (1040–1105 CE), who is the biblical and Talmudic commentator par excellence and is the starting point for many Jewish interpretations of the Chumash (Pentateuch), claims that the word "Elokim" signifies exacting punishment; "Elokim" invokes judges and adjudication. Rashi is actually stressing the uniqueness of the Ten Commandments. At times, the indication in the Torah is that people will not be punished if they do not observe volitional commandments.[8] From Rashi's perspective, people might have thought that there is also no punishment for not obeying these Ten Commandments. "Elokim" thus informs us, claims Rashi, that if people do not observe the Decalogue, the judge will adjudicate and people will be punished. The commandments are not optional here.

Rashi is working within a traditional interpretation of Elokim as stated in the Mekhilta, a classic rabbinic commentary on much of Exodus.[9] According to this earlier text, disobeying a command by Elokim causes punishment in one's life (rather than in the afterlife). R. Soloveitchik builds on these commentaries by the Mekhilta and Rashi by bringing us back to "Elokim" as used in the creation narratives of Genesis. For R. Soloveitchik, God's "dual relationship to creation" is expressed in two terms: Elokim and the tetragrammaton. Elokim stands for the ruler of nature; the tetragrammaton stands for the ruler of metaphysical laws.[10] Here, R. Soloveitchik refers to Rashi's comments on Elokim in Genesis: Elokim connotes "a shalit [the ruler of the cosmos] and shofet [the judge of the sociopolitical order]" (Rashi on Genesis 2:5). What does natural rule mean in this situation and how does this natural power of Elokim relate to the opening of the Decalogue? We can better understand natural law by focusing on the opening shots of *One*.[11] First, let us notice the focus on nature in the film's opening shot, which barely receives comment.[12] We must ask what significance imbues Kieślowski's mesmerizing depiction of the resplendent, organic complexity of nature, in the first moments of his *Decalogue*. The slow camera movement shows the partly frozen natural waters moving as if with massive, but inexplicit, meaning.

The partly frozen water, which has been altered by human intervention, indicates how people in the film have defied a crucial meaning of Elokim, or, as R. Soloveitchik explains the term in Rashi and the Mekhilta: *dayan le'hiparah* (a judge to exact punishment), that which legislates both cosmic and sociopolitical orders. Elokim signifies the principles of causality, mathematics, physics; moreover, a "violation of natural law always results in catastrophe" (*Nor'ot ha-Rav* 5:6). For R. Soloveitchik, this kind of violation also occurs when "modern technologically minded" people try to gain absolute control of the environment. Put tersely, "natural law is basically an existential law . . . [one] either accepts the natural law, or causes the termination of [one's] own existence. This is Elokim Shalit [judge]" (*Nor'ot ha-Rav* 5:8). In addition, Elokim is *shofet*, a lawmaker who legislates moral laws, and the outcome is similar: A violation of moral law causes catastrophe. R. Soloveitchik's reading of Rashi (and the Mekhilta) invites us to realize that Exodus 20 begins with Elokim to underscore that these "ten principles constitute the foundation for any civilized existence, and are placed on the same level as the laws governing nature" (*Nor'ot ha-Rav* 5:12).[13]

The term "Elokim" also refers to God's relationship with the universe and with man in the natural universe. In Genesis, for example, Elokim dominates the first chapter ("and Elokim said, 'let there be light,'" and so on).[14] One clear ramification of R. Soloveitchik's reading of Elokim in Exodus 20:1 and in the first chapter of Genesis is that the term refers to a judge who exacts swift punishment in the world that humans inhabit. Violating natural law, such as adding heated water to a frozen pond, will cause a swift effect: Ice will melt (causing Paweł to die). Let us note that in Kieślowski's screenplay, though not in the film itself, this form of natural causation is given as the explanation for the ice on the lake breaking. The justice of natural law is exacting (which is why Elokim is used in the creation story of Genesis 1, when different dimensions and beings of nature are brought into existence). From this perspective, Exodus 20 begins with Elokim to announce that the basic moral laws contained in the Decalogue are not volitional; if disobeyed, dire consequences occur in this earthly, natural, existence.

Our focus on "Elokim," however, is still insufficient to deal with Kieślowski's opening scene, for the partly frozen ice alongside the flowing water and above the natural world living beneath the icy surface ostensibly foreshadows the death of Paweł, the spilled ink bottle, and other haunting images. Indeed, it is not simply death that is foreshadowed, but natural life and death in sentient beings.[15] For instance, the animal kingdom appears in unexpected figurations in this film. The opening shot before we move to Paweł and his father focuses on birds; then we witness Paweł happily responding to the pigeons through the window; shortly thereafter, Paweł encounters the dead dog; then at school Paweł encounters the living guinea pig in the arms of a female peer. At this point Kieślowki switches to the father's lecture, which deals with translation and symbolic transfers of meaning. From this point in the film, animals become representations of animals.[16] For example, Paweł in bed looks at pictures of birds, and quite powerfully, in bed before the second half of the film, Paweł clutches his stuffed elephant. Indeed, this stuffed elephant echoes the unseen but mentioned Miss Piggy and Kermit—puppet creatures (but representing, however comically, animals) who inhabit the mathematical word-problem Paweł's father gives his son toward the start of the film. The father's response to the animal kingdom is exclusively symbolic; the son, though, in his first screen appearance, happily watches the natural drama of pigeons flying and taking crumbs. We can sense the joy on the boy's face. Why should Kieślowski intersperse all of these natural creatures into his metaphysical drama? Why should he move from images of real natural beings to images of either illustrations or fake natural beings?

I would like to suggest, based on the rabbinic interpretation of Elokim as exacting judge of natural laws, that Kieślowski's film intersperses, overlaps, and merges the Decalogue's earthly natural principles—causal, cosmic, earthly, animal nature, and sociopolitical, interhuman nature—with existential and spiritual principles. Just as we should not view part of the Ten Commandments in Exodus as being inherently more natural than other parts, we should not separate all the parts of Kieślowski's *Decalogue*. The films go together, and both the natural and mysteriously transcendent moments are experienced, and responded to, by the same characters. Unlike critics who want to divorce the rational character from the spiritual character, or the natural element from the spiritual element, we can more effectively recognize the honesty and complexity of Kieślowski's project by addressing the mixture of these parts "in our daily lives."

To better understand this idea from a rabbinic perspective, let us return to Exodus 20:1, but now let us focus on the word *kol* (all): "Elokim spoke all [*kol*] these utterances." The word "all," it turns out, displays an enhanced notion of parts existing together. Once again, R. Soloveitchik becomes an exegete of Rashi, who is an exegete of the Mekhilta. A close reading reveals that the biblical verse does not need to use the word *kol*; it is superfluous on the level of simple plot, so it means, for Rashi, that God pronounced all the words simultaneously, in one statement. From a halakhic perspective, R. Soloveitchik points out that *kol* has two meanings: It is a mathematical, additional, integrated sum total of something, and it denotes a gestalt, a wholeness, an intrinsic oneness of total unity. The total of the second is intrinsic unto itself, whereas the total of the first is integrative (adding parts up to a sum total).

The question, then, is what *kol* means in Exodus 20:1. R. Soloveitchik claims that God did not speak "all" as in an additive sum, where each part has its own priority over the complete sum of the parts; if so, then "all" would indeed be superfluous in the verse. Rather, the Mekhilta and Rashi demonstrate that God spoke *all* Ten Commandments in a holistic, gestalt manner. The Decalogue is not the sum of adding ten, mutually independent and unrelated parts, but is an "organic unity" (*Nor'ot ha-Rav* 5:18). The practical consequence of this reading—as Kieślowski might say, the influence on "our daily lives"—is that the "Decalogue is indivisible" (*Nor'ot ha-Rav* 5:18). When the Mekhilta claims that God says it "all" in one saying, the Mekhilta is asserting a powerful message to people: Accept "all" or none at "all."

Unlike critics who want to accept a stark division between science (or reason) and faith in *One*, or a stark division between a ritual or theological notions of morality and secular, humanistic notions of morality, or even a stark separation between each of Kieślowski's ten films, a rabbinic understanding of "all" in Exodus 20:1 would allow us to perceive that the very notion of the Decalogue itself is based on an "all" together or "none at all" attitude. Any question about God's participation in this world cannot be limited to abstract theological conceptions, or those that might be asked in the rooms governed by Paweł's father. Such a question must include Elokim's participation in all natural principles as well. In other words—and this is crucial for an effective response to all of *One*—we need not wait for Paweł's father to enter the church at the end of the film to start encountering the challenges of God's participation in creation and destruction. The opening scene of ice, water, fire, and birds, with the mysterious man staring directly at us, not to mention the crosslike image of the building as the camera moves upward, challenges us to respond to all that we witness (Figure 3–1). Indeed, we are placed in a postevent position at the start of the film, for the aunt, Irena (Maja Komorowska), cries in response to the filmed vision of Paweł, who has already died, on screen before her. The cross-cut to the mysterious man crying suggests that he too has experienced Paweł's death. The film's plot is over before the film begins. What matters is the history of responses and responsible memories, the human responses to others and to moments that suggest mysterious transcendence—even, or perhaps especially, in nature.

Figure 3–1. The mysterious man staring directly at us in *Decalogue One*.

The consequences of this reading, both of the verse and the film, are far-reaching. For R. Soloveitchik, the Mekhilta and Rashi promote a notion of the Decalogue that cannot be based on a secular, social morality that relies for its authority and commandments on either one's own judgment or the legislation of one's moral conscience. R. Soloveitchik quotes a famous passage in the Tosefta (a Tannaitic source from the times of the Mishnah)[17] to show that a Decalogue morality presupposes that "one does not steal from his neighbor unless he also denies the existence of God" (*Nor'ot ha-Rav* 5:20). Kieślowski's film enacts for us the following traditional dilemma: Should one accept authority and legislation of moral norms from outside of oneself, or should one attempt to create a moral conscience that strictly comes from one's own reasoning? *One* embodies the dilemma itself.

In fact, R. Soloveitchik's understanding of the Tosefta brings us to a strange narrative, one that speaks to Paweł's father's agnostic comments in the film about the soul and God. When considering the question of whom society should "consider a contemptible creature," the Tosefta says, "Rabbi Reuven answered that society should hate the atheist, the agnostic, the skeptic, one who denies the existence of his Maker. The philosopher did not understand. He asked, 'How is this so? Why should a non-believer be held in contempt and hate? Isn't faith the private affair of the individual? His skepticism is not harmful to society'" (*Nor'ot ha-Rav* 5:21). Tellingly, R. Soloveitchik emphasizes the social dimensions of a choice that the philosopher perceives affects only the individual: "Rabbi Reuven answered, 'Honor thy Father and Mother, Thou shalt not kill, Thou shalt not fornicate, Thou shalt not steal; there is no man who will violate these precepts until he has denied the existence of his Maker'" (*Nor'ot ha-Rav* 5:21). For this Tosefta, if there is no faith in God, social relations on all levels will disintegrate.

Kieślowski, though, is surely not arguing that we should hate Paweł's father or his skepticism. What he might be arguing is that in a society there might not be (typologically) Paweł's father without Paweł's aunt. How so? To better understand the social dimension here, let us move to R. Soloveitchik's interpretation of the traditional rabbinic stance against secular ethics in terms of the opening words of the Decalogue, and, of all things, Marxism, which brings to mind the political history and context looming behind the massive edifice that is the main structural setting for Kieślowski's film.[18] For R. Soloveitchik, "Marxism is fundamentally an ethical credo . . . [since the] underlying idea of Marxist econometrics is justice. Labor, according to Marx, creates the economic value system, and hence the so-called ibber-wurth belongs to the laborers and not to the investor or the Capitalist" (*Nor'ot ha-Rav* 5:24). Yet, based on his analysis of Russian Marxism, R. Soloveitchik claims that this "ethical doctrine turned into a gospel of brutality and tyranny" (*Nor'ot ha-Rav* 5:24), for without adherence to a moral power beyond oneself, without the first verses of the Decalogue, which stress human relations with the divine, there can be no adherence to the second half of the Decalogue, which stresses human relations with humans.[19]

The *kol* (all) of Exodus 20:1 turns out to mean an ethical principle: The Decalogue cannot be divided since it is a gestalt whole. One cannot respond to parts of the Decalogue without responding to all of the Decalogue. Theological faith must be integrated into secular morality: "Man cannot legislate his own moral laws" (*Nor'ot ha-Rav* 5:26). Moreover, argues R. Soloveitchik, ethos and ritual are so bound together that they are, for most purposes, identical. There is no opposition between the sacred and the mundane, the academic lecture hall or the hall of a house of worship. Sacredness, unlike what Paweł's father might think as he bursts into the church at the end of the film, is not limited to cultic gestures, to rituals, to the ecclesiastical. R. Soloveitchik even calls this attitude of strict separation "moral schizophrenia" (*Nor'ot ha-Rav* 5:29). Unlike such schism, the *kol* unity of the Decalogue means that no moral system can be divorced from faith. Kieślowski's film as a whole, not a specific character within the film, performs these very conflicts.

Not only should one not bracket *One* from all ten films, but one should also respond to the whole of *One* in terms of metaphysical, spiritual, and physical laws. In other words, the father's lecture on theories of translation needs to be applied to the film itself. Whether the film translates real birds into illustrations; animals into stuffed animals; natural calculation into seemingly unnatural events, frozen ice into melted ice; candle wax drippings on a painting into (possibly) real tears of the Madonna; human memory into computer memory (or even, in the academic lecture, "unlimited memory" of a translator); digital commands into locked doors and running water; Polish into English (Paweł is supposed to take English lessons, but his tutor is sick); or Hebrew verses on the Ten Commandments into Kieślowski's *Decalogue*: All of these translations suggest that responses to transcendence cannot be kept inside a single location (the walls of a church) or a single time (either of happiness, during the aunt's time with Paweł or Paweł's time with the birds; or of horrible sadness, during the time after Paweł's death, when the father's inward state is the focus of the screen or during Paweł's response to the

Decalogue One

dead dog). Just as the opening shot does not stay focused on fixed ice, but moves along frozen and flowing water, so too what was ostensibly mundane, even a bottle of ink, can suddenly translate into an intimation of mysterious transcendence and sacredness, and vice versa, as happens with the holy water turned into a block of ice in the shape of a tear on the father's head at the film's end.

Yet, while the array of responses is starting to come to the critical fore, the nature of this command is still not clear enough. That is because, in part, we have not yet addressed the last word in Exodus 20:1, *laymor*, which means "saying." In a simple reading, the word appears to be superfluous. If God "spoke all these words," then why should the verse add a word that means "saying as follows"? If, however, the act of saying became a performance by respondents, then the word accrues a constellation of meanings. God "spoke all these words" in order that the people respond by saying something in acknowledgment of "all" these words. As Rashi says, quoting Rabbi Yishmael's opinion from the Mekhilta, "this teaches us that the people would answer 'yes' to the positive commandments and 'no' to the negative commandments" (Rashi on *laymor* in Exodus 20:1). The Mekhilta itself, as R. Soloveitchik points out, also includes Rabbi Akiva's opinion that the people responded yes to both positive and negative commandments.

What parts of the verse troubled the Mekhilta? For R. Soloveitchik, there are two issues: one halakhic, the other semantic. In terms of Halakha, there are intricate legal procedures for a convert to undergo to accept "the yoke of the commandments" (*Nor'ot ha-Rav* 5:32). To accept this yoke fully, it was insufficient to say, "we will do and we will hear/learn" in response to the whole Torah. God required that each *dibur*, each saying, "each law, each principle, be accepted individually" (*Nor'ot ha-Rav* 5:32). In terms of semantics (the second issue), the word *laymor* in Hebrew often means "to be repeated" by someone (usually Moses) to an audience (usually the Jewish people). The exegetical problem here is that God addresses the people directly; God does not use Moses as a hermeneutic intermediary. Thus, *laymor* semantically appears to be logically irrelevant. The Mekhilta therefore claims that *laymor* actually indicates responsiveness, acceptance, assent, or confirmation by the people: "'laymor' has the connotation of being accepted, of taking upon oneself, of being committed, of responding to the great challenge" (*Nor'ot ha-Rav* 5:33).

With this hermeneutic of response in place precisely during the opening verse and scene of the Decalogue, we must ask what the difference is between Rabbi Yishmael's account and Rabbi Akiva's. Here, R. Soloveitchik explores the psychological, legal, and ethical distinctions between the two to such an extent that he connects this dispute to the critique of secular ethics whenever the concept of *chok* (commandments that human reason cannot rationalize) gets removed from practice "in our daily lives." According to Rabbi Yishmael (which is Rashi's only account), the Jews accepted, that is, responded to all the positive commands with the affirmative "yes": "I am your God"—"yes." The people accepted, that is, responded to all the negative commands with the negative "no": "You shall not accept other gods"—"no." On the other hand, according to Rabbi Akiva, the people responded "yes" to everything. Phrased in a modern philosophical manner, the foundation of this conflict emanates from different interpretations of "the philosophy of motivation" (*Nor'ot ha-Rav* 5:34). Here R. Soloveitchik provides a quotidian anecdote to explain the ancient dispute. If R. Soloveitchik were to tell his grandson Moshe not to play with another child because the child is poorly behaved, his grandson might respond either by saying "'No, Zeidy. I won't play with him,' or he may answer, 'Yes, Zeidy, I shall not play with him'" (*Nor'ot ha-Rav* 5:34–35). For R. Sloveitchik, what distinguishes this answer is whether his grandson agrees with his assessment, or whether he agrees to be obedient: "When Moshe tells me, 'No Zeidy, I shall not play with him,' he means to say that he concurs with me as far as my evaluation. . . . [But if] he answers 'Yes, I will not play with him' [it] means . . . 'I shall respect your wishes. I myself do not see any harm in fraternizing with Johnny. . . . However, your order will be carried out'" (*Nor'ot ha-Rav* 5:34–35). This fictional distinction of responses—narrated clearly in terms that affect our daily lives—embodies an essential question in Halakha and, for that matter, a question any individual who seeks to obey a commandment might ask: What motivates one's obedience to a law? Should a person follow Rabbi Yishmael—answering "No, I won't play"— out of an existential motivation that expresses an inward urge to agree with an ethical norm? Or should a person follow Rabbi Akiva, answering, "Yes, I will not play": an act of obedience that is imposed from without?

R. Soloveitchik's distinction applies to the two kinds of decrees uttered in the Decalogue. The majority of commandments in the Decalogue are *mishpatim*, usually defined as norms that one considers to be reasonable, not *chukim*, usually defined as ritualistic norms that do not have explicit reasons. The stereotypical division between *mishpatim* and *chukim* keeps these norms in mutually exclusive categories, if not in opposition. *Chukim* are not to be understood fully by means of rationally derived principles, but are to be accepted out of submission to the law. *Mishpatim*, such as the decrees that deal with interhuman relationships, are comprehensible by reasonable people. This, for R. Soloveitchik, is Rabbi Yishmael's philosophy of motivation: We use our reasoning to find negative acts, like stealing or killing, despicable, so we reject them.

However, Rabbi Akiva's philosophy of motivation presents a radically different psychology and ethics: We conform to the negative commands *because* of the normative decree.[20] For Rabbi Akiva, there is no motivational difference between the *mishpatim* and the *chukim*. Without using any Derridean language, R. Soloveitchik deconstructs the standard opposition between *chukim* and *mishpatim* to claim that a "clearly defined distinction between chukim and mishpatim is almost non-existent. It is a sheer illusion" (*Nor'ot ha-Rav* 5:41). Although R. Soloveitchik demonstrates that there are occasions when stealing or murder might be accepted by one's own conscience, and even acceptable by society, he claims that whether one truly understands the full nuances of the decree or not, the judge in these cases cannot be human criteria of ethics or justice: "Left to its own conscience, society, little by little, simply destroys the very fabric of its morality" (*Nor'ot ha-Rav* 5:45). Ethical reasonableness is an insufficient source for social justice; people cannot defer to their own sensitivity. The responses of hatred to the atheist (in the Tosefta) is not necessarily a hatred of a human being, but a hatred of an ideological ethics that remains grounded in pure inwardness, a rationality understandable by a person's own cognitive powers. Marxism as an ethical system is to be despised, from this perspective, because it attempts to base the ethics of the Decalogue entirely on human cognition: "It is not atheism that can replace God, but a new godless religion such as Communism" ("Aseret ha-Dibrot," 117).

In his own precise manner, Kieślowski's opening film presents this ancient debate about motivation for all (*kol*) the episodes to follow. What is the natural motivation behind both Paweł's father's and his aunt's beliefs, fidelities, trusts, and behaviors? The word *laymor* in Exodus 20:1 signifies acceptance by those who receive the Decalogue. The nature of this acknowledgment is precisely what Kieślowski demands of his viewers when he has his characters and his scenes dramatize the conflicting motivations. Instead of seeing *One* as only depicting a conflict between scientific and religious beliefs, which is a more traditional understanding of the film, I argue that we should now see the first episode as dramatizing the ethical tension of responses to noncognitive, nonrational experiences and obligations as well as to cognitive, rational, mathematically calculated experiences—particularly through the camera's intense focalization on facial responses of the natural father and aunt, the facial responses of the iconic Madonna mother (with her tears of wax), the facial response of the chess master to the father-son winning team, the facial response of a perplexed human to a computer screen that is "ready" for something, and the facial responses of the mysterious man at the fire.[21] As R. Soloveitchik claims, "God may be found in science, aesthetics, and morale, in crisis or in triumph" ("Aseret ha-Dibrot," 116); we might add, in an aunt's hug with her nephew. Even in an academic room, which ironically and sadly anticipates the father's silent rage and inward struggles at the front of the church, the camera lingers on the responses of the father's audience, and most intensely, on the young Paweł's directorial responses of framing his father from different angles and perspectives (all occurring as the professor discusses aesthetic potentials for computers and the problem of translating what might be untranslatable). When searching for a source of human morality, a response to scientific order is not, at base, that much different from a response to beauty. Moreover, if we understand R. Soloveitchik's interpretation of Rabbi Akiva, then as Kieślowski shows, human beings are fully capable of reasoning and killing, of cognitive rationality and immorality, of creating artificial systems of translations, computing, beliefs, and a felt sense of a divine gift in a human embrace. For Rabbi Akiva, though, the first way to stop murder is to submit to a force outside of oneself, to obey a divine decree that comes from outside human invention. Kieślowski films these philosophical differences to demand a response to it "all" from us, his film's respondents.

From this perspective, one in which, as the Mekhilta underscores, there are not ten utterances, but a single utterance by God, the entire series of films relies on our initial response to the natural opening and to these first characters' responsive and affective convictions and motivations. Kieślowski's film moves us to a crucial realization: Ritual commandments cannot be separated from commonsensical ethical ones. Building in incremental intensity, the frozen (natural) water that cracks and the freezing water that flows beneath the icy surface—the opening and simultaneously the absent narrative center of the entire film, since we never see the moments of Paweł's death in icy water—is also the frozen (spiritual) water that Paweł's father puts to his head at the end of the film. Natural cosmic orders cannot be separated from socioeconomic orders, which cannot be separated from social justice, which cannot be separated from the motivation behind a response. I would even claim that Kieślowski is, ironically, at his clearest when he does not film the event of Paweł's death: What better way to say to us that the film is about the responses to that event, from start, to middle, to end? Again, even the face of the watcher seen toward the start of the film—before we even see Paweł with his father—demands our response to a felt acknowledgment. Even without knowing ancient Talmudic and halakhic disputes, Kieślowski films the utterly intense, even horrific, resolve of human beings' responses to *chok*. Do we, those of us watching in the audience, want to say "yes" or "no" to Kieślowski's pronouncement?

> *I am God [tetragrammaton], your God [Elokekha], Who took you out of the land of Egypt, from the house of slaves. (Exod. 20:2)*[22]

The next verse is often quoted as the first official saying in the biblical Decalogue. It might at first seem more familiar to Kieślowski's critics, but the rabbinic exegesis will defamiliarize it by taking us to vastly different dimensions of divine expression and human conflicts, specifically, the relation between doubts and responses. The first word stresses the speaker's ethos—*Anokhi* (meaning "I")—by referring to a particular event, the exodus from Egypt and bondage, rather than to a universal emphasis on nature or genesis. Why, as classic Jewish commentators ask, does God not describe Himself as the Creator of the cosmos rather than as the Redeemer? Rashi provides multiple responses. First, he says, "taking you out of Egypt is sufficient reason for you to be subject to Me." This interpretation agrees with that of Ibn Ezra, who "quoting Yehudah Halevi, says that the reason for this was that the Jews had not experienced Creation but had experienced the Exodus" ("Aseret ha-Dibrot," 114–115).[23] They needed to respond to their personal redeemer. This personal experience might also help to explain why Kieślowski stresses the extremely personal experiences of his characters. Unlike a philosopher or theologian, Kieślowski does not film an abstract philosophical treatise on the powers of creation. His characters live in the ethical conflicts and emotional turmoil of their personal, daily lives. One cannot quite relate to the Decalogue if it does not address the intimately felt, lived experiences of human beings who suffer, who are in bondage, who are enslaved.

Rashi augments this explanation by observing the strangeness of the word *Anokhi* ("I"). In terms of the Hebrew language, one must ask why God does not use the more standard Hebrew word for "I," *Ani*. Here, R. Soloveitchik distinguishes the semantic valences of the two words for "I." One would use *ani* when "I" is the subject of the sentence, but the "emphasis [of the sentence] is on the action" ("Aseret ha-Dibrot," 115). One would use *anokhi* when one wants to proclaim and stress one's very identity. The verse, in other words, has God proclaiming that his identity is God. Why? Because people at the time, claims Rashi, encountered different appearances of the divine. During the exodus, at the parting of the waters, God appears "as a mighty warrior," but now, here at Mount Sinai, God appears "as an old man, full of mercy." Out of concern that the people would confusedly think that there are multiple divinities, God says "*Anokhi*"—it is I, the same God, the same identity. Crucially, what R. Soloveitchik claims we learn here is that "God's actions differ . . . since actions are in response to different needs, to different situations" (*Nor'ot ha'Rav* 12:109). Since *imitatio dei* in rabbinic discourses demands the human imitation of divine characteristics, we need to learn degrees of change and appearances in response to different confrontations. That is, unlike a perception of God as an actor fixed in the same motion or appearance constantly, R. Soloveitchik's interpretation shows how beings need to respond differently, to behave differently, depending on the situation and needs.[24]

It is precisely here (with God in both warrior and merciful guises), however, that our analysis brings us to a crucial difference between one of the film's notions of God (and the human response to the divine) as expressed by Paweł's aunt, and R. Soloveitchik's emphasis on rabbinic Judaism's conceptions of divine manifestations. After Paweł says that he feels love when embracing his aunt, his aunt says that that is where God is. This utterance by the aunt does not mandate that God is found exclusively in interhuman embraces, but her comment about God's location or felt presence does appear to emphasize love more than anything else. This particularly Christian view does not correspond with R. Soloveitchik's halakhic perspective. The divergence in the asymptotic relation I have created intensifies here. Namely, "Judaism, as a moral discipline, is not a homogenous discipline of love and compassion. Judaism is also very practical; it knows that man cannot protect himself with love alone" ("Asert ha-Dibrot," 115). In other words, complex moral discipline is precisely what the opening of the Ten Commandments stresses. When we consider the notion of *imitatio dei* or when we seek God's appearance in the world, we should understand that God assumes multiple guises on earth, at times a being who exacts punishment and justice, at times a being who is imbued with and expresses love and mercy.[25] The translation, so to speak, depends on the situation's responsible responses. The aunt's notions and expressions of love and God are not necessarily wrong, but they are insufficient to express or depict the manifold nature of the divine. It is not the case that we should leave the film insisting that only Paweł's father needs to add his sister's faith to his own existence; it is the case, rather, that the sister also needs to add her brother's understanding of the cosmos to her notion of God and love. In both cases, moments of violence and death would destroy any person's conception of the divine if the divine only includes a human sense of love in the living embrace of two humans. Human beings "cannot protect [themselves] with love alone."

Rashi does not leave us with just a focus on multiple responses and guises. He adds another interpretation, one that stresses difference in sound, voice, and direction. In turn, I argue, we can use his commentary to address the significant direction of technological sounds in the second half of *One*. The people at Sinai might have been confused about multiple identities of God due to His different actions and appearances ("Aseret ha-Dibrot," 115). Thus, the Decalogue teaches people to resist a fixed position; as part of the injunction to imitate the divine, we must learn to adapt to needs and circumstances. In addition, claims Rashi, the people might have also been confused "because [they] heard many sounds [during the revelation], as it says 'the sounds' (Exodus 20:15) coming from four directions and from the heavens and earth" (Rashi on Exodus 20:2). Here, the potential doubt in the people's responses addresses the relation between identity and difference: Because voices were coming from all directions—the word *kolos* in Exodus 20:15 is in plural—people might have inferred that there are many divinities. Hence, God announces "*Anokhi*"—I, with my unique identity—am the only God speaking. R. Soloveitchik claims that the multiple directions "demonstrate . . . the universality of Jewish law [which] is not bound nor confined to one area" (*Nor'ot ha'Rav* 12:111). Speaking in America and aware of the Diaspora, R. Soloveitchik posits that regardless of location, people must abide by identical commandments.

Whereas this interpretation explains the four directions, it does not account for the additional claim of two directions and voices "from heaven and earth." For this reason, R. Soloveitchik shows a dialectic that, I argue, works effectively to explain Kieślowski's need to have both the sister and the father respond to Paweł, as well as his need to have Paweł's father and sister respond, each in different locations and at different times, to screens (television and computer) and representations that point to the divine (the picture of the Pope and the artwork representing the Madonna). Additionally, it turns out to address the multiple sounds that play such crucial roles in the transformations of the father's ethos and the narrative structure. God's voice needs to come from above, or the heavens, to respond to people who wish to live the lives of saints, lives "in defiance of society" (*Nor'ot ha'Rav* 12:113), for Torah principles and an ethical existence. At the same time, God's voice needs to come from the earth below to respond to people who live within society, in an earthly, carnal existence—people who do "not work to surrender nor withdraw from joys of this world" (*Nor'ot ha'Rav* 12:113). In other words, God does not only address the saintly life of the Pope in Irena's picture; God also addresses those who toil in the frozen earth and water, those who need to light fires for warmth and for heating water (which includes both Paweł and the mysterious man).

Thus, for R. Soloveitchik, when God announces "*Anokhi*/I am God [tetragrammaton], your God," God is asserting that there are multiple ways for people to reach the divine. On the one hand, for example, one can be a great scholar and academic, demanding the most from one's intellect in order to use one's intellect to reach the divine. Indeed, one of R. Soloveitchik's major contributions to Jewish notions of *imitatio dei* (developed extensively in *Halakhic Man*) is the obligation to imitate God's creativity; thus, R. Soloveitchik is a major advocate of advanced, intellectual creativity and self-creativity.[26] One might even say that R. Soloveitchik's heroic paradigm for the typological halakhic person is the mathematician who calculates an ideal system, who desires to bring the divine down to earth, much more than the emotionally zealous religious figure who desires to leave this natural existence and reach the divine. On the other hand, one can approach the divine more experientially and emotionally, not just as Paweł's aunt suggests, but also as Paweł's father does in the last scenes of the film, in which the force of the film arrives not in the viewer's clarity of whether or not the father finds God or finds answers, but rather in the poignant approach of this human being who has been forced to acknowledge a clear limitation of human existence. Kieślowski has us ponder an act of rebellion (overturning the table, or even coming into the church at all) if one does not believe at all in a divine transcendence. Kieślowski does not show us that there is no atheist in a foxhole (the cliché of turning to God in times of duress); in a more challenging way, he takes us on the inward journey of the father's range of responses.

Indeed, it is at this turning point in the film's narrative, once the living Paweł no longer appears in the film (though he will reappear on the taped film shown on the television monitor at the end), that we should listen to the sounds of the film. Kieślowski's critics have brought much critical acumen to bear on the ink bottle and spreading ink, but what of the sounds the father starts to hear while he tries to wash all the ink off his hands? From this point until the father realizes it is Paweł who had died beneath the ice, we hear the sounds of a plane, an ambulance, a helicopter: technological sounds announcing a terrible revelation. This indeed might be the film director's own translation of the first two biblical verses immediately following the Decalogue in Exodus: "And all the people could see the sounds [*kolos*] and the flames, the sound of the shofar and the smoking mountain; the people saw and they moved and they stood from afar. They said to Moses, 'You speak to us and we shall hear; let God not speak to us lest we die'" (Exod. 20:15–16). The aesthetics of synesthesia (seeing sounds), the mixture of sense perceptions, is precisely what Kieślowski has us witness as both the start of the father's recognition, and the heterogeneous, experiential, inward journey that the father endures for the rest of the film. Indeed, the rest of the narrative is structured as a response to terrible technological sounds that reverberate in, and confront, this parent's very being. His changing facial expressions and speeds, his decisions to take the stairs or the elevator, his emotionally wrenching stare, are all responses to the mixed sounds and sights that announce a profound encounter with absolute limitation, not just a revelation. The long stretches of silence and haunting sounds from a wind instrument on the soundtrack not only contrast with the extensive use of logos by the father (not to mention his lecture on language) in the first half of the film, but set up the confrontation with the divine in the church.

Before I accentuate this notion of limitation in the film and in the biblical Decalogue further, we should ask how Exodus 20:2 might lend credence to this rabbinic emphasis on each person's response to the divine, and the divine's address to each individual. It turns out that the grammar of the verse provides potential support for such a claim. In Hebrew, the Decalogue in Exodus (and in Deuteronomy) has God use the singular "Elokekha" (your God); however, those commandments and phrases from the Decalogue that appear in Leviticus, starting in chapter 19, have God speak in plural "Elokeikhem" (your God). The grammatical difference stands out even more when one reads what God says after the Exodus Decalogue: "You have seen that from the heavens I have spoken" (Exod. 20:19). In Hebrew, "You have seen" is plural, yet the Decalogue is in the singular. Why? Basing himself partly on the Ramban's exegesis of the verses, R. Soloveitchik reinterprets the Ten Commandments in terms of the classic conflict between an individual and a social group (the one and the many).[27] A person should not assume that God only addresses the group of people in the plural. If an individual disobeys, the individual will be punished. Similar to the halakhic analysis of *kol*, the analysis here relies on the halakhic sense of "following the majority." For R. Soloveitchik, one cannot rely on what the majority accomplishes. Every individual is unique and must observe the law "regardless of what the members of society do" (*Nor'ot ha'Rav* 12:120). The singular form of the Decalogue addresses each and every individual personally. For each respondent to Kieślowski's film, the obligation addresses not the group of critics or academics; it matters not what the majority rules about the film. The personal response to the film is an integral part of its haunting power.

In addition, a rabbinic approach in the manner of R. Soloveitchik must also stress the strong force on limitations, on retraction and contraction. How does this emanate from the multidirectionality of divine voices, which complicates the relationship between diversity and unity? For R. Soloveitchik, God, omnipresent, contracts in order to create the revelation at Mount Sinai: "Just as God presents himself in both modes, so man must emulate him in both expression and in self limitation. Man is duty bound to manage his own moral law as modern man is inclined to do" ("Aseret ha-Dibrot," 116). Is there a more effective response to the very first spoken words in Kieślowski's film? Unlike critics who ignore the complicated and resonant beginnings of the film, again, the first spoken words by Paweł and his father present to us in quotidian, experiential terms, this exact conflict between human self-creation/expansion and human self-limitation/negation. The first words uttered by Paweł's father are numbers: He is counting aloud his push-ups, a physical enactment of self-creation and expansion. Paweł announces clearly and nicely, "That's my limit." The boy recognizes and articulates his limitations. From this perspective, the film contains the narrative of the boy's actualized limitations, including the literal embodiment of human finitude. The father confronts, and must respond to, a dramatic, horrific law of limitation that as a modern man he might have been too disinclined to apply up to that point.

This stress on singular, personal responses, though, is only part of the biblical emphasis. To account for the locations of "Your God" in the plural form, R. Soloveitchik argues that this plural grammatical number is also crucial, for it teaches us an ethics of responsibility, namely, one for others: "The plural form binds us all to one another" ("Aseret ha-Dibrot," 116). In other words, introspection, repentance, and self-creation are all obligations, but too much introspection neglects the significance of the obligations each individual has to others. This distinction between group and individual comes forth powerfully in at least two scenes that contrast Paweł's father with larger groups. One encounter occurs when Paweł's father goes outside to test the ice on the lake personally. As he walks he encounters first the face of the mysterious man staring back at him (suggesting a potential epiphany, however quotidian it might be) and then "a nighttime gathering of silent men and women in front of a church (a wake, perhaps? A political gathering? Whatever it is, the occasion is solemn, and the people holding hands)" (Kickasola 173). While apt, Kickasola's description misses a significant inference: At the very least, "people holding hands" indicates a group. Kieślowski has filmed Paweł's father, the introspective, cognitive, modern man, encountering a group that could provide a responsible response. No such response appears from the solitary father.

Another encounter that accentuates the stark contrast between the individuality of modern man—Paweł's father—and the larger group appears when the camera films the utterly painful inward response by the many and one to Paweł's dead body. While Kickasola astutely notes the juxtaposition between the group's response to kneel, and the father's refusal to kneel (173), I suggest that this reverential movement invokes the people's awe-filled response at Mount Sinai (Exod. 20:15–16). I would argue that Paul Coates's description here manages to express part of the scene's significance: "The . . . piercing wind instrument breathes mystery and mortality . . . mournfully marking the fishing of Paweł's body from the icy water as the crowd sinks to its knees to acknowledge the *mysterium* of the event."[28] The critic's language of "fishing" and "sinking" marks precisely the response of acknowledgment to the "*mysterium*." Krzysztof's face and actions wonderfully portray his encounter with the self's limitation when confronting the *mysterium* of existence. He is still not ready to acknowledge any meaningful relation with a group (other than possibly his *tzimtzum* students, with whom he clearly holds a position of power). Dramatized before us, this threshold demands our own responses to the film. How will we respond to a nearly inexpressible exhibition of an ethical norm: Will we engage in *tzimtzum*, in contracting, in kneeling, or will we continue to count onwards, building up our bodies and minds (like the father does with his push-ups)? In what context might one response be more effective than the other?

This brings us to the last words of the second verse in Exodus 20: "Who took you out of the land of Egypt, from the house of slaves." Why are the last two words necessary (*mi-beis avadim*, from the house of slaves), and are they not implied in the previous phrase? First, R. Soloveitchik offers Rabbi Hirsch's distinction between two types of slaves: a free individual who is sold into slavery, and an individual who is born into a family and heritage and tradition of slavery.[29] The first individual knows to detest slavery and explicitly desires freedom. The second type of slave does not necessarily know what freedom means. It was not until these slaves suffered physical tortures that they cried out to God, but even then they did not truly understand freedom. Therefore, God says, in Exodus 20:2, according to R. Soloveitchik's exposition of Rabbi Hirsch, "You never asked for freedom, because you did not know what freedom meant. Yet, I took you out of the house of bondage" (*Nor'ot ha'Rav* 12:133). This reading provides an additional insight as to why the Decalogue is addressed in a personal, experiential manner rather than from a voice reminding the people exclusively of the narrative of creation in Genesis. It also announces a clearly political dimension to Kieślowski's seemingly apolitical film. Do the Polish people reveal an awareness of their political state of existence? Are the people of this concrete complex asking for freedom from the current Polish state, for release from physical duress, for human acknowledgment, for clear answers? Is Kieślowski subtly suggesting that Poland is caught in generational bondage, or is he filming a free individual who is suddenly experiencing existential bondage? Here, too, the film's respondents are obligated to provide their own responsible responses.

R. Soloveitchik, however, makes these questions more emotionally poignant and relevant to modern people, for he does not leave the verse alone with Rabbi Hirsch's exegesis. Instead, he adds Rashi's perspective to connect the verse to political torture, to totalitarian and Nazi regimes. According to Rashi, one can be a slave to the state or a slave to a private citizen. Whereas an individual master might be slightly generous, inclined to practice ethical laws, and merciful, according to R. Soloveitchik, the state, state officials, state taskmasters, "are generally sadists, murderers, and criminals, who find joy in torturing people" (*Nor'ot ha'Rav* 12:133–134). The correspondences to Poland's history are an intrinsic part of Kieślowski's implicit vision for us to acknowledge and to which we must respond.

Before we leave the second verse (Exod. 20:2) and its implied pronouncements concerning bondage and suffering, as well as personal relationships, let us focus on one more word to help address the film's famous scene with the portrait of the Madonna: *hotzeitikha*, which means "who took you out" (of the land of Egypt from the house of slaves). According to traditional rabbinic sources, this can be translated syntactically to mean: "'I [God] have gone out with you from the land of Egypt.' We both were oppressed. We both were in bondage. We both gained freedom. This singular relationship which binds [God] with man, within one fellowship, is a result not of creation [hence, verse two does not refer to God the creator of the cosmos]" (*Nor'ot ha'Rav* 12:48), but of redemption and freedom from Egyptian bondage and slavery. God was, in this figurative sense, in bondage with the people, feeling and experiencing the suffering, humiliation, pain, and degradation right alongside each person. Indeed, this reading links back to the notion of *tzimtzum* or contraction. Based on the Ramban's exegesis, R. Soloveitchik asserts that God "contracts," as it were, to be—in suffering, in oppression, in bondage—with the individuals who are unaware of the meaning of freedom (*Nor'ot ha'Rav* 12:50).

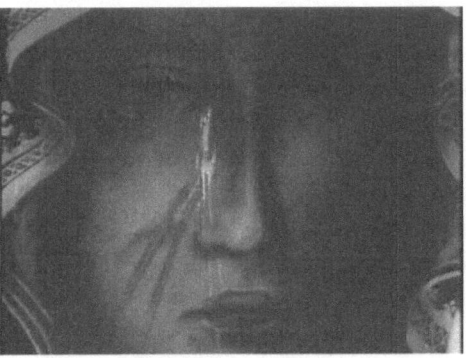

Figure 3-2. Dripping tears in *Decalogue One*.

Perhaps the most understudied response in the film, one that aptly demonstrates the rabbinic tradition of God's Transcendent Presence, is the explicit framing device of the aunt's facial response. Critics tend to use Catholic and Protestant frameworks to focus on the father's response. For Haltof, Krzysztof "in frustration purposely destroys the makeshift altar with the icon of the Black Madonna of Częstochowa (*Matka Boska Częstochowska*) ... The dripping wax forms a few 'tears' on the Madonna's face and she looks as if she is crying" (83) (Figure 3-2). For Coates, the "miracle of the Weeping Virgin is both bitterly and poignantly ironic: her hot tears are wax, and it is really the father who weeps" (96).[30] Kickasola suggests, "Perhaps the Madonna does cry, symmetrical with the tears of Theophanes [the mysterious man/angel figure]: a film beginning and ending in divine grief. Such would be the Catholic perspective; a Protestant might reflect Coates's interpretation: she could not protect the child because 'perhaps she is mere mortal.' Garbowski suggests the tears are not for Paweł, who now has 'all the answers to his innocent questions,' but rather for Krzysztof, 'the one who is most in pain'" (173–174).[31] But what would a response informed by a rabbinic tradition look like? While the Madonna herself would not be part of the picture, Kieślowski's perfectly ambiguous, magically realistic, depiction of wax and tears, responds nearly directly to the rabbinic tradition that has God "contract" to be with those who suffer physical, metaphysical, social, familial, and personal devastation and abrupt, utter, unexpected duress, finitude, and limitation. Moreover, God is not simply with those who suffer; God "contracts" for those others. Exodus 20:2 expresses God's words as utterances signified by the Redeemer who also joined the people to gain freedom. The wax tears are perhaps the limit-test of what Kieślowski can intimate through filmic representation of the unrepresentable. It is not necessarily a deity crying tears of grief over "His Creation affected by the Fall" (Kickasola 174). It is not the relation to Genesis here; it is the personal relationship experienced by those who suffer now, in their daily lives. In addition, whereas Kickasola presents a persuasive argument for connecting the tears to Kieślowski's respondents, I would further develop this claim. Transcendence is with and for us in suffering, but the divine commands us to respond. We, the respondents, should perform an act of *imitatio dei* by contracting and creating ourselves. Therefore, unlike Kickasola's question, which asks the Divine for justification—"Why haven't you done anything about this?" (174)—my own question tries to emulate a contraction of self: Why have I (not "you") not done anything about this? What can I do for the other who suffers?

Kieślowski accentuates the creation of mechanisms that might mollify other people's suffering, from Paweł's comments about helping others to the father's technological advances, which Paweł proudly displays to his aunt.[32] Along with R. Soloveitchik, Kieślowski asks us to consider that the "logos can easily be stretched in various directions.... Without chok, every social and moral law can be rationalized away" (Shapiro, *Rabbi Joseph B. Soloveitchik on Pesach, Sefirat ha-Omer and Shavu'ot*, 238). A responsible ethical response demands that one's obligation to respond emanates from a decree beyond one's own rationalized conscience. Before one "rationalizes away" rituals and the "grandeur of religion [which] lies in its mysterium tremendum, its magnitude, and its ultimate incomprehensibility" ("Sacred and Profane," 6), one might achieve more by limiting oneself, acknowledging the *chok* that cannot be rationalized away.

"Religion . . . deepens the problems [of life] but never intends to solve them," writes R. Soloveitchik ("Sacred and Profane," 6). Kieślowski might indeed be a major religious filmmaker who seeks to deepen the problems of life and what we experience as incomprehensible. To redeem those who are slaves—to the state, to an individual human master, to a computer, to oneself—the director and the Orthodox rabbi use different expressions and traditions to articulate how and why people respond to the Decalogue's principles. If we maintain a fundamental division between the mundane and the sacred, we might continue our present, agonizingly inward journey, a movement that fails to limit constructively one's ego or to create oneself. Indeed, as Kieślowski states, we have already "become too egotistic, too much in love with ourselves and our needs, and it's as if everybody else has somehow disappeared into the background" (*KK*, 145).

NOTES

The first epigraph, by Rabbi Joseph B. Soloveitchik, comes from "Sacred and Profane," in *Shiurei HaRav: A Conspectus of the Public Lectures of Rabbi Joseph B. Soloveitchik*, ed. Joseph Epstein (Hoboken, N.J.: Ktav Publishing, 1994), 6. Further references are cited in the text. The second epigraph is from the film *Decalogue One*, in *The Decalogue*, DVD, directed by Krzysztof Kieślowski (Chicago: Facets Video, 2003).

1. Halakha, often defined as the ideal normative legal system of Judaism, can refer to the entirety of Jewish law, or the legal decision after a discussion, or one particular law. Yet, for Rabbi Soloveitchik such definitions are too static and atemporal; Halakha "is best understood as a mode of thinking, a way of interpreting man and his environment" (*Shiurei HaRav*, 130). Etymologically, "Halakha" comes from "halakh," going, walking, or being underway.

2. Krzysztof Kieślowski, "An Introduction," in Krzysztof Kieślowski and Krzysztof Piesiewicz, *Decalogue: The Ten Commandments*, trans. Phil Cavendish and Susannah Bluh (London: Faber and Faber, 1991), xiii–xiv. Hereafter cited in the text.

3. Born in Pruzha, Poland (Pruzhana, Poland/Belorussia) in 1903, Rabbi Soloveitchik studied at the Free Polish University in the early 1920s. My essay thus functions as a comparative analysis of two Polish commentators on the Decalogue. See R. Aharon Lichtenstein, "Rabbi Joseph Soloveitchik," in *Great Jewish Thinkers of the Twentieth Century*, ed. Simon Noveck (Washington: B'nai B'rith Books, 1963), 281–298; and "The Rav at Jubilee: An Appreciation," in *Rabbi Joseph B. Soloveitchik: Man of Halacha, Man of Faith*, ed. Menachem D. Genack (Hoboken, N.J.: Ktav Publishing, 1998), 45–60; and Aaron Rakeffet-Rothkof, *The Rav: The World of Rabbi Joseph B. Soloveitchik* (Hoboken, N.J.: Ktav Publishing, 1999), 2 vols.

4. I rely upon audio recordings first given as lectures by R. Soloveitchik in the late 1960s and early 1970s collected by Rabbi Milton Nordlicht. See B. David Schreiber, *Nor'ot ha-Rav* (New York: B. D. Schreiber, 1997), 5:1–58; *Nor'ot ha'Rav* (New York: B. D. Schreiber, 2000), 12:107–134; David Shapiro, *Rabbi Joseph B. Soloveitchik on Pesach, Sefirat ha-Omer and Shavu'ot* (Jerusalem: Urim Publications, 2005); and *Derashot HaRav: Selected Lectures of Rabbi Joseph B. Soloveitchik*, summarized and annotated by Arnold Lustiger (Edison, N.J.: Ohr Publishing, 2003). Further references are cited in the text.

5. Rabbi Joseph B. Soloveitchik, *Halakhic Man*, trans. Lawrence Kaplan (Philadelphia: Jewish Publication Society, 1983), 17. Further references are cited in the text.

6. Paul C. Santilli, "Cinema and Subjectivity in Krzysztof Kieślowski," in *Thinking Through Cinema: Film as Philosophy*, ed. Murray Smith and Thomas E. Wartenberg (Malden, Mass.: Blackwell Publishing, 2006), 149.

7. Out of respect to the traditions I am working with, I intentionally print "Elokim" with a "k" rather than with (the more appropriate, at least phonetically) "h."

8. R. Soloveitchik provides examples of commandments to be observed only when "the conditions specified are present," whose fulfillment is voluntary: If I choose not to have a doorframe, I will not be punished if I do not put a mezuzah on my doorpost (*Nor'ot ha-Rav* 5:53); if "one wants eggs from a nest, he must first send the mother away" ("Aseret ha-Dibrot," *Shiuri HaRav* 112).

9. The exact date of the Mekhilta of Rabbi Yishmael is unknown, though Jewish tradition estimates its redaction around the second or third century CE.

10. The root of Elokim (aleph-lamed) "always suggests power or might" and the tetragrammaton root (*heh-vav-heh*) "means 'existence'" (Shapiro 227). The latter signifies mercy; Elokim signifies judgment. God's "immanence [is] represented by Elokim, and His transcendence [is] represented by [the tetragrammaton]" (Shapiro 228).

11. Natural law signifies laws that make nature what it is and what it does (physics, mathematics), not the philosophical discussion of the "natural law" of cultures.

12. Marek Haltof, *The Cinema of Krzysztof Kieślowski: Variations on Destiny and Chance* (London: Wallflower, 2004), 81–82. See also Joseph G. Kickasola's description in *The Films of Krzysztof Kieślowski: The Liminal Image* (New York: Continuum, 2004), 167. Further references are cited in the text.

13. Unlike Elokim, the tetragrammaton addresses not the natural but the metaphysical person. In other words, the latter term is used with commandments that do not save "natural society from disintegration, but . . . raise natural society to [a] committed covenantal community. Those mitzvos [commandments such as shofar or not eating the fat or blood of animals] hallow and redeem the human spiritual personality" (*Nor'ot ha-Rav* 5:12–13).

14. In the second chapter of Genesis, when a closer relationship develops between God and humans, the tetragrammaton and Elokim are both used.

15. Critics often focus on the image of the dead dog when they discuss the foreboding opening (see Haltof 82). This focus ignores Kieślowski's subtle focus on animals. In fact, as Annette Insdorf notes in a parenthetical statement, "Paweł's pigeon suggests danger: spots of blood can be glimpsed on its side." *Double Lives, Second Chances: The Cinema of Krzysztof Kieślowski* (New York: Miramax Books, 1999), 74. Further references to Insdorf's work are cited in the text.

16. There are also sounds of a dog in the background noises during the scene at the lake when Paweł's father (and the crowd of people) await the

Decalogue One

news, but the animal certainly does not get any clear time on screen. For Insdorf, even the mysterious man played by Artur Barciś "is part of this landscape, the furry collar of his coat adding a primitive, animal look" (73).

17. Many Tannaitic texts were not included in the Mishnah. One such "supplementary" text is called a Tosefta.

18. Here I think Santilli is right to underscore what might be one standard critical reception of Kieślowski's work: "All ten films of *The Decalogue* are set in the same massive apartment complex in Warsaw at a time when Polish society was still suffering from the spiritual and economic deprivations of communist rule" (149).

19. Because I focus solely on the first two verses of Exodus 20, this is not the place to address R. Soloveitchik's claims about communism. For those who wish to embark on such an enterprise, they might note that the third verse states, "You shall have no other Gods before Me." According to R. Soloveitchik, "We must not think that avoda zara (idolatry) is limited to idol worship. Whenever anything that is not God is given an absolute value, we have avoda zara. . . . [If] Jews worship avoda zara, it will betray them. One modern example of this is Communism. Many Jews worshipped Communism. But Russia later betrayed them and all Jews. 'Al Panai' ('before my face'). Onkelos translates this as 'bar mene' ('to replace Me,' 'before Me'). Interestingly, there are many injunctions against idol worship, but none against atheism. When man revolts against God, he may think himself free; but soon, even he will build his own idol. It is not atheism that can replace God, but a new godless religion such as Communism" ("Aseret ha-Dibrot," *Shiurei HaRav* 117).

20. Here R. Soloveitchik relies on his understanding of the halakhic system to state that if it were up to him, he would "rule as Rabbi Akiva whenever he disagrees with one of his contemporaries, but not when he disagrees with many of his contemporaries" (*Nor'ot ha-Rav* 5:41).

21. Kieślowski underscores the revelatory resonance of the computer's "ready" and the human responses by changing the usual computer prompt of "ready" to include the biblical "I am" in the English onscreen prompt "I am ready" (thus echoing God's response to Moses in Exodus). If the father (and perhaps the son) thinks he can store Paweł's biological mother in the computer's memory (which the aunt shows, with the question about the mother's dreams, is quite insufficient a notion), then after Paweł's death, the computer may be "ready" to store the son as well. From this perspective, the father's poignant response to the computer at the end includes a fundamental questioning of his beliefs in computers, memory, and human identity.

22. "Why, after all, was it necessary at this moment to refer to 'what I did to Egypt?' The answer: 'From the viewpoint of Elokim, all the miracles

which transpired in Mitzrayim [Egypt] could not have taken place.' In Elokim's relationship with the world, 'there is no departure from the laws of nature. Not a single particle will act in violation of its natural law' (Shapiro, *Rabbi Joseph B. Soloveitchik on Pesach, Sefirat ha-Omer and Shavu'ot*, 234). This explains why, when God mentions his role as Redeemer from the house of bondage, the name of God as the tetragrammaton appears.

23. Ibn Ezra (Abraham) (1089–1164) was a poet, philosopher, grammarian, and biblical commentator. Judah Halevi (c. 1070–1141) is one of the great Hebrew poets and philosophers, especially famous for his theological and philosophical work, the *Kuzari*.

24. This rabbinic notion of multiple appearances stands in stark contrast to the stereotypical perception of God in Hebrew Scripture. On this note, Kieślowski and R. Soloveitchik are worldviews apart. Kieślowski admits that he tends to consider "the God of the Old Testament [to be] a demanding, cruel God; a God who doesn't forgive . . . [who] leaves us a lot of freedom and responsibility, observes how we use it and then rewards or punishes, and there's no appeal or forgiveness. . . . And that's what a point of reference must be, especially for people like me, who are weak, who are looking for something, who don't know." Krzysztof Kieślowski, *Kieślowski on Kieślowski*, ed. Danusia Stok (London: Faber and Faber, 1995), 149. This passage almost sounds as if Kieślowski is commenting on the differences between Elokim and the tetragrammaton. It suggests that Kieślowski the filmmaker is a much more sophisticated thinker than Kieślowski the essay writer. Such stereotypical thinking is precisely what *One* forces respondents to question. Further references to *Kieślowski on Kieślowski* are cited in the text using the abbreviation *KK*.

25. The notion of God the merciful father is based in part on the language used in Exodus 24:10 (see Rashi on Exodus 20:2). If one etymological root of the aunt's name is the Greek *eirēnikos*, from *eirēnē* (peace), then Kieślowski might move closer to R. Soloveitchik's position. Irena, being irenic, appears to be full of peace and conciliation when she is with the live Paweł, but love alone might not be enough to create lasting peace. Perhaps the implication here is that, sometimes, for people to achieve peace, people must become militant, but without losing mercy and love.

26. The usual paradigm for self-creativity, in R. Soloveitchik's thought, is the act of repentance.

27. Nachmanides (1194–1270), known by the acronym Ramban (Rabbi Moshe ben Nahman), was a classic halakhic, biblical, and Talmudic scholar.

28. *Lucid Dreams: The Films of Krzysztof Kieślowski*, ed. Paul Coates (Trowbridge, UK: Flicks Books, 1999), 95. Further references are cited in the text.

29. Rabbi Samson Raphel Hirsch (1808–1888) was one of the great rabbinic leaders in Germany during the nineteenth century.

30. Coates nicely relates the Madonna's tears to Paweł's mother's absence. However, this point should not obscure Kieślowski's depiction of Paweł's aunt crying at the start and at the end of the film. She frames, and is framed by, the screen.

31. Kickasola quotes from Coates's "Kieślowski and the Antipolitics of Color: A Reading of the "Three Colors" Trilogy," *Cinema Journal* 41, no. 2 (Winter 2002): 45, and Christopher Garbowski's *Krzysztof Kieslowski's* Decalogue *Series: The Problem of the Protagonists and Their Self-Transcendence* (Boulder, Colo.: East European Monographs; New York: Columbia University Press, 1996), 92.

32. In this regard, respondents can acknowledge the film's earlier scenes of joy between Paweł and his aunt as he uses the computer to lock the door and turn on the water.

CHAPTER 4

Visual Reverberations:
Decalogue Two and *Decalogue Eight*
Eva M. Stadler

Each of the films in Krzysztof Kieślowski's *Decalogue* calls into question the certitude implicit in the word "commandment." As a result, the relation of each film to the biblical commandment is often ambiguous and has been the source of disagreement and discussion among critics.[1] Kieślowski himself insisted that he did not intend to teach a lesson or set forth a moral point of view in these films. Rather, his aim was to start a conversation with the spectator. As he explained: "I am someone who does not know. . . . Someone who searches. I like to observe the fragments of life and I like films that examine a small segment of life, without knowing how it began or how it will end."[2]

In this essay I will explore the formal elements the filmmaker uses in *Two* and *Eight* to establish his dialogue with the spectator, and consider how meanings are suggested through *mise-en-scène*, through patterns of close-ups and long shots, through editing and lighting, through the configuration of filmic space, and through unusually constructed soundtracks.

In an interview given after completing the *Trois couleurs* trilogy, Kieślowski noted that "there were a lot of connections between the films of the *Decalogue*," and added that these were far more numerous and more important than those between the films of the trilogy.³ There are indeed many links among these ten films which are all shot in the same large, gray housing complex in Warsaw. Characters reappear from film to film, often in walk-on roles reminiscent of the recurrent characters in Honoré de Balzac's *Comédie humaine*. Many of the protagonists are highly educated professional people: doctors, professors, musicians, scientists. Questions of the role of religion in everyday life are raised and issues of family relations and education often play a central role with a particular focus on the lives of children. One of the most interesting links, both thematic and formal, is the role of a nameless, silent "witness," played by the actor Artur Barciś, whom we see in almost all the films. His appearances are brief and his look intense and indecipherable. His diegetic role varies from film to film. Annette Insdorf likens him to characters in Wim Wenders's *Wings of Desire* who are "pure 'gaze,' able . . . to record human folly and suffering but unable to alter the course of the lives they witness."⁴ According to Kieślowski, "he has no influence on the action but he leads the characters to think about what they are doing. He is an engine for thought. His intense gaze on the characters leads them to question themselves."⁵ As we shall see, his role is also a powerful device to engage the spectator in the action of the film.

Two and *Eight* present an additional interesting thematic link. Among the ethical problems to be discussed by a Polish professor's students in *Eight* is the dilemma faced by a woman whose husband is in all likelihood dying. She is pregnant, though not by her husband, and her decision as to whether she should have an abortion depends on whether her husband lives or dies. This is also the story of *Two*. "For me time is very important," Kieślowski told an interviewer in 1991. "What I call discourse, the way of telling a tale, evolves in time. Camera, montage, actors, music, are the means of telling the tale, the discourse."⁶ Depending on montage and the other elements of film language, the "same" story can be told in many different ways. This is an issue of particular interest to Kieślowski, and nowhere in *The Decalogue* is this impact of formal cinematographic constituents on meaning more striking than in a comparative analysis of the often abstract visual style of *Two* with the almost documentary quality of *Eight*.

A grave yet theoretical philosophical problem in the ethics class in *Eight* is presented in *Two* as a pressing, living, practical, and deeply emotional decision which has to be made not only by the woman, Dorota (Krystyna Janda), but also by the old doctor (Aleksander Bardini) who treats her dying husband (Olgierd Łukaszewicz), and whom Dorota confronts directly for advice. Ethical and religious issues, as well as questions of the relation of language and truth, underlie the conversations between these two protagonists, but they are never explicitly articulated. They are reflected in the poetic visual style of the film. Moral ambiguities are suggested in the structuring of space and time, the use of camera movement and close-ups as well as the gestures of the characters: Dorota's unrest and nervousness, the doctor's weariness. The film is a brilliant illustration of Kieślowski's mastery of montage and his special brand of realism where the invisible is invoked and the unfathomable attained through minute scrutiny of material reality.[7]

The opening shot of *Two* focuses on the grim, colorless reality of the gray buildings of the housing project. In the foreground, a custodian, raking leaves, finds a dead rabbit. He looks up, and the camera follows his eyes with a long tilt (vertical tracking shot) up the side of the building to an enclosed terrace. The camera enters the apartment and reveals the ordinary, everyday life of an old man who tends to a plant, uncovers a bird cage, turns on the radio, and puts several pots of water to heat on the stove. The doorbell sounds, interrupting the English-language broadcast. Before opening the door, the old man faces the camera, and we catch a first glimpse, in close-up, of his weary face, which will become a visual motif in the film. The rabbit is not his, he tells the custodian, turning to feed the caged bird. The dead rabbit provides entry into the building and into the story, *in medias res*. This is the first of several instances in the film where the tracking camera allows unfettered movement through space, often skipping over expository information.

After another brief scene in the apartment, we see the old man walking down the hallway, toward the camera; he nods to an attractive woman standing in the hallway, seemingly waiting for something. After he leaves, she throws her cigarette on the floor, and the camera focuses on her shoe putting out the cigarette. It is the first of many close shots of cigarettes and the first example of the technique Kieślowski uses to transform the banal into a visual motif through often unexpected repetition of close-ups.

When the old man returns, the blond woman is still standing in the hallway, smoking. She comes to his door, introduces herself as Dorota Geller, and tells him that her husband is a patient on his ward at the hospital. She stands in the doorway, not entering the apartment, and, after a brief but tense conversation, leaves. The camera, now in her apartment, cuts to the close-up of a telephone answering machine, and then tilts up the wall over photographs of mountains and mountain climbers. On the soundtrack, we hear the recorded voice of a woman leaving a message for Dorota. The camera then focuses on a medium shot of Dorota standing alone and isolated among the attractive modern furnishings of her apartment.

The camera cuts back to the doctor's apartment, where it pauses on a photograph of a young woman and two small children. We briefly listen to a conversation between the doctor and his housekeeper, and the camera pauses on the doctor's face before cutting to Dorota in the hall and another cut to Dorota in her apartment. She turns on recorded classical music, looks out the window through the horizontal slats of a blind, and begins tearing the leaves off a plant standing on the window sill; she cannot break the stem, and the camera holds briefly on the plant, which seemingly refuses to die.

Her gesture underscores the difference in temperament between Dorota and the doctor. He nurtures his plant, while she—in apparent frustration—tries to destroy hers. There is also a striking contrast between their two apartments. The doctor's apartment, with its traditional furnishings and family photographs, seems to reflect a solitary, old-fashioned life committed to work, while Dorota's reflects a youthful modern style: white walls hung with large abstract-looking photographs, a telephone answering machine, clean-lined furniture. The young woman's contemporary taste is also reflected in her fashionable clothing and hairstyles, and her constant smoking. Casting the star Krystyna Janda in the role gives Dorota an added aura of seductiveness and glamour.

These elements of *mise-en-scène*, including in particular the photographs we are shown in the two apartments, reflect not only aesthetic differences in décor and life style but also seem to suggest additional diegetic information not otherwise articulated. They function as texts within the text of the film which, as Yuri Lotman suggests, can transmit information, intensify and accentuate meaning.[8] These incorporated texts as well as the detached voices entering the space of the story via the telephone and the answering machine serve as mirrors and reflections. The voices reframe Dorota's dilemma by allowing others to briefly become part of the text of her story. The photographs, which reflect her husband's interest in mountaineering, visually frame Dorota's dilemma. For the doctor, the photograph of his family frames the quandary that results from the intersection of his professional responsibility and his personal sense of loss.

When Dorota visits the doctor's apartment and fully explains her situation—she is pregnant, and loves both her husband and her lover, the father of the unborn child—the dialogue is shot in alternating close-ups of Dorota and the doctor. When he says that he really does not know the prognosis for her husband, she nervously tries to put out her cigarette in a matchbox. The camera focuses on the flare of the small fire she creates. Dorota asks the doctor if he believes in God, and he replies that it is a very personal God, only for him. After she leaves, he covers the bird's cage and looks at the picture of the young woman and the children. The camera pauses in a lengthy close-up of the photograph, which occupies the full screen.

Background information about Dorota's life is revealed by suggestion or indirection in several short sequences. We learn that her husband is a mountain climber when a colleague waits in the hallway in front of her apartment to return mountaineering equipment. A little later, during a brief scene in a café, we learn that her lover is a musician, on tour in a foreign country. The camera often lingers on Dorota, silent and alone; the objects around her, shown in close-up—the plant, the cigarettes, the glass of tea she slowly pushes off a table—significantly evoke her feelings. One sequence begins with a close-up of a cigarette in an ashtray, then a close-up of Dorota in the dark. The phone rings, she turns on the light, finally answers the phone and tells her lover that she will have an abortion, that she knows that it is all over between them. The camera focuses on the receiver she puts down before he says that he loves her. Music begins as the camera then tilts up the wall to a close-up of a large framed photo of a mountaineer whose face is partially masked but evidently that of Andrzej, her husband. The music and the photograph quite literally frame Dorota between the two men she loves.

The camera cuts to the apartment of the doctor who waters his cactus, then moves to a close-up of coffee poured into a glass. The doctor is again sitting at a table with his housekeeper and finishes the story of how his wife and two young children were killed during a bombing raid, many years before, during World War II, while he was working at the hospital.

Earlier we had seen the doctor, in his laboratory looking into a microscope. The slides he studies occupy the screen in close-up. These slides present a new text introduced within the space of the narrative. This text is completely unreadable to the spectator and perhaps also to the protagonists. While the doctor and an associate try to interpret the meaning of the slides in the context of Andrzej's illness, the witness, who in this film plays the role of a technician or orderly, stands in the doorway and looks on. "It's progressing," the doctors ambiguously agree.

As the stories of the doctor and Dorota seem to reach a critical climax, it is worth noting the degree to which all the elements of film language—editing, the startling juxtaposition of spaces, the intense focus on banal objects—have relativized what "was externally stable, set and ready-made."⁹ We seem to be in the "carnivalized" world Mikhail Bakhtin describes in Dostoevsky's novels, a world where "everything is taken to the extreme, to its outermost limit . . . shown in a moment of unfinalized transition" ("Characteristics," 167). The encounters between Dorota and all other protagonists, including the doctor, almost always occur on thresholds, in hallways, corridors, doorways and other transient, intermediary spaces. The doctor's first glimpses of her are in the hallway of the apartment house and, in the hospital, from the corridor, through an open door as she looks at her motionless, comatose husband. Bakhtin characterizes this organization of space and time in works of fiction as a "chronotope of crisis and break in a life," and continues to explain that the

> word "threshold" itself already has a metaphorical meaning in everyday usage (together with its literal meaning), and is connected with the breaking point of a life, the moment of crisis, the decision that changes a life (or the indecisiveness that fails to change a life, the fear to step over a threshold). In literature, the chronotope of the threshold is always metaphorical and symbolic, sometimes openly but more often implicitly.[10]

In this film, the witness also watches from doorways: first the doctor and his colleague looking into the microscope, and later Dorota at her husband's bedside in the hospital. A slow dripping sound is heard and images of a leaking pipe alternate with close-ups of Andrzej. The camera tilts down the wall from the pipe to a basin filled with bloody liquid. We are reminded of an earlier sequence where the drab elements of everyday reality at the run-down hospital intrude on the narrative and invite suggestive readings. After Dorota is told that her husband's situation looks bad, we are shown an astonishing montage: a series of disorienting cuts, first to a water pipe dripping, then a close-up of Andrzej, semi-comatose, then peeling plaster as the camera slowly moves down the wall. Camera and soundtrack point to physical instances of neglect and disrepair surrounding the gravely ill man. The montage intimates other layers of meaning: Do doctors have any control over the lives of patients? Can only a miracle save this man? Slavoj Žižek suggests that *"if we want to reconstruct 'all' of the narrative content, we must reach beyond the explicit narrative content as such, and include some formal features which act as the stand-in for the 'repressed' aspect of the content"* (58, emphasis in the original).

This manner of reading the film is patently relevant in considering the closing sequences. When Dorota again confronts the doctor, asking him to tell her with certitude if her husband will live or die, he tells her not to have the abortion. Her husband will die. At her insistence, he swears it. He then tells her that he would like to attend one of her concerts. For the first time, we learn that she is a musician, a violinist with the Philharmonic. Music begins, and not a word is spoken during the entire very beautiful and abstractly structured sequence that marks a resolution of the crisis, the closing events for which there is no rational explanation. We see Dorota standing before her window, again looking out through the horizontal slats of the blind (Figure 4–1). The camera then travels slowly down an exterior wall of the building in a movement opposite to the opening of the film. We see a close-up of the doctor's reddish face seemingly suspended against a black background. Is he at the concert, in his own private world, in a world imagined by Dorota? The camera tracks horizontally to the right. Andrzej, in his hospital room, opens his eyes, looks up, and, for the first time, observes his surroundings as the camera continues to move horizontally until it halts and focuses on a drinking glass of red liquid and a bee caught there, struggling not to drown. After a long close-up of the bee's struggle, the camera cuts back to Andrzej, who now seems to be watching intently. This is followed by another close-up of the bee, which finally frees itself. An abrupt cut shows Dorota playing the violin as a faint smile seems to move across her lips. Another abrupt cut shows Andrzej, now dressed and looking healthy, standing in the doorway of the doctor's office. He has come to thank him, and he tells him of the added joy that he and his wife are going to have a baby. "Do you know what it means to have a child?" he asks the doctor, who answers, "I do."

Figure 4–1. Dorota through the horizontal slats of the blinds in *Decalogue Two*.

This surprising closing sequence, followed by the coda of Andrzej's visit to the doctor, summarizes all the aspects of film language that have contributed to the extraordinary impact of *Two* on the spectator. Camerawork, editing, emotionally charged close-ups, image, and soundtrack converge and point to the element of mystery in human experience. As Kieślowski explains, "I don't film metaphors. Only people perceive the images as such and that is very good. I want to move people, I want to bring them somewhere, I want to touch them in a certain way" (Biró 28).

At the end of *Two*, the spectator is not only deeply affected but left with many unresolved issues. Many questions remain in addition to Andrzej's miraculous cure. Did the doctor lie about her husband's prognosis when he advised Dorota not to have an abortion? Was this advice given to save the child? Was it tied to his own life experience? To his religious beliefs? Does Andrzej's question to him in the last scene resolve any of this? Finally, will Dorota and her husband live the lie of the paternity of her child?

When Dorota's story is presented as an ethical problem in the lecture hall of *Eight*, the issues seem to be more narrowly defined, somewhat simplified: The doctor is Catholic, it is a true story and we are told from the start that the child lives. The focus seems to be, to a large extent, on abortion and that issue is resolved. It seems fitting that a problem presented for discussion in a philosophy course should be more circumscribed in its outlines. It is also inevitable that theoretical analysis will somehow misrepresent the living, deeply emotional situation as it is described in *Two*.

Eight is one of the most philosophical and, visually, one of the most beautiful of the films. A Polish American researcher, Elżbieta (Teresa Marczewska), attends a lecture in an ethics course at Warsaw University. Specific ethical problems are presented for reflection and discussion, among them a "hypothetical" story, raised by the visitor, of a Jewish child who was refused shelter from the Nazis in 1943. After class, Elżbieta approaches Zofia (Maria Kościałkowska), the ethics professor, and identifies herself as the little girl whom Zofia had refused to shelter during World War II.

After the scene in the lecture hall, there are three lengthy verbal confrontations between Zofia and Elżbieta: in the hallway outside the classroom, in the car in front of the house where Zofia lived during the war, and finally in Zofia's apartment after a dinner they share. Quite opposite to the technique used in *Two*, the conversations in this document-like film explicitly articulate questions about the meaning of truth, the relation of the individual to the community, the guidance that religion may or may not offer in ethical matters, and most centrally, the responsibility all bear for protecting children. "Nothing is more important than the life of a child,"

Zofia admits to Elżbieta after a very tense conversation and confession. "Try to understand the woman," Zofia had earlier told her students to encourage them (and the spectators) to think about the problems raised by Elżbieta's story as well as, by implication, Dorota's story.

Long wordless sequences accompanied by music and/or sound effects are another distinctive aspect of the style of this film. When they alternate with scenes of profound dialogue, they not only underscore the drama, but also allow time for the spectator to reflect. This editing technique is visually paralleled by the intense focus on faces captured in lengthy close-ups or sweeping tracking shots, as in the lecture hall scene where Elżbieta tells her story. The focus on people, which most often accompanies dialogue, alternates with wordless, long, often deep shots, frequently in darkness—at night, through tunnels, in narrow streets or alleyways—as if the camera, the characters, and the spectators are seeking enlightenment. Again, contrary to the technique used in *Two*, film language here seems to support the possibility of attaining resolution.

The credits are shot against a disorienting and deeply moving sequence focused on an adult leading a small child by the hand, in twilight or early evening. It is only later that we come to realize that this scene represents a retrospective to a time some forty years before the action of the film. However, the close shots of clasped hands shown in this episode establish an important visual motif in *Eight*, and, as is so often the case in Kieślowski's work, the close-up shot itself is central to the grammar of the entire film. After the credits, a straight cut brings the viewer to another close-up, this time of a beautiful flower in bright daylight, and then the camera reveals a long shot of a park while it tracks a jogger at her morning exercise. We see this elderly woman in close-up and look at her hand in close-up, and then the camera accompanies her to the gray housing complex, now familiar to viewers of *The Decalogue*, where she lives. Not a word is spoken until she briefly greets a neighbor. While the credits and the scene from the past are accompanied by a musical score, the outdoor scene and the later scenes of Zofia in her apartment are accompanied by postsynchronized sound effects, the few words of dialogue as she greets her neighbor, and ambient sounds.

After the somewhat disconcerting opening sequence, the film seems to document the present-time trajectory of Zofia's ordinary day: jogging and exercise in the park, collecting the mail, activities in her apartment, the drive to the university, the greeting of the students, the visit to the dean's office and finally in the lecture hall with her class. During this daylight trajectory, there is some evidence of disorder in Zofia's orderly and organized life. She has difficulty lighting her stove and starting her car, and a painting in her living room will not hang straight. Nevertheless, the spectator experiences the continuity of what Bakhtin calls "biographical" space (*DI*, 252–253).

In the lecture hall, Zofia announces the topics of the class discussion as examples of "ethical hell." A student tells the story of the pregnant woman who must know whether her husband will die in order to decide whether she should have an abortion. The student who tells the story emphasizes that the doctor believes in God. As the camera tracks over the faces of the other students, it seems to halt momentarily on Elżbieta fidgeting with her necklace. As the student continues that it was up to the doctor to decide on the life of the child, Zofia finishes the story by saying that she knows that the child lives and that this is the most important aspect of the story. As Zofia gives information about the child, Elżbieta rises from her chair and moves forward in the lecture hall, asking if she could tell a story since the life of the child is so important. The camera frames her in close-up as she begins her story and then moves slowly over the faces of the students.

When she refers to the young Catholic couple whose apartment the child and her guardian visit, there is a momentary interruption by a drunken student who bursts into the lecture hall. After the intruder is asked to leave, the camera returns to a close-up of Elżbieta who continues her story by noting that the woman said that she had to go back on her promise of acting as a godparent to the Jewish child, since she could not bear false witness before God. The camera stops on the witness, played by Artur Barciś, whom we see in this film as a student in the lecture hall. He looks pensive, and stares straight into the camera, toward the front of the lecture hall and the professor. The camera stops more than once to allow us to contemplate his indecipherable look while other students comment on the complex moral issues. Does his look convey secret knowledge? Consternation?

The camera tracks back to Elżbieta and to Zofia's tense and nervous face. Before she finishes the story Elżbieta says that she remembers that it was getting dark, that a green lamp was not lit and that she was offered tea in good but unmatched porcelain cups. After a brief discussion of the possible motives of the woman who went back on her promise, Zofia dismisses the class and asks the students, in preparation for the next class discussion, to try to understand the woman. After Zofia leaves the lecture hall, the camera focuses on Elżbieta, who stays seated as the students leaving class pass in front of her, and extradiegetic music begins, as in the prologue. There is an abrupt cut as the camera, in a lateral pan, moves over a shelf of books and a telephone until it stops on the face of a pensive Zofia sitting in her darkened office. As the music continues, the camera cuts to a medium shot of Zofia walking down a barely lit corridor toward Elżbieta, seated and seemingly waiting. After a tense conversation, Zofia invites the American to dinner and the camera cuts to a long shot of a car moving down a dark street. The car stops in front of a building, and in a brief conversation in alternating close-ups between the two women, we learn that "this is the place," as the music begins again.

Elżbieta walks into the dark courtyard as the camera follows her; she looks briefly at a small chapel where candles flicker on an altar, she moves on and then hides as the camera focuses on Zofia who gets out of the car and starts calling Elżbieta's name. The sound track reverberates with music, the echoes of the name of Elżbieta, and the sharp sound of steps that accompany Zofia's desperate search. "Is there another exit from this courtyard?" she asks an attendant in the building. She seems lost. Is she trapped, has she lost Elżbieta again?

When she returns to her car, she finds Elżbieta sitting there. During a brief conversation in the darkness, the faces are occasionally lit by passing cars. The women seem to agree that they analyze but do not understand. They drive off into the dark street. There is an abrupt cut to a close-up of the brightly lit shade of a table lamp in Zofia's apartment. After the long nocturnal trajectory of Zofia and Elżbieta, this is the first sign of hope and it dramatically underscores the moral implications of Kieślowski's use of light and darkness in *Eight*.

After dinner and a long conversation between the two women, other visual signals of redemption and forgiveness begin to appear in the film. Most striking of these is that Zofia and Elżbieta are now shot together in the same frame, in a two-shot, whenever they speak to each other. Prior to this, earlier in the film, all conversations between the two were either in shot-reverse shot showing the face of one and then the other, or in alternating close-ups.

This stylistic shift occurs during a rather unusual series of shots that seem to fall between a classic shot-reverse shot and a two-shot. Elżbieta is seated and Zofia stands behind her with a hand on her shoulder. The camera moves up and down, focusing on one and then the other during this tense conversation. When Zofia again says that nothing is as important as the life of a child, the camera focuses on her hand, which rests on the younger woman's shoulder as Elżbieta raises her own hand to clasp Zofia's (Figure 4-2). This close-up of the clasped hands parallels the opening shots of the film and seems to mark visually the moment of forgiveness. It is followed by a prolonged medium two-shot of the two women sitting

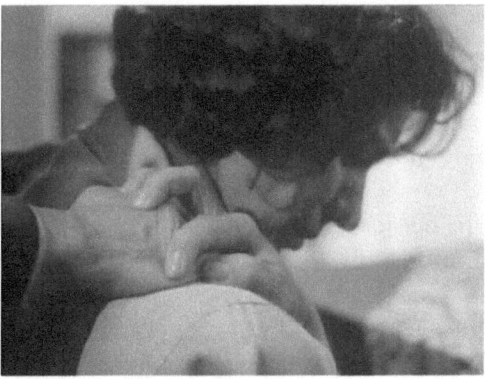

Figure 4–2. Clasped hands in *Decalogue Eight*.

next to one another discussing what they can, as philosophy professors, teach their students about themselves, about good and evil, about the existence of God. At this point, a neighbor, the same man Zofia had greeted at the beginning of the film, briefly visits. The flow of everyday life interrupts philosophical speculation just as the intrusion of the drunk had in the lecture hall. The interruption also serves to release tension and allow the viewer to reflect on the difficult issues raised.

Zofia asks Elżbieta to spend the night in her apartment in the room of her son, whom Zofia has not seen for a long time. In a brief shot, the spectator and Zofia observe Elżbieta kneeling in prayer, in the darkened room, before going to sleep. This is immediately followed by a cut to Zofia again jogging in the park in bright morning sunlight. Her meeting with a contortionist offers comic relief, the intrusion of an unusual aspect of everyday life, which could also be read as a graphic representation of the ethical twists and turns of the story we have been watching.

During their conversations of the previous evening, Zofia had revealed the reason that caused her to turn Elżbieta away during World War II. The man who was to shelter the child was suspected—falsely, it turned out—of collaborating with the Nazis, and Zofia, a member of the Resistance, was afraid to put the movement at risk. In the morning, Elżbieta asks Zofia to take her to meet the tailor (Tadeusz Łomnicki) whom the resistance fighters had unjustly suspected of collaborating with the Nazis.

On the way to see the tailor, at the end of the film, the two reconciled women ride together and their car is shown moving through a dark tunnel with light at the end. Elżbieta goes into the tailor's shop, but he refuses to talk about the past. After she leaves, we see a close-up of the tailor as he looks through the window at the two women on the street. The image is cut horizontally, thus reframing Zofia and Elżbieta talking, embracing one another. The camera returns to the face of the tailor, expressionless or puzzled at what he observes. The two women come to terms with the past while the tailor does not speak or cannot put his predicament into words.

Like all of Kieślowski's films, the ending of *Eight* leaves the spectator with a sense of the mystery of the human condition, an acknowledgment of the secret areas which lie within each individual. "I try to be as close as possible to the protagonist," Kieślowski explains. "The closer I am to him the more I discover mystery, fantasy, imagination, philosophy. All this is within ourselves" ("De Weronika à Véronique," 117). Yet, as we have noted, formal elements used in this film—editing, the configuration of filmic space, lighting—give a sense of documenting real experience, of a more positive access to meaning. There seems to be light at the end of the tunnel.

Because of its focus on the impact of past decisions on present day lives, Kieślowski considered *Eight* one of the most important films of the *Decalogue* series ("Je cherche," 102–103). Other thematic resonances between *Eight* and Kieślowski's oeuvre can also be noted. When Zofia tells her visitor, after the neighbor leaves, that every house is interesting, she underscores a theme important to Kieślowski as a filmmaker. "If you look through any window you will see people," he told his interviewers in 1989. "If you are willing to look closely there is something very interesting about them . . . inside each one there is something interesting" ("Je cherche," 94). Insdorf sees a similarity between Zofia's words and the language Kieślowski himself uses in interviews, and she concludes that "it is hard not to see Zofia . . . as Kieślowski's mouthpiece, espousing a skeptical humanism rooted in spiritual belief" (113). René Prédal suggests that *Eight* can actually be seen as a formal model for the other films of *The Decalogue*: "*Decalogue Eight* conceptualizes the procedure used in the entire series by proposing a method of reading: like the filmmaker, the ethics professor presents situations drawn from everyday life in her classes . . . the ethical problem is born out of the story, the idea is expressed through flesh and blood protagonists, the concept is never separated from human substance" (82–83). *Eight* thus documents not only human experience for both the filmmaker and the characters he creates but also serves as a model for structuring and reading the *Decalogue* films.

The relation between *Eight* and *Two* is ultimately not more substantial than the many connections that bind all the component films in the *Decalogue* series. However, the thread of Dorota's story allows us to juxtapose and compare the formal elements of these two films, which brilliantly demonstrate the range and the virtuosity of Kieślowski's style as a filmmaker.

NOTES

1. Joseph G. Kickasola notes the differences between the Roman Catholic and the Protestant numbering of the commandments, suggests that it is very clear that Kieślowski is using the Catholic system, and even provides a chart showing the relation of each film to the biblical commandment. *The Films of Krzysztof Kieślowski: The Liminal Image* (New York: Continuum, 2004), 161–164. Slavoj Žižek, on the other hand, reads philosophical significance in what he calls "the shift of gear" that is operated between each film and the corresponding biblical commandment. He titles an entire chapter "Displaced Commandments," and in a lengthy footnote summarizes other conjectures about the relationship between the Ten Commandments and Kieślowski's *Decalogue*. Žižek, *The Fright of Real Tears: Krzysztof Kieślowski between Theory and Post-Theory* (London: British Film Institute, 2001), 111–135 and 196–197 n. 1. Further references to Žižek's work will be cited in the text.

2. Cited by Yvette Biró, "*Le Hasard*: petite grammaire du hasard," in *Études Cinématographiques: Krzysztof Kieślowski* 203–210, ed. Michel Estève (Paris: Lettres Modernes, 1994), 29. Further references will be cited in the text. Translations of all texts from the French are my own.

3. Cited by Emma Wilson, *Memory and Survival: The French Cinema of Krzysztof Kieślowski* (Oxford: Legenda, 2000), 91.

4. Annette Insdorf, *Double Lives, Second Chances: The Cinema of Krzysztof Kieślowski* (New York: Miramax Books, 1999), 73.

5. Krzysztof Kieślowski, "Je cherche l'explication de tout," interview by Michel Ciment and Hubert Niogret, *Positif* 346 (December 1989), repr. in *Krzysztof Kieslowski*, ed. Vincent Amiel (Paris: Positif/Jean-Michel Place, 1997), 99. Further references to this interview will be cited in the text using the abbreviated title "Je cherche."

6. Krzysztof Kieślowski, "De Weronika à Véronique," interview by Michel Ciment and Hubert Niogret, *Positif* 364 (June 1991), repr. in Amiel, *Krzysztof Kieslowski*, 111. Further references will be cited in the text using the abbreviated title "De Weronika à Véronique."

7. See René Prédal, "*Le Décalogue*: Une esthétique du silence et de l'obscurité," and Agnès Peck, "*Trois Couleurs Bleu/Blanc/Rouge*: Une trilogie européenne," in Estève, *Etudes Cinématographiques*, 65–84 and 147–162, respectively.

8. See Yury M. Lotman, "The Text Within the Text," *PMLA* 109 (1994): 377–384.

9. Mikhail Bakhtin, "Characteristics of Genre and Plot Composition in Dostoevsky's Works," in *Problems of Dostoevsky's Poetics*, ed. and trans. Caryl Emerson, vol. 8 of *Theory and History of Literature* (Minneapolis: University of Minnesota Press, 1984), 101–180. Further references will be cited in the text using the abbreviated title "Characteristics."

10. Mikhail Bakhtin, *The Dialogic Imagination*, ed. Michael Holquist (Austin: University of Texas Press, 1981), 248. Further references will be cited in the text using the abbreviation *DI*.

CHAPTER 5

Remember the Sabbath Day, to Keep It Holy: *Decalogue Three*

Joseph W. Koterski, S.J.

According to an old legend, there were originally fifteen commandments. But at one point when Moses was carrying the tablets down the mountain, he is said to have tripped and fallen, shattering one of the stones on which the laws had been inscribed. When he met the people assembled at the base of the mountain, he explained: "I've got good news for you, and bad news. The good news is that there were fifteen commandments, but now there are only ten. The bad news is that adultery is still on the list."

Smile as we might at this rather curious way of breaking the commandments, the story reinforces one of the points that Krzysztof Kieślowski illustrates throughout his series of films on the Decalogue.[1] The dictates of the Law that were given by God to Moses are precisely that—divine commandments, not merely human rules. They have a definite content and a divine purpose. One might try to interpret them in a legalistic way as stating the bare minimum of what one must do and what one must not do in order to keep God at bay. But that would be to miss the real thrust of the Ten Commandments. Understood more deeply, they are divine prescriptions for how to order one's loves rightly. They are a gift from on high, designed to lead people to exercise their freedom well, so as to live according to God's providential plan for human well-being and happiness.

Each of Kieślowski's ten films displays an artist's quest to understand the full import of the commandments. The stories told in his *Decalogue* are ways to explore the contents of each statute in full, without interpreting their requirements according to some legal minimalism. By his creative cinematic vision, Kieślowski is trying to discern what the purposes of the Almighty may have been in formulating the details of the moral law in the way we find them. The third of these films is no exception. Even *Three*'s interesting way of expressing the third commandment ("Remember the Sabbath day, to keep it holy"), let alone the plot that unfolds in the course of the film, gives witness to the nature of the filmmaker's quest for deeper understanding of these matters.

The Third Commandment

In the history of Judaism and Christianity, there have come to be a number of ways to enumerate the commandments. In part, these differences have arisen from the choices in regard to translation and the grouping of phrases in the text that were made over the course of time—choices about just what the proper interpretation and emphasis should be. But certain features of the controlling biblical texts have also played a role here.

Within the book of Exodus, the Ten Commandments (the Decalogue) are found as part of the divine theophany that Moses experienced at Mt. Sinai, as described in chapter 20, verses 1–17. The Decalogue is contained in a section of the text that runs from chapter 19 to chapter 24, which tells the story of Israel's experience of God in this part of their desert journey from slavery in Egypt to the land that God had promised them. Deuteronomy recounts much of the same material that is found in Exodus, but this book is structured as a series of addresses by Moses to the people of Israel. The Commandments (Deut. 5:1–22) are found within the second of these Mosaic discourses, which begins at 4:41 and continues until 28:69.

The Catholic tradition of interpretation takes the material in Exodus 20:2–6 and Deuteronomy 5:6–10 together as the first commandment, a requirement of monotheistic worship. It regards the second commandment as prohibiting any profanation of the name of God: "You shall not take the name of the Lord your God in vain" (Exod. 20:7; see also Deut. 5:11 RSV). Protestants have tended to see the first commandment as expressed in the single verse at the head of both biblical accounts (Exod. 20:2; Deut. 5:6) and then to regard the prohibition on graven images when treating the following passages (Exod. 20:3–6; Deut. 5:7–10) as the second commandment. What Catholics have treated as the second commandment is generally taken as the third commandment in Protestant lists. The material that is at issue in the third film of Kieślowski's *Decalogue* is what Catholics regard as the third commandment (the fourth in Protestant versions). The numbering differences continue until the end of the list, where Catholicism sees the final verses (Exod. 20:16–17; Deut. 5:21) as containing two distinct commandments that prohibit covetous desires for the neighbor's spouse and for the neighbor's goods; Protestants read this verse as giving a single commandment.

The traditionally Catholic culture of Kieślowski's Poland makes it natural that he uses the standard Catholic way of numbering and articulating the various commandments, including his decision to put the focus of the third film where he does. This decision in no way circumscribes or forecloses his artistic quest to explore and appreciate the content and purpose of this commandment ("Remember the Sabbath day, to keep it holy"). In Polish translations, the object of remembering is "the Sabbath" while the idea of "keeping it holy" is relegated to the subordinate clause. In English translations, the emphasis tends to be somewhat different. The most familiar renditions of the third commandment for English speakers put a certain emphasis on what we are supposed to remember to do, namely, to keep something holy, and the reference to the Sabbath provides the context of a special day of the week on which to do this. Consider, for example, the way in which the commandment is rendered in the *New American Bible*:

Remember to keep holy the Sabbath day. (Exod. 20:8)

Take care to keep holy the Sabbath day as the LORD your God commanded you. (Deut. 5:12)

The stress in translations like these on our obligation to respect the holiness of the Lord's Day is typical, especially given the Christian understanding of what day this is. Early Jewish Christians not only tended to honor the seventh day (what we usually call Saturday) as the Sabbath, in keeping with traditional Jewish customs, but also to call the first day of the week (Sunday) the Lord's day and to make it a special day of worship, in memory of the day of Jesus's resurrection from the dead. In the Jerusalem Bible, the Gospel of Matthew, for instance, begins its record of the resurrection thus: "After the Sabbath, and towards dawn on the first day of the week" (Matt. 28:1; see also Mark 16:1, Luke 24:1, John 20:1).

Jewish traditions treat the Sabbath as a time for remembering God's creation of the world. Exodus 20:11, for instance, explains: "For in six days the Lord made heaven and earth, the sea, and all that is in them, and rested the seventh day; therefore the Lord blessed the Sabbath day and hallowed it." It was also a day for calling to mind God's liberation of Israel from bondage in Egypt (see Deut. 5:15: "You shall remember that you were a servant in the land of Egypt, and the Lord your God brought you out thence with a mighty hand and an outstretched arm; therefore the Lord your God commanded you to keep the Sabbath day"). Israel thus understood the Sabbath as a sign of God's irrevocable covenant (Exod. 31:16), a day that was holy and set apart for praising God's work of creation as well as God's saving action on Israel's behalf. This act of remembering divine work was seen to have direct implications for human conduct—if God rested on the seventh day, so too human beings ought to rest and be refreshed (Exod. 23:12 and 31:17). Keeping the Sabbath meant a halt to everyday work.

The Gospels recount numerous incidents when Jesus is accused of having violated the law of the Sabbath. While he never failed in respect for the holiness of this day, he clearly offered a distinctive interpretation of what it means to keep the Sabbath that Christians regard as authentic and authoritative, beginning with his remark that "the Sabbath was made for man, not man for the Sabbath" (Mark 2:27). In the Christian understanding of the Gospels, it is out of compassion that Christ asserts that the Sabbath is reserved for doing good and not harm, for saving life and not killing (Mark 3:4). The Sabbath is to be a day of mercy (Matt. 12:5; John 7:23) and a day for honoring God, for "the Son of man is lord even of the Sabbath" (Mark 2:28).

Once Christianity experienced a vast expansion by the influx of many people who were not of Jewish origin, there was a growing tradition of amalgamating the Sabbath and the Lord's day. As a way to honor Jesus's prophecy that "a day will come . . . when true worshipers will worship the Father in spirit and truth" (John 4:23), there emerged a tradition of conducting a weekly eucharistic liturgy that synthesized elements of the Jewish Passover meal with remembrance of the events of the passion, death, and resurrection of Christ. Further, while Christians felt excused from some of the regulations that had governed Jewish conduct on the Sabbath (the restriction on travel, for instance, to a Sabbath day's journey), they tried to honor the spirit of the commandment by stressing the importance of making this a day for family rather than for labor. In this way the Christian observance of the Lord's day attempted simultaneously to include worship, rest, and family.

The Third Commandment in Kieślowski's Decalogue

By choosing Christmas Eve and Christmas Day as the setting for this film, Kieślowski is already at work exploring the meaning of the third commandment. In Polish culture, the celebration of the traditional "Wigilia" on Christmas Eve is especially important, and the protagonist's choice to leave his family in the middle of this celebration risks profaning something very sacred. The episode's actual title—*Dekalog, Trzy (Decalogue Three)*— remains enigmatic and does not definitively link the film and the third commandment. Yet a number of critics seem quite rightly to align the film with the third commandment and the films' American distributor, Facets Video, uses such correlations between the films and the commandments as a marketing strategy.[2] While the actual title does not provide a definitive meaning, it allows the filmmaker to explore the range of options within the ambit of the third commandment: The film focuses on the question of keeping or profaning the holiness of the holy day—that is, in a sense, on the obligations of Sunday as the Christian Sabbath.

In the film, we are presented with the feast of Christ's birth as the temporal setting, and thus a focus on a day that is the Lord's in a very special way. When we ponder this aspect of the third commandment in any of its possible translations, it is not likely that anyone would think first of Christmas Eve or Christmas Day, and yet there is an interesting connection between this feast and the idea of the Lord's Day. The Christian way of coalescing the traditions of the Sabbath with the remembrance of Christ's resurrection introduced something quite new into the picture, and the practice of setting aside a day on which to honor Jesus's birth readily suggested that Christians ought to recall the wholly new order of history that came with Christ's appearance on the earth. So, in a remarkable way, Christmas Day is the Lord's Day and the Sabbath in a paramount fashion.

The commandment, of course, contains two directives: to remember the Sabbath and to keep it holy. The protagonists of the story, however, find themselves struggling to stay mindful of the sacredness of this feast (e.g., when trying to keep their mind on the Christmas Eve services once their gaze meets in the church). Sometimes they simply seem to forget what feast this is or even what time of day it is (e.g., as they race around in the taxicab all night in the process of visiting various hospitals and government offices). At other times, they do seem mindful of the feast (as in the Christmas toasts), but even then they struggle in the efforts that keeping it holy require, as during the scene within the apartment that nearly turns into a moment of seduction. Ironically, the need to remember what day this is provides both the source of the problem and the key to its resolution. What should one do to remember and keep a day holy, and this day in particular? And how should one do this, especially when one's memory is tinged with lives that are as broken and conflicted as are the lives of the characters in this film?

The film presents us with Ewa (Maria Pakulnis) intruding upon the quiet Christmas Eve of Janusz (Daniel Olbrychski), a man who was once her lover. She claims that her husband Edward is missing and pleads with Janusz to help find him. This story eventually proves to be fabricated, but Janusz—perhaps out of pity, perhaps out of some residual affection for her—chooses to help. Unwilling to explain what happened to his wife (Joanna Szczepkowska), Janusz decides to tell her that his taxi has been stolen and that he must go out to search for it. His nervousness, however, makes this lie implausible, and his wife even sees him speaking with Ewa.

When Janusz returns briefly to explain that he must hunt for the taxi, she says nothing about what she has seen. In vain she tries to give Janusz an honorable way to remember his duties to his family: "Perhaps it's not worth it to search for the taxi." Janusz insists that "it's our living"—a double entendre that suggests that not only his job as a taxi driver is at stake, but something much more profound about their marriage.

Janusz and Ewa proceed to drive around the city in search of Edward. The night they spend together is surreal—they visit a hospital, a morgue, and even an alcoholic center in what proves to be a fruitless quest (Figure 5–1). By morning Eva confesses to her somewhat reluctant helper that he has saved her life, for she had been terrified about spending Christmas

Figure 5–1. Janusz and Ewa at the morgue in *Decalogue Three*.

Eve alone and would surely have killed herself. It has been a night of talk, sometimes tender and sometimes bitter, a night of not infrequent lies, and a night of crude attempts at rekindling a lost love. By the end of the film Janusz returns to his wife, whom he finds sleeping on the couch.

Do the characters of this story remember the Sabbath and keep it holy? The film begins in an abstract way. There are splashes of color, flares of the camera lens, recollections that are distorted, and dabs of blue and white light that have an impressionist feel. There are several shots of the city from above—perhaps this is supposed to be a divine point of view—as well as scenes from a church during the vigil Mass on Christmas Eve. The pillars block our view from time to time, in much the same way that the daily struggle with life and love can obscure one's sense of the sanctity of this day or the moral implications of the commandment to keep the Lord's Day holy. One gets the impression that Ewa in particular is on the outside, trying to gaze inside so as to see the holy. She catches the eye of Janusz, and it is clear from early on that she is obsessed with the project of engaging his attention.

His own muddled affections are evident in the way that he strains to look for her when she moves out of sight. He is visibly moved by the traditional Polish carols, and especially by the singing of "*Bóg się rodzi*" ("God is born"). But as the story unfolds, it is clear that this film is not a traditional Christmas tale. When we hear the carols sung in the church, it is actually the second time that they occur in the film. The first time was in the haunting voice of a drunk, who is seen pulling along a Christmas tree and forlornly asking where his home is. Later in the film we will see the same man, who has apparently been arrested and tossed into a holding cell, being abused by a sadistic orderly. Kieślowski may well be asking where mercy is on this sacred night. Janusz's kindness in accompanying Ewa on her search makes their entire trip, in one sense, an errand of mercy, but his mixed motives during the course of the night nearly lead him at certain points to rekindle an old romance that would utterly ruin the charity of his decision.

The domestic scene of Janusz's home on Christmas Eve suggests his mindfulness of the need to play his part in keeping this day holy, but we might well feel unconvinced that he is doing anything more than playing a part. Dressed in a Santa Claus suit, he brings in the children's gifts. He unplugs the phone and drinks a toast with his wife and her mother, who seems to bore him with her chattering about times long before. We are given the impression that he would like this to be an intimate family evening, one that has been carefully protected from intrusion from the outside. The buzz of the intercom disturbs their peace, and Ewa's desperate desire for communication interrupts their plans.

Perhaps there is some measure of mercy in Janusz's compliant agreement to join Ewa's desperate search. But his motives are never wholly clear at any point in the film—certainly not to the viewer, and presumably not entirely to Janusz. His prima facie duties are at home with his family, but Ewa's plea for his help suggests another Christian duty, to help those in need. But it is not simply that he is torn between duties, for the fires of an old flame make his response ambiguous. Is he being compassionate, or is he secretly hoping that there may be a temptation lurking here to which he may find an occasion to yield? We see Janusz increasingly irritated by Ewa's awkward efforts to play the part of an old friend who is distraught about her missing husband and simultaneously that of a temptress whose loneliness has driven her to this desperate strategy.

It is not clear at first to Janusz—or to the viewer—that Ewa has made up the whole story. He seems to suspect that she is frustrated about something and is trying to manipulate him. Even as his suspicions grow, he still plays along. She expresses sadness when she sees an adult rush out after a young child who has run outside into the snow, without a coat, to see the red lights of a Christmas tree on a nearby traffic island. She has no child to chase this evening. We are brought to a kind of sympathy for her when we see her paying a visit to an elderly aunt in a nursing home. The camera lingers over the limp leather gloves that Ewa had brought her aunt as a present. The aunt cannot seem to understand or even stay awake, let alone to acknowledge the gift.

Like many of the other car scenes in the film, the sequence in which Ewa's car leaves the nursing home suggests futility and almost complete hopelessness. We see her car enter a traffic circle and pass the red lights of a Christmas tree. She drives aimlessly while considering the unlikely possibility that she may be able to enchant Janusz. The predominant red color of many of these scenes mingles one of the traditional colors of Christmas with the color of hellfire. Later in the film, their drives across the city have an in-built futility—Ewa has no husband for them to find—and her only goal for the trip is to cling to Janusz for company until dawn breaks.

The institutions that Ewa and Janusz visit are utterly bleak. At the morgue the night clerk callously reads out the gory description of a nameless corpse, without any concern for the possibility that this unknown man might be Ewa's missing spouse. A bit later, it appears for a moment that they have found the man they are seeking. When shown a corpse whose face is torn apart beyond recognition, Ewa starts violently and throws herself into Janusz's arms. The viewer would naturally suppose that this was a reaction of grief, but instead she bursts into a rage about her hatred for all the men she has loved: "I wish it was him. . . . or you. How often I've pictured your faces crushed by truck wheels." Whatever compassion was growing for her predicament immediately disappears.

By juxtaposing these stark and hate-filled images with Ewa's crying need for love and understanding, Kieślowski shows us a mixture of brokenness and hatred. In the decision of Janusz to leave his family on Christmas night, we see a mingling of compassion and danger. The lies that Ewa tells Janusz and those that Janusz tells his wife risk wrecking their lives. On the screen the danger is concretized by the curious scene in which Janusz drives so recklessly that a police car cannot help but give chase. The viewer is subjected to a bruising rush of lights and the horror of a near collision with a streetcar. The streetcar is driven, incidentally, by the character who appears from time to time in Kieślowski's films as a quasi-chorus—he speaks no lines and shows no fear, but simply looks at the crazily speeding vehicle as if the outcome (a collision or a near-miss) will be their choice. Will they tempt death? Is a deliberate crash their way of escaping from the tangled web of deceptions and disordered love in their lives? Eventually the police do stop them, but then let them go with the reminder, "It's Christmas." Remembering the Lord's special day and sanctifying it require them to make decisions that thus far they have avoided only by swerving around obstacles as dangerous as the bus and the truth of their situations.

Ewa's plotting brings them to her apartment, on the pretext of phoning in a report about her missing husband. We are left to speculate about whether she wants to seduce Janusz, or perhaps to explain everything, including her despair. She initially instructs Janusz to wait downstairs, just in case her husband has returned home. But she uses the time alone to try to make it look as though her husband has been living there, including her placement of a man's shaving brush. When he does come up from the car, she pretends to file an accident report over the phone, but her hasty efforts to deceive him fail. She had not thought to change a razor so rusty that Janusz can now confirm for himself that no man has used it for a long time.

Yet, he does not confront her with her lie. Is he still hoping to be seduced? They sit down for a cup of tea and begin to talk more honestly. They recall their decision to end their affair when Edward had walked in upon them while they were making love. Was it that Janusz himself had alerted Edward, to force her to choose? She explains that she had chosen Edward, but all of her actions this Christmas night suggest that it is Janusz she still wants.

The tortured and conflicted Ewa cannot keep in character. Having just turned from a distraught search for her husband to a desperate attempt at rekindling an old flame, she suddenly turns again to blaming Janusz. If he has managed to make such a happy life for himself, she must be the true victim. He does not know what to say—to return to her now would mean betraying his family, even if the present status of his family life is not everything he might want. She vacillates between truth telling and lies: "It's Christmas Eve . . . sorry I lied to you." But then she returns to her deceit: "I am with him [Edward] in the usual way." They break a stick of gum in the very way that any Pole would find reminiscent of the Christmas custom of the breaking of *opłatki* (wafers)—a ritual in which family members wish one another peace and forgiveness. But just as the viewer is expecting them to embrace, the buzzer alerts them to children at the door, caroling badly off-key and in funny costumes. The way in which Ewa romantically cuddles up close to Janusz during the song allows her for a brief moment to act out a fantasy. We cannot but be struck by how easy self-deception can be.

The spell now broken, they continue their search by heading for a detoxification center, a reminder of the terrible problem with alcohol that has long plagued Poland. The drunk whom we saw dragging the Christmas tree earlier in the film is still pitifully asking, "Where is my home?" The attendant at the center, whose appearance and whose morbid curiosity about the ethnic origins of his charges suggests the inhumanity of the Nazis, sadistically douses the men lying naked in the cell with cold water so that Ewa and Janusz will be able to see if they recognize anyone. With a cruel laugh, he tries to amuse the visitors ("See how they jump?"), but in another act of mercy for these poor souls Janusz rips the hose from his hands.

Janusz has now had enough of this deceitful and manipulative evening: "It's senseless, I'm going back . . . I'm going home." What will he find there? Ewa first tries to calm him by laying her hand on his leg. When he is unresponsive, she grabs the steering wheel and the car jumps off the road, right into the Christmas tree on the traffic island that they drove by earlier that night. The scene is filled with red light—is it the color of Christmas or are they still in a hell of their own making? Her desperation is clear, and she pleads with Janusz to drive her to one more place—maybe her husband is in the train station. Or perhaps she is still looking for the courage to take her own life and end the pain.

In the desolate train station, the camera centers on a Christmas tree standing alone. The scene is surreal—a security camera pans the eerily empty station while the guard sleeps. All of a sudden, another guard, a young woman on a skateboard, noisily rolls in and shows them her creative way to stay awake during her watch. When Ewa catches sight of an electric clock that moves from 7:02 to 7:03, Ewa finally tells Janusz the truth. What she has been dying to explain suddenly comes tumbling out: She had found it impossible to be alone, especially on Christmas night, when everyone else has a family and a home. Edward left her years ago and now has a family of his own in Kraków. She explains that she thought that she could keep from killing herself if only she could make it until seven o'clock.

Even while she is explaining, we see in the background the child whom we saw earlier in the film. Apparently it was not one of his own parents who had caught him racing toward the Christmas tree, but a hospital attendant who was chasing him when he had tried to escape. The boy is now being caught in the same place where they have arrived, a train station. Ewa has finally managed to escape—at least for one night—from her horrendous fears. A train station is a place of departures as well as arrivals, a place of transitions from one place to another. Having watched the torturous trip that Ewa has undertaken this night, the viewer can only wonder where she is headed next.

The final scene for Ewa and Janusz involves taking leave at the traffic signal where she had left her car at the start of the night. There is no kiss and no embrace, but they flash the headlights of their cars toward one another—a wordless communication that manages to speak something of the truth about their affection, but at a safe distance.

At home, Janusz finds his wife asleep on the couch (Figure 5–2). She will not pretend that she does not know at least something of what has happened, and so she asks: "You'll be going out again in the evening?" If there was anything noble or merciful in his decision to leave their home that night, if there was anything compassionate or charitable in his ac-

Figure 5–2. Janusz returns to his wife in *Decalogue Three*.

tion, she offers no complaint. But by her question she reminds him that true compassion cannot spring from adultery or from the abandonment of his home. What she offers him is the peace and stability of a family and a household, but he must give up the stimulation of Ewa. The viewer may know that Janusz has not been unfaithful to his wife. But there is every reason to think that he had fantasized about the possibilities and perhaps even hoped for seduction. He needs to decide whether he will indeed live out the choice that his wife now offers.

The Third Commandment, Again

A well-told tale can make the questions of religion and morality come alive in a special way. The third of Kieślowski's *Decalogue* films provides the occasion and the incentive.

The Sabbath, the Lord's Day, and especially the feast day of Christmas are all sacred times. They require true worship of God, but the God who commanded that these be days of authentic worship also expects that we will learn to keep these sacred days holy in the full sense of holiness. The scriptural texts that record the obligations of the commandments speak of rest from work, and of turning our attention to home, to family, and to the commitments that we have made in love. But those love commitments are difficult and it is easy to stray. It is always possible to turn the leisure intended for our rest and family devotion into occasions for indulging ourselves and rationalizing our duties by the most minimal and legalistic understandings of what religion and morality really require.

Kieślowski wisely refuses any moralizing tone, but he presses the moral questions. Mindful of the foibles of the human heart, he shows us the plight of those with mixed motives. Perhaps there never was a motive that was not mixed. The task is to sort our motives out and not be carried over dangerous shoals by easy rationalizing. Even on a day of a sacred nature, a day consecrated to the memory of the birth of the Savior and a day supported in the Polish setting of this story by timeless customs of family and worship, the protagonists of this story move by motives almost too mixed to sort out.

Does keeping holy a day that God has directed us to sanctify mean taking the risks necessary to do an act of compassion, or declining to do so because of the temptations that the person being asked to show compassion will almost certainly feel? Do the pressing needs of someone who does not know how close she stands to suicide have a claim on an old lover now trying to live out his duties as a husband and a father? Could not Janusz have asked his wife to join him in having the desperate Ewa as a guest in their home on Christmas night? There are countless ways in which we can hope that we ourselves would have shown the needed compassion, and real life will not leave us without opportunities to test our mettle.

But the explorations of the artist here give us reason to say what we have learned from his storytelling. There is a need for distinguishing between true and false compassion. There is reason for insisting that the commandments must never be taken extrinsically in the fashion of a legally acceptable minimum. And there is an incentive for undertaking a fresh examination of conscience on this commandment, as on the others to which Kieślowski has turned his cinematic gaze. Have we remembered the Sabbath, to keep it holy?

NOTES

1. There are many fine studies on the films of Kieślowski. I would like to acknowledge, in particular, two books for the insights they have provided about the interpretation of various scenes in this film: Christopher Garbowski, *Krzysztof Kieslowski's* Decalogue *Series: The Problem of the Protagonists and Their Self-Transcendence* (Boulder, Colo.: East European Monographs; New York: Columbia University Press, 1996); and Joseph G. Kickasola, *The Films of Krzysztof Kieślowski: The Liminal Image* (New York: Continuum, 2004).

2. See, for example, Marek Haltof, *The Cinema of Krzysztof Kieślowski: Variations on Destiny and Chance* (New York: Wallflower Press, 2004), and "The Ten Commandments and the Decalogue" in the booklet accompanying *The Decalogue*, DVD, directed by Krzysztof Kieślowski (Chicago: Facets Video, 2003).

CHAPTER 6

Decalogue Four: The Mother up in Smoke, or "Honor Thy Father and Thy Mother"

Gabriella Ripa di Meana

A young woman of twenty who lives alone with her father informs him one day that she has found a secret envelope that he has been hiding from her for years. The envelope contains a testamentary letter from her mother, who had passed away a few days after giving birth to her. The father has kept this letter, addressed to his daughter, inside another envelope containing, in turn, his own testament to her. On this envelope, the father, with the conscious intention of delaying its dreaded opening and disclosure for as long as possible, wrote these words: "To be opened after my death."

In this way, the man, who had both evaded and feared the content of the letter, has now learned, from the daughter's provocative account, that he is not her father. This revelation has upset him. The family system has broken down. The relationship between them has blown up. The incest taboo has wavered. The father and the daughter have now become ensnared by desire.

It is only after a period of tumult between them that the young woman admits that she totally fabricated the contents of the maternal letter, and that she had, in fact, never opened it. This finally snuffs out the morbid curiosity with which the two had guarded the mysterious message for years. Their spirits thus soothed, they decide to burn the letter. Only a few scorched fragments remain to recall the message that is now permanently lost.

The Oedipal Trap

Between the father and the daughter lies, hidden, a mysterious yellowish envelope on which the father has written by hand, "To be opened after my death." When the two are separated for a few days, the yellow envelope remains at the bottom of a common-use drawer. One day, the father, who is about to travel somewhere, appears to forget it there, careless in a way he has never been before. Thus the amnesia of the father, Michał (Janusz Gajos), puts the daughter, Anka (Adrianna Biedrzyńska), under pressure. She takes the initiative and arrives at a solution. She only has to cut the yellow envelope open to discover the truth of the father's postmortem injunction.

She indeed executes that cut, thus breaking the enclosure of the paternal word. Within it, however, she finds no revelation other than yet another sealed envelope with the words, "For my daughter Anna," written on it. This time, the writing belongs to the mother who died giving birth to her. Thus, Anka finds a secret within a secret, a cut following a cut. Meanwhile, Anka, holding a pair of scissors and the letter in her hands, vanishes from the film viewer's field of vision against a brilliant white canoe that a man approaching from the water carries over his shoulders (Figure 6-1).

We see her again when she furiously recites her mother's arcane message to the father: "My darling daughter . . . Michał is not your father."[1] There is a slap in the face, some broken glass, and the two find themselves

Figure 6-1. The mother's letter within the father's in *Decalogue Four*.

speaking of desire, jealousy, and love. What happens then is a sort of game of truth or dare, which follows all the conventions, mannerisms, and terrors of truth itself.

We see Anka cry hysterically, now undressing to seduce her father, now curling up on her own—adolescent—bed, while he quivers with unexpressed desires. And yet, neither knows what to do with such an outpouring of emotions, revelations, and accusations. In all of this, eros is only but a fragment of their truth. Exhausted, Michał leaves. Anka, upset, follows him. What ensues is another moment of half-truth. Anka confesses to her act of mise-en-scène. She has not opened the letter. She has plotted her deception and laid an Oedipal trap. She is a theater actress and has staged a truth . . . but only one of many possible truths.

Together they have always thought that the content of the mysterious letter—sanctioned by the dead mother, whom she never knew—would delegitimize their bond as father and daughter. Perhaps they have always suspected that they were victims of some sort of (male)diction by the mother, who disappeared too soon not to be jealous of the end of her own youth at the birth of the bond between her man and that little girl. But with time, their suspicion turns into a dark desire to know the Truth. And a similar desire leads them to invent ambiguous tricks to both reveal and conceal that letter. In any case, the letter always remains in the middle between them, like a mystery and a condemnation. Meanwhile, with the passing years, father and daughter work out, but do not communicate to each other, a form of shared knowledge rooted, day by day, in the mysterious origins of the relationship that binds them. For this reason, Anka cuts open the father's sealed envelope, but confronted with the unknown of the mother's white envelope does not cut it, preferring rather to unleash the obscure, infernal forces of incest.

Nevertheless, despite her jolts and agonizing recognitions, and despite pathetic moments of seduction by this frail and reckless girl, Michał does not give up his desire to be a father. At the same time, the daughter's staging of this fiction is a fearless and absolute filial act. Actually, while the father looks fearfully at the presumed maternal verdict, which undermines and denies everything their father-daughter bond is based on, Anka elects to give up her mother's truth, whatever it may be. In fact, she dares to uncover and provoke precisely the unknown aspect of that truth, a truth that had threatened them both until then, nailing them to each other not by filiation but by negation.

Anka thus decides to burn the letter that she had yearned for so long, in order to honor her father and her mother. The film ends by leaving the truth of the matter unresolved. Perhaps the letter enclosed the truth that they had imagined; perhaps it did not.

The pure and simple knowledge of the facts (whether Anka was or was not Michał's biological daughter) would not have triggered the dark and indomitable forces of their subjective truth so powerfully. These forces break out precisely because that type of knowledge had remained impossible. And this impossibility was always attested to by the presence/absence of the hermetically sealed envelope.

There is no truth without concealment, as there is no filial honor that has not somehow traversed the deceptions and pitfalls of truth. That sort of *discovered* truth, bequeathed as a legacy by the mother, needed to be, precisely, *re-covered* or covered again, not only by the husband through the yellow envelope and the lengthy deferral, but also by the daughter, by means of lies and by fire.

The Knowledge of Origins

Therefore: a letter that contains but another letter; a message that holds but another, mysterious, message. The first message is written in the father's handwriting: "To be opened after my death." A deferment, a threat, a desire. Anka has her first glimpse of the envelope, by chance, at fifteen. The other is the message the father imparts to her whenever he takes the envelope with him when he travels, so that the daughter would not be tempted to open it if she found it. An unknown, a seduction, a betrayal. But these messages fall apart when one day, the father leaves the letter in the drawer, not absentmindedly but rather intentionally. And so the father's desire comes into the fore, in its duplicity as both the desire to be a father to this girl and the desire of the man-father for the girl-daughter.

Another mysterious message is the one from the dead mother who writes on the envelope: "For my daughter Anna." This message alludes to at least two things: the desire for a direct contact with her, lost in childbirth, and the unveiling of a secret. All in all, the father seems unable to communicate to the daughter what only the mother can know and communicate to her, that is, the knowledge of her origin. It is knowledge that, according to an ancient biological hypothesis, only the mother is supposed to possess (*mater certa, pater incertus*).

If the father's desire for the daughter is too intense and if his defenses against it are organized in a way that is too rigid or dismissive, the daughter runs the risk of forfeiting the knowledge of her origin, for she can no longer trace her ancestry if her mother is no longer there to attest to the generative act. Therefore, for a son or a daughter to be able to honor his or her father and mother as his or her parents, or *procreators*, it is necessary that the parents themselves also recognize their symbolic positions.

On the contrary, in this situation, Michał must fight against an initial disavowal—that which emanates from the sealed envelope of his woman, Anka's mother. Apparently, just before dying, she had undermined the symbolic terms of Michał's paternity, not only and not so much by deceiving him, but rather by implying on her deathbed that he is not her little girl's father, while at the same time entrusting her to his fatherhood. This sets up an atmosphere of symbolic uncertainty that strikes a blow at the father's heart as well as his paternal function.

Moreover, what certainty could there be about paternity and filiation? For that matter, is there such a thing as symbolic certainty about maternity? As *Decalogue Two* shows, these are open questions for everyone. But here Michał confesses to his daughter that he has always suspected, although he was never certain, that he was not her "real" father. Therefore, from the beginning, Michał has lived a paternity always threatened by doubt, which, for the duration of the more dangerous period of the Oedipal stage, he decided not to resolve. Instead, he essentially drew from it the symbolic energies to love Anka as a daughter, to protect her and to guide her in her life. It is only when she finds a boyfriend that Michał decides to "forget" the mysterious letter and to take the risk of clearing up his doubt.

Anka literally declares to her father that, in her teenage years, she was deeply alarmed when she found out that there could be something that would be revealed to her only after his death. Anka would have to learn something mysterious about her origin and her identity after the death of both of her parents. Michał's "oversight" predisposes his daughter to and sets off in him a veritable syndrome of failure. Therefore, once the alleged recognition is staged, there follows, inevitably, Anka's question to her father: "What shall I call you now?" "I don't know," Michał, the dishonored father, replies.

But the mother is also dishonored, as father and daughter throw themselves on her modest and fragile secrets, greedily rummaging through her papers in the cellar, blinded by the idea of finding the Truth there. Yet, in the end, the mother's letter is put to flames. With it, the phantasms of delegitimization it was able to incite are also gone. But this resolution becomes possible only when Anka drops the deception inherent in her fiction. This is the only way she can honor the father again: by again recognizing the father's symbolic function.

On the other hand, for this function to be recognized by the daughter, Michał in turn must succeed in resisting Anka's explicit and implicit seductions and remain resolute in his paternal position, with regard to which the last words of his wife had weakened and disoriented him. In reality, by burning the letter Anka ends up, exactly, paying respect to her mother's word, the word by which she had entrusted Anka's paternity to Michał. In fact, the revelation of a presumed "biological truth" was perhaps nothing more but the dead woman's revenge against her man, the man who would become a parent at very little cost of life or death, while she lost her parenthood in dying. And who knows? Perhaps that allusive, disquieting message was also an unconscious act of retaliation of the mother against her daughter, the daughter who, in being born, killed her.

Maternal envy does exist. It makes no sense to idealize things, and Kieślowski does not idealize. With his film, the agnostic Polish director seems to suggest that the act of honoring one's father and one's mother must traverse a similar terrain of knowledge. It is the knowledge of the profound imperfection of those who have brought us into the world: not only of their imperfection as subjects and individuals, but first and foremost of the imperfection of love, upon which our utopias go up in smoke.

The Dead Letter

To burn the letter enclosing the mother's secret appears, then, to be the most profound way to honor both the father and the mother. The mother's secret can never be identical to the daughter's secret. Instead, Michał enacted a morbid system of concealments and insinuations around that letter, and contributed to transforming what was a weak maternal message into a powerful Message from the Mother. But whatever the mother's knowledge, which constitutes the secret of her identity as a woman, may be, it must remain a dead letter to the daughter. It is only upon this condition that a daughter can succeed in piecing her own story together, that is, the story of her desire and, ultimately, her own secret knowledge, in its uniqueness, peculiarity, and difference. In a sense, we could infer from this filmic narrative that in order to obey the fourth commandment, it is necessary to let go of the possession of the mother, or of the maternal Thing. And this can only happen if the Oedipal law functions well. But in order for this law to work, the father must identify both the limitation and the inadequacy of his position. And the film shows this masterfully.

In other words, the father is *incertus* and remains such. He can function as father only within a nuclear, symbolic nexus of this kind.

In conclusion, to *honor thy father and thy mother* means to live one's life and one's death fully, which one's father and one's mother have consented to inaugurate in the very act of birth. Therefore, the mysterious letter—which should be opened only after the mother's death and, subsequently, only after the father's death—materializes the spiritual *viaticum* whereby the subject of desire is allowed to experience the life of his or her life and the death of his or her death. For this reason, Anka rightly threw that letter into the fire. The material existence of this message made the peculiarity of its origins appear disturbing and mysterious because of the allusive power of a secret that would be sooner or later unveiled. But burning the unopened letter eliminated this illusion once and for all. There cannot be any unveiling of our destiny: It is only from its ashes that we are born to the mystery of our identity.

Like everyone else, Anka is destined to experience some ontological uncertainty and some psychological precariousness if she wants to achieve her own individuation or, better yet, to attain her sexual difference. This seems to be the only way she can truly honor her father and her mother.

In the Form of an Enigma

Elsewhere, I have pointed out the particular structural positioning of the title in each of the ten films of Kieślowski's *Decalogue*.[2] And, surely, we have had and will still have much to learn from their original articulation in relation to the story and the techniques of each film. The director's words highlight the essential arbitrariness of each title with regard to the merit and content of the individual story each film is based on.

"To be honest," Kieślowski asserts, "I did not follow any rules because I simply wanted to relate ten stories. Their connection with the Ten Commandments is not binding. . . . All good books can, in the end, be traced back to the Ten Commandments . . . . Essentially, any book about human or metaphysical nature can be related to one or more commandments. The same thing is true for theater and the figurative arts because these norms exist and, when we speak about our existence or human relationships, we end up implicating them."[3] There is no necessary relation between any given commandment and any given story, and there are alternative associations one can think of. Nevertheless, the director continues: "We [Kieślowski and Piesiewicz] wrote the screenplays in such a way that a link existed, however tacit or veiled, but we did not aim for a simple illustration at all" ("Perché siamo qui?" 29). Therefore, each film's relation to the relevant commandment does not implicate its content, nor does it have any prescriptive, summative or definitive function with regard to the story that is being told. Rather, it has a maieutic and productive function. Thus, the commandments do not so much embody the moral message of Kieślowski's films as constitute a signifying trace within each of them. And as we speak of signifying traces, let us put to rest any hypothesis of moralistic decryption and make way for the subject of ethics. The latter, on account of its subjection to language and desire, acts and suffers from sin, guilt, pleasure, and sanction, and, on occasion, even happiness.

Having articulated this premise, we are now left with the task of validating it in the case of the fourth commandment: "Honor thy father and thy mother." The film's story, style, and language seem to assert the failure of this powerful ethical principle following a sequence of this kind: Dishonor the truth by means of Anka's fiction; dishonor the father by seducing him; dishonor the mother by burning her letter.

A different reading is, however, possible, one that exfoliates the metapsychological levels of narration and that seeks out the paradoxical knots within which the symbolic law is articulated. We already mentioned in the introduction that, according to the psychoanalyst and mathematician Daniel Sibony, the paradox of the symbolic law is that it pretends to offer a universal cohesion to human beings but entails the impossibility of conforming to it.[4] And this reading allows for clarification and articulation of some semantic connections between the style in which the story is narrated and the antirhetoric that is also immanent in the fourth commandment.

Even according to theological exegesis, "Honor thy father and thy mother" does not accentuate the aspect of the child's submission to his or her parents, but rather the opposite.[5] From a more unconventional perspective, to honor the father and the mother becomes an act of differentiation and autonomy by means of which a child fulfills the most productive aspect of his or her parents' desire of filiation. This desire comprises both a voracious and destructive maternal/paternal component that tends toward the absorption of the child into sameness and a strong aspiration toward the alterity and difference of their progeny.

However, we can observe something more in *Four* if we treat the title as a meaningful card laid on the table during the aesthetic and ethical game that we are playing with the author. It is almost by chance that the fourth commandment corresponds to this episode, rather than the sixth ("Thou shalt not commit adultery"), the eighth ("Thou shalt not bear false witness against thy neighbor"), or the ninth ("Thou shalt not covet thy neighbor's wife"). Yet, when you see the film through the prism of this card, its system of meanings coalesces around those signifiers—"Honor thy father and thy mother"—to offer some pathways to knowledge that is unfamiliar, perhaps, even to the author himself. All this makes Kieślowski's entire film arbitrary like the Saussurean sign and allows the subject of the unconscious, rather than the moral or moralistic subject, to emerge. Whereas the moral subject has the function of filling the message with meaning, the subject of the unconscious adds meaning only in the form of an enigma.

How can Anka honor her father and her mother?

First of all, by freeing herself from the unconscious desire for her father's death, which until that moment represented to her the necessary condition of opening the mysterious envelope. Only in this way can she liberate her mother's letter from the paternal interdiction. This letter, once liberated from the yellow envelope that enclosed it, is capable of destroying, by its mere presence, the relative harmony between Michał and Anka, most likely because the prolonged state of repression, which it had been under until then, is suddenly lifted at that moment. Michał feared that the letter furnished evidence that he could not be the father: ultimately, his paternal dishonor. It was, therefore, necessary for the daughter to seize the "letter" of his message to escape this dead end. It was explicitly a matter of life or death: What was written on the envelope ("To be opened after my death") set things up in these terms.

What could be done, then? One could put a stop to the agony of ambivalence and accept the enigma. At the same time, Anka also took her mother literally: "*You are my daughter*" is implicit in her mother's exact words, "For my daughter." This is enough of a signal for Anka to shift her mother's position from that of an imaginary avenger to that of the symbolic mother who recognizes her. The very fact that the daughter could perform such a shift of register with regard to the subjective ethical value of the forbidden letter is sufficient to compel Michał to assume both the weight and the renunciations of his self-legitimation as a father.

All in all, the Maternal Message does not exist for the subject of the unconscious of "Honor thy father and thy mother." However, if the father, by fearing it, brings the Message into being and gives it authority, he ends up being condemned to having to vacate his function as a father.

The Desire of/for the Cut

In the first part of the film, Michał and Anka perform a love game with water, in which there are clear echoes of an imaginary complicity, founded on a phallic bond between them. The relation between father and daughter appears to be sustained by a mutual tension directed at the avoidance of limits and of lack, of that foundational lack by virtue of which the object of desire, between father and daughter, exists only in gaps and defects.

After all, by using the expedient of fiction and by exercising the more or less hidden pressures of mastery, Michał and Anka attempt to hide from each other the degree to which the questions of origin and acknowledgment dig a void and signal a mystery in the constitution of their respective identities. Thus, both maintain a relationship of omnipotent control with regard to that sealed envelope, which is, for each, both a condemnation and a chimera.

The second part of the film brings to light, as do all the episodes of Kieślowski's *Decalogue*, the explosive power of the effort to make the impossible possible. The impossible is that dimension of the *real* around which the subject revolves and, around which it, for the most part, runs in circles. The term "the impossible" indicates, in this instance, that phantasm of revelation that ties around the fetish of the sealed letter like a knot. The phantasm of revelation, in turn, refers to the obscure auspices and prophetic expectations that envelop the unknown message, hidden as well as revealed, of the father and of the mother.

In any case—whether the powerful utopia about the truth of origins takes hold, eliminating any dimension of mystery; or the presumed dogma of the letter eradicates any enigmatic root of the subject; or the power of absence and death invades the living space of the two protagonists—we always deal with the maternal Thing, of which it is impossible to say or predicate anything.

And so, in this story, the confines of the impossible are trespassed in at least three different areas: in the field of Truth, in which minor vestiges of language and meaning remain; in the field of Dogma, where mysteries vanish and the intermittences of the heart dissolve; and, analogously, in the dizziness of Absence, where loss allows for a few flashes of bodily presence to persist. In this way, the maternal Thing predominates.

In other words, Anka decides, in the name of the Mother's dead end, immediately to marry a man whom she does not love. She does so under the aegis of the maternal Dogma, which holds the key to annulling paternity at any moment. Michał, for his part, falls into the all-powerful hole of Absence, kicking and screaming like an automaton. The visual frame is then filled by the dazzling white shape of a canoe, carried by a featureless man, at the very moment when Anka is about to cut the mother's envelope.

Figure 6-2. The diamond-shaped canoe in *Decalogue Four*.

It is an asymmetrical diamond form that simply draws on the screen four enigmatic and disquieting polarities (Figure 6-2).

Only later do we find out that Anka, following this vision, in fact refrains from the act of unveiling as if she understood, right at that moment, its impossibility or its fundamental uselessness for her soul. For Anka to cut open the father's envelope meant to undercut the extortion over origins and to weaken her imaginary complicity with him; on the contrary, to cut open the mother's envelope would be equivalent to making the mother's absence intrusive, thus filling in the void of her lack.

In the third phase of the film, father and daughter sink into anguish. Their situation effectively illustrates how the fantasy of touching the truth of the mother is, simultaneously, an irresistible temptation and an insufferable experience.

At this point, the fourth phase of the film begins. The imaginary triangulation, at first constructed around the phallic pole of the avoidance of lack, later develops, once it has suffered the cut inflicted by Anka, into another pole predicated on the symbolic components of insufficiency and void. This is the only mental space in which the inscription of desire and language is possible. In short, the triangulation of complicity closes ranks around the void that the maternal letter has created, once it is accepted that it always remains unknown.

The magic and the logic of absence now begin to exert an effect. And so Anka's incestuous desire dissolves into the mystery of origins. Perhaps this mystery will permit her to find herself. The father's incestuous desire—which initially overflowed, by identification with the much hoped for and much feared maternal verdict—now begins to flow within the embankments of an intense and difficult paternal desire. The squaring of these

Figure 6-3. Anka's resolution in *Decalogue Four*.

triangles opens up the space of the lost object, the object that is lost precisely because it has never been possessed. This space opens up in the film at the moment when Anka admits that she did not open the letter and that she ignored the truth therein. Therefore, the truth that until then she had boasted to have held in her hands was nothing but a dose of that lost truth, never ever possessed.

At the very moment when Anka makes this admission to her father, the man with the canoe passes by again. But, for us, the image is no longer the same from a logical and metapsychological perspective. What has happened? It is now time for the white diamond of the canoe to be wounded (Figure 6-3).

Although its whiteness is untouched and its geometry unchanged, the absoluteness of its silhouette against the space is even more essential because it has sustained what I would like to define as a transversal cut through/of lack. This cut breaks the phallic bond and introduces an element of openness and contamination into the integrity and invulnerability of the original Object.

To Honor the Truth

In conclusion, Kieślowski's *Four* ends with a signifier that burns. The unknown of the unconscious emerges in the very act of signifying itself.

"Honor thy father and thy mother" corresponds, for Michał, literally to a fire that still burns him: "The letter is burning (me)." In this way, Michał is surprised by his own enigma, with which, in the end, he will not be able to do anything but continue living: "Is he or is he not the father of that daughter?" In truth, there is a barrier that resists meaning and divides the signifiers of the unconscious from the semantic body of signification. As for us, in the last frame we leave Michał before the fire, while he is incinerating, with that letter, that which still inflames him in vain.

"Honor thy father and thy mother" corresponds, for the dead woman, literally to a fire that goes beyond her own demise. It is a fire of love and hate, a flame that makes her soul migrate without giving her peace: "May the letter burn (you)!" The echo of another enigma lights up in this message: the enigma of that which burns the heart of a mother.

"Honor thy father and thy mother" is, for Anka, the signifying materialization or, better, the letter of her desire to be: "I burn (for) the letter." In other words: "I yearn for the letter that holds the secret of my identity." In all truth, the letter of identity rises from the ashes of incestuous desire: an unreal desire that mutates, leaving in the hands of each individual only the unknown with which they honor both the progeny and the progenitors.

"Honor thy father and thy mother" is "the letter" of *Four*. What is written in it is that the symbolic weight of origins is our most immanent mystery. And, thus, all this talk about it only weaves our stories together (up) in smoke.

Translated by Eva Badowska
and Francesca Parmeggiani

NOTES

This essay was first published in Italian as "Madre in fumo: Onora il padre e la madre," in Gabriella Ripa di Meana, *La morale dell'altro. Scritti sull'inconscio dal Decalogo di Kieślowski* (Florence: Liberal Libri, 1998), 95–116.

1. Krzysztof Kieślowski and Krzysztof Piesiewicz, *Decalogue: The Ten Commandments*, trans. Phil Cavendish and Susannah Bluh (London: Faber and Faber, 1991), 97.

2. [Ripa di Meana first addresses the relationship between the Commandments and Kieślowski's cycle in the introduction to her volume on *The Decalogue*. She observes that the Commandments are present tacitly as numbers—rather than as moral laws—in the title of each episode. This as if obliterated presence of the Commandments in *The Decalogue* activates the plurality of meanings within each story. In other words, the Commandments, as *The Decalogue*'s missing titles, function as "signifying traits" that set off the working of interpretation rather than provide each story with content or moral meaning (*La morale dell'altro*, 15–16). — Trans.]

3. Małgorzata Furdal, interview with Krzysztof Kieślowski, "Perché siamo qui?," in *Kieślowski,* ed. Małgorzata Furdal and Roberto Turigliatto

(Turin: Museo Nazionale del Cinema, 1989), 29. Further references will be cited in the text.

4. Daniel Sibony, *Jouissances du dire. Nouveaux essais sur une transmission d'inconscient* (Paris: Grasset, 1985), 14.

5. See Valdo Benecchi, *I dieci comandamenti: avventura di libertà* (Turin: Claudiana, 1994).

CHAPTER 7

Decalogue Five: A Short Film about Killing, Sin, and Community

Michael Baur

Decalogue Five tells the story of Waldemar Rekowski (Jan Tesarz), a jaded taxi driver, Piotr Balicki (Krzysztof Globisz), an idealistic, newly-licensed attorney, and Jacek Lazar (Mirosław Baka), a young and troubled drifter, whose lives intersect with one another as a result of fate, or contingent circumstance, or some combination of both. With brutal detail and detachment, the film depicts Jacek's seemingly aimless wanderings through Warsaw, his senseless killing of Waldemar, his interactions with Piotr (his court-appointed attorney), and his eventual execution after a failed defense in court. Like other films within the *Decalogue* series, *Five* illustrates what happens when human beings are forced to confront ethical dilemmas (and thus are forced to confront themselves as responsible moral decision makers) in a world that seems to offer little in the way of moral direction, meaning, purpose, and community with others. Discussing the overarching aim of the *Decalogue* series as a whole, Krzysztof Kieślowski refers to the sense of alienation, aimlessness, and loneliness that often describes the human condition:

> *Decalogue* is an attempt to narrate ten stories about ten or twenty individuals, who—caught in a struggle precisely because of these and

not other circumstances, circumstances which are fictitious but which could occur in everyday life—suddenly realize that they're going round and round in circles, that they're not achieving what they want.[1]

Of the three main characters in *Five*, two in particular—Jacek and Waldemar—seem to illustrate the directionless, alienated form of existence that constitutes the subject matter of the *Decalogue* series as a whole. Paul Coates describes Jacek's aimless and menacing wanderings throughout the city as the wanderings of someone who "stalks Warsaw like an edgy, existential angel of doom."[2] While Waldemar appears to be better off in some respects—he is married and employed, after all—it is apparent that he does not share much affection with his fellow citizens. When we first meet Waldemar, we see him walking around the housing complex where he lives and narrowly escaping being hit by a clump of wet, dirty rags thrown down at him from a resident above.

In general, Jacek and Waldemar seem not to care much about the world that surrounds them, and the world, in turn, seems to care little about them. Neither Jacek nor Waldemar is especially likable, and both are seen to be capable of violence and callousness as they interact—or fail to interact—with their fellow citizens. For example, we see Jacek attack another young man in a public restroom and throw him violently into a urinal, all for no apparent reason. Also for no apparent reason, Jacek runs into a crowd of pigeons being fed in a public square, scaring the pigeons away from the woman who had been trying to feed them. While on a highway overpass, Jacek places a rock on the overpass ledge and nudges it until it falls off into traffic below, causing what sounds like a serious and perhaps even fatal accident. After finishing his coffee and cake in a local café, Jacek leaves a large dollop of spit in his empty coffee cup; then, before leaving the café, he flings a large spoonful of leftover food at the café's window, where two little girls had been standing and looking in on him.

Although Waldemar is a more established and gainfully employed member of society, he also has his moments of callousness and cruelty. While washing his taxicab, Waldemar takes his time and shows no sympathy or concern for the couple (Dorota and her husband from *Two*), who, after asking for a ride, waits patiently for him at the taxi stand. Once he is finished washing his taxi, he drives off without saying a word to the couple, leaving them stranded in the cold. While driving his taxi, Waldemar honks his horn at a man and his two dogs as they pass by, for no reason other than to witness the frightened reaction of the man and his dogs. In another scene, while Waldemar waits near the taxi stand, we see him ogling the young girl at the nearby vegetable kiosk and trying to look up her skirt as she reaches to receive vegetables from a delivery truck. And in a selfish act that will indirectly lead to his demise, Waldemar quickly drives off rather than giving a ride to an obviously inebriated man being helped by a friend to the taxi stand. In so doing, Waldemar keeps himself available to pick up Jacek as his next and—as it turns out—final passenger.

While both Jacek and Waldemar are unlikable in many respects, they display at least a few redeeming qualities. For example, Jacek shows genuine affection for others, especially for young girls, as is evident from the way he pensively observes the images of young girls being displayed in the window of the photography shop, and by the way he thoughtfully looks on as the street artist draws a portrait of the young girl sitting for him. There is at least a hint of genuine humanity and kindness in Waldemar when he decides to share half of his sandwich with a hungry stray dog. However, we should not think that these better and worse impulses reside in Jacek and Waldemar alongside one another as two entirely distinct and separable sides of their characters. It is an undeniable fact of human nature and psychology that some of our cruelest and most antisocial impulses are intimately bound up with our impulses toward genuine affection and community with others. Thus, Jacek's flinging of food in the direction of the little girls at the café window may certainly be understood as a sign of aggression, but just as plausibly it may also be understood as an attempt—though perhaps an awkward one—at sharing a laugh with them. The dual character of Jacek's act is clearly indicated by the ambivalent reaction of the little girls. As they turn to run away from the café window, the girls laugh, but their laugh is not an entirely comfortable one; while they laugh, their faces also show the uneasy awareness that Jacek's act of flinging food in their direction was not just (potentially) funny, but menacing and aggressive as well. A similar duality can be seen in Waldemar's act of sharing half of his sandwich with the stray dog. On the one hand, Waldemar's act may be understood as a sign of genuine kindness and concern for another needy, living being. On the other hand, as the film makes clear, the sandwich that Waldemar shares with the stray dog is a sandwich that had been prepared for him by his wife; and so, this very act of sharing might equally be understood as a sign of disdain for the wife, as if Waldemar were telling himself that the sandwich prepared for him by his own wife is really only fit for a dog.

Of course, we cannot be entirely sure what to make of these acts by Jacek and Waldemar. They are acts that seemingly and inextricably bind together cruelty and kindness. But this seems to be one of the points that Kieślowski wishes to make about the human state. Given our alienated and warped

Decalogue Five

condition, it is often the case that we humans simply do not know how to actualize our better impulses without also giving reign to our worse impulses. That is, we simply do not know how to reach out to others and seek community with them, without also introducing into our actions certain elements of callousness, cruelty, or aggression.[3] Indeed, one of the overriding lessons that emerges in *Five* and in the rest of the *Decalogue* series is that the systems or institutions which we humans have created for ourselves—systems that are supposed to enable us to achieve our better aspirations and goals—often conspire to frustrate our better strivings and to convince us that our strivings are in vain. In *Five*, the problematic systems within which we live—including our political systems, our systems of modern science and technology, the system of incentives and punishments known as the law, and the system of organized religion—are visually hinted at through Warsaw's Inflancka housing complex, which is the setting for much of the action in the *Decalogue* series as a whole. Like the housing complex, these systems often give people shelter for living, but not for living well; like the housing complex, they allow large numbers of people to live together, but they often frustrate our strivings for genuine togetherness and community. And so we often find ourselves trying to actualize our better impulses precisely in ways that seem destined to fail; and thus in ways that lead to a sense of frustration, aggression, and lack of direction. Just as Kieślowski said of the characters in *The Decalogue*, we too find ourselves "going round and round in circles" and "not achieving what we want" (*KK*, 145).

The Roman Catholic tradition (including the tradition that is very much part of Kieślowski's native Poland) has a name for the mechanism by which systems of our own making regularly frustrate, stunt, and warp our better aspirations toward genuine sharing and community with others. The tradition's name for this mechanism is original sin. Of course, we should be very careful about attributing to Kieślowski a theological outlook that is foreign to his own. It is well known that Kieślowski did not feel great attachment to the Roman Catholic Church, and—as one critic has observed—he did not have "much use for institutional Christianity" in general.[4] But in spite of his own critical self-distancing from institutional religion in general and from the Roman Catholic Church in particular, it is possible that Kieślowski's view of the human condition does indeed reflect certain views espoused, though in some cases also misunderstood, by proponents of institutionalized religion.

The point of original sin—as opposed to sin that is not original—is that it affects us in our very beginnings, our very origins, our very coming-into-being. It is not the kind of sin that arises out of misjudgments or bad choices by the individual alone. It is original in the sense that it characterizes the human condition through which we have our very being. But what is this human condition? Significantly, the human condition is a condition of interpersonal interdependence and socialization. The philosopher Alasdair MacIntyre has described the human condition as the condition of "dependent rational animals":[5] We depend on others not only because our biological needs have to be met (though that is certainly the case), but also, and more important, because we need others in order to acquire the virtues without which we could not be the rational, human agents that we aspire to be. The human being is by nature a social animal, and thus we humans need others in order to become what we truly are as human beings. When we do not have the help and support of others, we quite literally do not have ourselves. I have my being and my humanity by virtue of the communication, mutual support, and sharing that I have with others, but because of this, if there is any failing, perversion, or distortion in the means and mechanisms of my sharing and communicating with others, there is equally a failing, perversion, or distortion in my very own being. This is what original sin refers to: the perversion or distortion that is inscribed in my very being, insofar as my very being depends on systems of communication and sharing that are themselves perverted or distorted.

Furthermore, original sin cannot be eradicated through the initiative of individuals (even if this initiative were widespread or even universal among individuals) to treat each other better and more humanely. The point of original sin is that the failed, alienating systems within which we live will always persist at disguising themselves, justifying themselves, and co-opting for their own ends the very weapons that we might fashion in order to oppose them. The problem of original sin is helpfully explained by Herbert McCabe, one of the twentieth century's most refreshingly creative and yet reliable expositors of the Roman Catholic faith. As McCabe writes,

> The point is that we are born into a society which in various ways fails us as we stand in need of love. And for this reason we are born crippled (using the word "born" in a more extended sense). And our society does not fail us simply because of the ill will of individual members but because of the structures it represents, because of the role it assigns these members. You could be born and brought up in a group who were all individually saints and you would still be subject to the deprivation we call the Sin of the World.[6]

We depend on others for our own humanity, and yet the systems that we create for our own humanity systematically fail us, not because of any particular shortcoming on the part of individuals, but because of the distortions and perversions embedded within the systems and media through which we relate to each other and communicate with each other. These systems cannot be corrected by better, kinder decisions by individuals, because the distorting powers embedded in these systems exceed our ability, individually and collectively, to control them. They will always co-opt our best efforts to counteract them, since each of us (dependent on such systems of communication and socialization for our very humanity) cannot escape operating from within the means provided by these systems themselves.

The problem is illustrated by the change in Piotr's thinking over the course of *Five*. Near the beginning of the film, Piotr suggests that the law (or "the application of justice") might "correct the mistakes" of "a giant machine" which tends to dominate our lives. By the end of the film, however, Piotr has grown to realize that the law itself has been co-opted by and made to do the bidding of this giant, anonymous, and ineluctable machine.

It is worthwhile to say more at this point about the connection between original sin and our need to live within systems of socialization and communication with others. On one level or another, all material beings in the universe interact with their environments, which is to say that they exist in community or in communication with other material beings. But the character of such interaction and communication varies, depending on the degree of excellence represented by the kind of being in question. In general, the higher or more excellent kinds of material beings are capable of more excellent kinds of communication (more complete and more intimate kinds of sharing) with other beings. But it is precisely because of their more excellent and higher degrees of communication with others that such higher beings also face greater risks, greater vulnerabilities, and greater chances for failure and perversion than lower beings do. One might say that there is a dialectical relationship between degrees of excellence and degrees of risk within the universe of material beings, and it is this dialectical relationship that helps us to better understand what original sin is, and how it is shown to manifest itself in *Five*.

Consider, for example, the ways in which animate beings are more excellent than inanimate beings and thus capable of greater degrees of communication and sharing with other beings. Unlike inanimate things, living beings maintain themselves in existence (*qua* living) precisely by not limiting themselves to being determined by the material components that happen to constitute them at any given moment, but instead by actively engaging in the process of metabolism, or the ongoing exchange or sharing of energy and matter with beings in the surrounding environment. Compared with nonliving things, living beings display a greater degree of excellence or a greater degree of immateriality, that is, a greater degree of freedom from being determined by their underlying material conditions. It is by virtue of this greater degree of excellence and immateriality that living beings are capable of sharing and communicating with other beings more fully and intimately. Thus, living beings maintain their existence, not by insulating themselves against the physical and chemical intrusions of other beings, but precisely by inviting such intrusions, or by making themselves relatively permeable and by participating in an ongoing process of material and caloric exchange with the environment. But because of their greater degree of excellence and immateriality (and thus because of their greater capacity for communication and sharing), living beings also face greater risks, greater vulnerabilities, and greater chances of failure or perversion than nonliving beings do. Simply stated, there are more things that can go wrong with the living being; the living being can fail in many more ways than nonliving beings can. Thus if the living being should cease to engage in the active exchange of energy and matter with its environment, it will die, which is to say that it will fail at being a living being. By contrast, nonliving beings maintain themselves as what they are, precisely by being inert, by not engaging in the exchange of matter and energy with their environments. The difference between living and nonliving beings helps to illustrate why a greater degree of excellence and immateriality entails a greater capacity for communication and sharing with other beings, but also a greater degree of vulnerability and a more daunting set of challenges for succeeding at being the kind of being that one is.

The same general observation can be made about the contrast between sentient living beings (animals) and nonsentient living beings (plants). When compared with plants, animals display a greater degree of excellence and immateriality, and thus a greater capacity for communication and sharing with other beings. Unlike plants, animals are capable of acquiring sensory knowledge about other beings in their environment. This sensory knowledge, in turn, allows animals to direct themselves toward sources of nourishment and away from sources of danger. On account of such motility, animals are not limited to nourishing themselves (they are not limited to engaging in metabolic exchanges) with material resources that happen to be contiguous with their own bodies. Because they are sentient, animals can also be motile, which is to say that they can move under their own power away from the spatial regions in which they immediately find themselves, and into regions where the ongoing availability of nourishment will depend not just on what the environment provides, but also on the animal's riskier and less assured performance of several higher-order, sensory-based interactions with the environment. Thus, in order to survive, the animal must be attentive at the right times, it must be able to move about in its surroundings with relative ease, it must be able to find food and evade predators; notice that the success of the animal's interactions with the environment will depend, crucially, on what other animals do as well. To extend an observation made earlier: There are simply more, and more varied, ways in which the animal can fail at being an animal than there are ways in which the plant can fail at being a plant. Because of its greater degree of excellence and immateriality, the animal communicates and interacts with its environment in a more excellent way than plants do, but also, on account of its greater degree of excellence, it also faces greater risks and dangers. Animals purchase greater freedom, greater self-determination, and a greater capacity for interacting with other beings, but only by exposing themselves to the possibility of failing more miserably, and in more ways, at being the kinds of beings that they are.

The preceding set of observations can now be extended to illustrate the difference between nonrational (nonhuman) animals and rational (human) animals, and to explain the significance of this distinction for the notion of original sin. When compared to nonhuman animals, humans display a greater degree of excellence and immateriality, and this, in turn, entails a greater capacity for communication and sharing with other beings. Thus, it is on account of their rational (i.e., their conceptual or linguistic) capacities that human beings can understand and share in meanings and perspectives that would be entirely closed off to them if left to their own devices as merely sentient beings. Human beings become genuinely rational and free, that is, they become capable of apprehending the nonparticularized meanings of particular things or events, only because of their capacity to communicate with others conceptually and linguistically.[7]

Now we saw above that living beings succeed at being what they are (they remain alive) only by maintaining themselves as active sites for the processing of material and caloric resources that are drawn from environments that are not of their own making and not subject to their exclusive control as individuals; hence the unavoidable risk and vulnerability attendant upon all animate beings. In a similar fashion, we can say that human beings succeed at what they are (they are rational and free) only by maintaining themselves as active sites for the processing of conceptual and linguistic resources which are drawn from traditions and communities that are not of their own making and not subject to their exclusive control as individuals. A mind that is not open to the give-and-take of such engagement with other minds is a mind that is not fully rational or free. But it is precisely because of the human being's greater degree of excellence and immateriality—the human being's openness to sharing in the narratives, meanings, thoughts, and theories of others—that the human being is also subject to greater risks and dangers. We have seen that the animal's own heightened degree of freedom and self-determination (its ability to move itself) made the animal more vulnerable to the workings of its environment and to the potentially destructive activities of other animals. We can now see that, in a similar way, the human being's own heightened degree of freedom and self-determination (its ability to share and participate in the meanings and narratives afforded by other human beings) also makes the human being more vulnerable to the potentially perverting and destructive effects of those meanings and narratives that he or she unavoidably shares with others. As human beings, we depend intimately and inescapably on the thoughts and narratives of others for our own rationality and our own self-understanding. But it is this more intimate and more complete kind of sharing and communication, which makes us truly free and rational in the first place, that also makes us vulnerable to being co-opted by the distorting, demeaning, and alienating systems of meaning within which we find ourselves and which we as finite rational individuals can neither control nor altogether abandon. The condition of being dependent and vulnerable in this way is the condition of being tainted by original sin. The sin is original because it is an infirmity that penetrates to the core of our being as rational and free beings; but it is still a sin, because it is not something that happens to us apart from our own agency, but rather something that we bring upon ourselves as the dependent, rational beings that we are.

Five indirectly addresses the problem of original sin—though without the off-putting doctrinal label—when the film raises the question of how seemingly random and insignificant events can play such an important role in determining the trajectory of a person's life. In a scene that follows Jacek's conviction and death-sentence, Jacek sits down with Piotr and speculates about why he has become the destructive, self-loathing person that he is. Five years earlier, Jacek and a friend had been drinking together. While drunk, the friend climbed into a tractor and ended up killing Jacek's younger sister as a result of his reckless drunken driving. Jacek clearly feels that he is at least partly to blame for the death of his sister, and openly wonders whether things might have been different for him if the fatal accident had not occurred. On the face of it, it may seem silly to wonder whether such a random accident could have turned Jacek into the directionless, nihilistic, murderous person that he has become. But that is not the point of Jacek's rueful musings about the accident; these are not the musings of a detached scientist or philosopher wishing to know more about how one random event might bring about a chain of other, seemingly unrelated events in our causally ordered world. Rather, the point of Jacek's speculations is that seemingly random and insignificant events in our lives (such as the act of getting drunk with a friend) can engender unbearable meanings for us, meanings that exceed our capacity for coping and for making sense of things. Such meanings can exceed our capacity for coping and for making sense of things, not because of the intrinsic character of the events out of which they arise, but rather because the events take place within systems of socialization and communication which are distorted and inadequate, and thus incapable of helping us to actualize our proper strivings as human beings. When those strivings are frustrated or distorted, they do not cease to exist altogether; rather, they become strivings for the wrong sorts of things: domination, destruction, and self-aggrandizement at the expense of others.

One of the systems of socialization and communication that has a regular tendency to frustrate and distort our true strivings is the legal system, which is ostensibly the primary subject matter of *Five*. The film opens with an image of Piotr as he prepares for his final law-licensing exam, accompanied by a voiceover of Piotr discoursing on the nature and purpose of law. In the voiceover, Piotr argues,

> The law should not imitate nature, the law should improve nature. People invented the law to govern their relationships. The law determined who we are and how we live. We either observe it, or break it. People are free; their freedom is limited only by the freedom of others. Punishment means revenge, in particular when it aims to harm, but it does not prevent crime. For whom does the law avenge? In the name of the innocent? Do the innocent make the rules?

Like the other systems within which we must live, the legal system also has a tendency to pervert and distort our proper strivings as human beings. The law does not make people better as it should (it does not "improve nature"), but in fact makes people worse by reinforcing their destructive, antisocial behaviors (it "imitates nature," and in particular the human being's baser nature). Since punishment—and in particular, the death penalty—does nothing to prevent or deter crime, the only justification for it can be retribution. But retribution, Piotr suggests, amounts to little more than revenge, which is destructive of human beings and their nobler aspirations toward love and community.

After Jacek's trial, conviction, and sentencing, we can see how the retributive, vengeful character of the law harms Jacek and destroys the last remaining shreds of humanity that he is trying to salvage in himself. In response to his being convicted and sentenced to death, Jacek rightly infers that the overriding message of the law is that he is altogether worthless and thus unworthy of continued existence as a human being. Piotr tries to correct Jacek by distinguishing between the crime and the criminal, but Jacek will have none of it:

JACEK: They were all against me.

PIOTR: Against what you did.

JACEK: Same thing.

Rather than help Jacek to be the human being that he ought to be, the legal system—like so many other systems that mediate our socialization and communication with one another—only serves to reinforce Jacek's self-loathing and self-destructive behavior.

Jacek is not the only victim of the legal system. *Five* shows us how the legal system can begin to take its toll on people, like Piotr, whose calling is ostensibly to dedicate themselves to the law itself. At the beginning of the film, we get to know Piotr as someone whose sense of meaning and direction seems to make him very different from Jacek and Waldemar. Piotr, after all, is an idealistic lawyer who believes in the higher goals that the law apparently professes for itself; and, as we learn a bit later in the film, he is a proud new father. As the film progresses, however, we begin to wonder whether the legal system is not also conspiring to undermine Piotr's idealism and sense of purpose. After Jacek's trial, conviction, and sentencing, Piotr realizes that he has failed to save a human life from the death penalty, even after he had given what, according to the judge, was "the best argument" against the death penalty that had been presented in a long time. At the very end of the film, we see Piotr sitting in his car in a grassy field and shouting in anger and desperation, "I abhor it!"—apparently referring to the legal system that has failed him and failed Jacek. But while the legal system has failed him, Piotr feels that he too has failed. Thus he asks the judge whether Jacek's case might have turned out differently, if he had made a stronger case for Jacek or if the case had been assigned to another defense lawyer. When Piotr learns that he was dining in the café precisely at the time that Jacek was in the same café planning his crime, he begins to wonder whether he himself could have acted differently then in order to help Jacek. Like Jacek, Piotr has come to show the beginning signs of self-doubt and self-loathing, wondering whether things could have turned out better if he had only acted differently. Once again, Piotr's musings about what might have been are not the detached, speculative thoughts of someone wishing to know about how the causal laws of our universe operate; they are the musings of someone whose idealism and sense of direction are being slowly warped and crushed by our ever-distorted and distorting systems of interpersonal communication and socialization.

It was suggested earlier that original sin refers to the perversion or distortion inscribed in our very being as individuals, insofar as our being as individuals depends on systems of interpersonal communication and socialization which are themselves perverted or distorted. The odd thing about original sin is that it reverses our otherwise healthy strivings toward communication and community, and turns them into their virtual opposite; thus, original sin has the tendency to isolate us and drive us away from each other. But insofar as we are alone and isolated, we are deprived of community and the nurturing support of others, and thus ultimately deprived of what we need to be our true selves. It is altogether appropriate that one of the Christian tradition's greatest representations of hell—Dante's *Comedy*—portrays the most forlorn in the inferno (Lucifer) as entirely silent and cold, chest-deep in ice and possessing three mouths which are stuffed with the bodies of other sinners (Judas Iscariot, Brutus, and Cassius).[8] In the inferno, Lucifer appears to be in the presence of others, but he is utterly unable to enjoy any real community or communication with them. For the Catholic tradition, hell is not other people (as Jean-Paul Sartre would have it) but rather, complete separation from other people, the complete failure of community with others.

But when we are alone, when we fail to achieve genuine community with others, we also fail to achieve ourselves; we fail to be who we are. Thus, there is an intimate connection between sin and self-loathing; and in turn, there is an intimate connection between self-loathing and self-deception. McCabe makes the point nicely:

> The root of all sin is fear: the very deep fear that we are nothing; the compulsion, therefore, to make something of ourselves, to construct a self-flattering image of ourselves we can worship, to believe in ourselves—our fantasy selves. I think that all sins are failures in being realistic; even the simple everyday sins of the flesh, that seem to come from mere childish greed for pleasure, have their deepest origin

in anxiety about whether we really matter, the anxiety that makes us desperate for self-reassurance. To sin is always to construct an illusory self that we can admire, instead of the real self we can only love. It is because we fail in realistic self-love that we fail in love for others. So sin, too, means being terrified of admitting that we have failed.[9]

It might be added here that if sin is rooted in the fear of being alone, it is equally rooted in the fear of not being with others and not being loved and accepted by others for who we really are. This fear of not being loved for who we are is what leads us to manufacture false selves that we try to sell to others. Even if we succeed in winning the attention and affection of others through such false selves, we nevertheless remain fundamentally alone—and we are often obliquely aware of this aloneness—because what we have offered to others for their love and acceptance is not our true self, but rather an idol or image that allows us to remain fundamentally hidden, isolated, and alone.

It follows from this that sin or sinfulness represents a kind of slavery or thralldom. In our sinfulness, we enslave ourselves to false images, and, correspondingly, to false gods that we manufacture for the sake of covering up our nakedness, our fear and our need. The discovery of the genuine God, the God who stands opposed to all forms of idolatry, is the discovery of a God who calls us out of such thralldom and invites us to the freedom of accepting ourselves and others for who we and they are, even in our and their neediness and failure. As McCabe explains:

> The only true God is the God of freedom. The other gods make you feel at home in a place, they have to do with the quiet cycle of the seasons, with the familiar mountains and the country you grew up in and love; with them you know where you are. But the harsh God of freedom calls you out of all this into a desert where all the old familiar landmarks are gone, where you cannot rely on the safe workings of nature, on springtime and harvest, where you must wander over the wilderness waiting for what God will bring. This God of freedom will allow you none of the comforts of religion. Not only does he tear you away from the old traditional shrines and temples of your native place, but he will not even allow you to worship him in the old way. You are forbidden to make an image of him by which you might wield numinous power, you are forbidden to invoke his name in magical rites. You must deny the other gods and you must not treat Yahweh as a god, as a power you could use against your enemies or to help you succeed in life. Yahweh is not a god, there are no gods, they are all delusions and slavery.[10]

Decalogue Five

Figure 7–1. Saying prayers before the execution in *Decalogue Five*.

At this stage, another word of caution is in order. For we need to be careful about attributing to Kieślowski any theological views or metanarratives that are foreign to his way of thinking. As noted above, Kieślowski maintained a critical distance from institutional religion in general and from the Roman Catholic Church in particular. He believed that the systems within which we live and have our being, including the system of institutionalized religion, are often the problem rather than the solution. For Kieślowski, institutionalized religion, like the other systems within which we have our being, has a tendency to distort and frustrate our longings for meaning and community with others, and so it is not surprising that the only priest we encounter in *Five* says prayers just before Jacek's execution and thus lends an air of divine approbation to the heinous act of killing (Figure 7–1).

Furthermore, through Jacek's final conversation with Piotr, the film reminds us about the Church's traditional policy of denying Catholic burial rites to certain people, thus suggesting that Jacek's praiseworthy yearning for community with his deceased sister (i.e., his desire to be buried near her) might well be thwarted, in the end, by the requirements of institutionalized religion. This is not to say that Kieślowski denied that there may be some system or metanarrative (religious or otherwise) within which we might find some genuine meaning and liberation. But even if there is such an overarching system or metanarrative, Kieślowski seems to hold that the meaning provided by any such system or metanarrative, whatever it might be, remains just beyond our grasp.

The existence of an overarching yet ever-elusive meaning-providing metanarrative is suggested by the recurring appearance of a character identified in the script only as "the young man" (Artur Barciś). At decisive moments in eight of the ten *Decalogue* films (he is absent only from *Seven* and *Ten*), "the young man" appears as a silent, detached witness who seemingly observes or understands the purpose that mysteriously escapes the comprehension of those who are being portrayed in the film, and us who are watching the film. In *One*, "the young man" sits at a campfire near the pond where a young boy will later drown; in *Two*, he is a worker in a hospital where the film's protagonists are confronted with issues of birth, life, love, fidelity and death; in *Three*, he drives a city tram that narrowly misses colliding with and killing the protagonist; in *Four*, he is seen kayaking on the Vistula River and then later carrying the kayak on his back shortly before the protagonist makes her fateful decision about whether or not to open a mysterious letter; in *Five*, "the young man" is seen first as an inspector surveying the road that Waldemar traverses on the way to being killed by Jacek, and then later as a ladder-carrying painter in the prison where Jacek is to be executed; in *Six*, he appears first when the protagonist is joyously running home after learning about an upcoming date, and then a second time when the protagonist runs home after he has been humiliated by the date; in *Eight*, he is a student who listens as the protagonist presents a lecture; and in *Nine*, he is a cyclist who witnesses the attempt by the film's protagonist to commit suicide.

The regular appearance of "the young man" at decisive moments throughout the *Decalogue* series serves to convey the important message that there may indeed be an overriding (theological) purpose at work in our fallen and alienated world. But his mysterious expression and strange silence also convey the sense that any such metanarrative or purpose—assuming that one is discernible at all—may inescapably remain beyond the scope of all possible comprehension by us. Furthermore, *Five* adds a sinister and unique complement to this character who silently witnesses events as if from a God's-eye perspective. In the episode, the appearance of "the young man" is echoed and perhaps undermined by the appearance of another silent witness: the hideous ornament—a disembodied head with a toothy grin—dangling from the windshield of Waldemar's taxi. At key moments in the film, the camera's perspective calls our attention to the presence of this small, silent witness, as if to suggest that the purpose to be observed or the metanarrative to be told about the event taking place is not a benevolent one at all. As we observers view the regular, silent presence of Waldemar's windshield ornament, we are led to wonder, as Robert Frost wonders in his poem, "Design," whether the purpose behind the seemingly random confluence of events, if there is any such purpose at all, might not be malevolent rather than benevolent: "What but design of darkness to appall?—/If design govern in a thing so small?"[11]

Decalogue Five

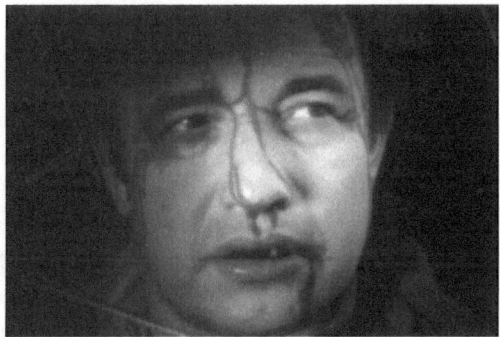

Figure 7–2. Waldemar's Christlike bloody face in *Decalogue Five*.

In spite of the ambiguity confronting us in regard to the overarching system or metanarrative that might give *Five* its meaning, there is no doubt that Kieślowski makes use of overt religious imagery and wants us to think about the possibility of an overarching religious system or metanarrative. Thus, when Jacek is in the midst of carrying out his murderous deed, Waldemar's bleeding, upturned face presents us with an undeniable image of the crucified Christ (Figure 7–2).

As Christopher Garbowski observes:

> In the face of the cabdriver victim, who has been strangled and clubbed on the head with an iron bar, we seem to see the face of the crucified Jesus with blood streaming down his face as if from a crown of thorns. The victim appears to look at the murderer as if to forgive him. After the deed, the slayer eats the victim's food, just as the soldiers cast lots for Christ's clothes.[12]

In response to the Christ imagery that is present in Waldemar's face, Jacek utters the words, "Oh, Jesus" in amazement and in apparent recognition of the terribleness of his deed. But instead of halting his deed, Jacek reacts with renewed violence and uses a large stone to finish off what he started. In response to the unconditional love and acceptance represented by the Christ figure, Jacek tenaciously holds on to the false gods and false, antisocial sense of purpose that he has created for himself. In this respect, he is like the rest of us. As McCabe writes:

> As a matter of history one of the peculiar things about man is that when he is left to do exactly what he likes he straight away looks around for someone to enslave himself to, and if he cannot find a master nearby, he will invent one. The Hebrew discovery of God (or God's revelation of

himself to them) begins in their recognition that man historically is a slave, and enslaved by his own preference. The true God reveals himself as he who summons man out of this degradation that he clings to, who summons him to the painful business of being free. (*Law*, 115–116)

For Kieślowski, as for the Judeo-Christian tradition, the only remedy for our sinful condition is the saving grace of a God, but not one who would save us by giving us the falsely comforting shelter of a security blanket. The true God is the God who liberates us to face the appalling fearfulness of our neediness and our finitude head-on. Kieślowski seems to be saying—as Martin Heidegger says in his famous aphorism—"only a God can save us."[13] But also like Heidegger, Kieślowski does not have the metaphysical confidence to assert that such a God actually exists. His reticence about making any such theological pronouncements is rightly motivated, for religious talk about God can all too easily devolve into the idolatrously comforting talk about gods. If there is to be salvation for us, it is to be had—Kieślowski seems to be saying—only if we undertake the frightful but fulfilling activity of entering into genuine community with others. For what is the kingdom of God, announced so often in the gospels through the image of a wedding party, other than such community with others?

In *Five*, Jacek's thoughtful yearnings for his deceased sister convey a similar message. Jacek's desire to have an enlarged photograph of his deceased sister implies the desire to bring her back to life (to see her grow again), and thus to be in community with her once again. Other moments in the film similarly illustrate Jacek's desire to resurrect his sister and reestablish the only form of community that he ever knew. As we viewers watch the film, we, like Jacek, are forced to confront the challenges and possibilities of genuine community. We are forced to ask ourselves whether Jacek, in spite of his terrible crime, is someone in whom we can recognize our own humanity, and thus someone with whom we might see ourselves in community. In asking these questions, we are in effect asking whether Jacek Lazar is alive or dead to us, or, perhaps better, whether his seemingly lost humanity, like that of his namesake Lazarus, can be resurrected for us. Like the photograph that Jacek wishes to have enlarged, Kieślowski's film depicts the outward manifestations of a human individual who may be alive or dead to us. And just as Jacek suggests with regard to the photo, it is impossible to discern from the film alone whether the individual depicted is alive or dead; everything depends on how we view the film, and how we allow ourselves to be affected by it.

NOTES

1. Krzysztof Kieślowski, *Kieślowski on Kieślowski*, ed. Danusia Stok (London: Faber and Faber, 1993), 145. Further references will be cited in the text using the abbreviation *KK*.

2. Paul Coates, "Anatomy of a Murder: *A Short Film about Killing*," *Sight and Sound* 58, no. 1 (1989): 63.

3. This feature of the human condition is illustrated especially well in *Six*, in which Tomek seeks to connect with Magda but does not know how to do so except by peeping at her through a telescope.

4. See Christopher Garbowski, *Krzysztof Kieslowski's* Decalogue *Series: The Problem of the Protagonists and Their Self-Transcendence* (Boulder, Colo.: East European Monographs; New York: Columbia University Press, 1996), 7.

5. See Alasdair MacIntyre, *Dependent Rational Animals: Why Human Beings Need the Virtues* (Chicago: Open Court, 1999), especially 8–9.

6. Herbert McCabe, "Original Sin" in *God Still Matters*, ed. Brian Davies (New York: Continuum, 2002), 171–172.

7. On the account being presented here, to say that the intellect apprehends the universal is to say that the intellect apprehends what is in principle shareable and thus communicable; by contrast, the sensory faculties apprehend what is particular, which is to say that they apprehend what is isolated and not shareable except in an indirect way (i.e., what is sensed is shareable indirectly, and not through the sensory faculties themselves, insofar as we can talk about what we sense).

8. See Canto XXXIV of Dante's *Inferno*, for example, in *The Divine Comedy of Dante Alighieri: Inferno*, trans. Allen Mandelbaum (New York: Bantam, 1980).

9. Herbert McCabe, *God, Christ and Us* (New York: Continuum, 2005), 17–18.

10. Herbert McCabe, *Law, Love and Language* (New York: Continuum, 2003), 118–119. Further references to this text will be cited using the abbreviation *Law*.

11. Robert Frost, *The Poetry of Robert Frost*, ed. Edward Connery Lathem (New York: Henry Holt, 1975), 302.

12. Christopher Garbowski, "Krzysztof Kieslowski's *Decalogue*: Presenting Religious Topics on Television," *The Polish Review* 37, no. 3 (1992): 330.

13. It was during an interview that Heidegger made his now-famous observation, "*Nur noch ein Gott kann uns retten.*" The interview was published shortly after Heidegger's death, in the May 31, 1976, issue of *Der Spiegel*.

CHAPTER 8

States of Exception: Politics and Poetics in *Decalogue Six*

Eva Badowska

When the state of exception (*stan wyjątkowy*), also known as the state of war (*stan wojenny*), was declared in Poland on December 13, 1981, Krzysztof Kieślowski sought to "record the tanks, clandestine news-sheets, and anticommunist slogans daubed on walls."[1] Trained in the venerable tradition of Polish documentary cinema, Kieślowski was driven by the documentary impulse—the desire to stand witness—even long after he had shifted entirely to making fiction films. In 1981, the director aimed to chronicle political trials that took place under martial law: Thousands of political activists were "interned" in makeshift prisons and detained for long periods before they were brought to trial, often in military courts that bypassed even the Soviet-style court system. Courts were handing out severe sentences for minor infractions, such as painting anticommunist graffiti, participating in public assemblies, leaving home without proper identification, or breaking the curfew, and the filmmaker was "keen" to capture "the faces of both accusers and accused" (*D*, ix).[2]

The authorities, however, took a long time to grant him permission to enter the courtroom with his film crew, and Kieślowski did not begin filming until November 1982. When he did, something unexpected took place. Instead of playing the role of passive witness, the camera became an actor in the proceedings, and even a "desirable and welcome presence" for the accused (*D*, x). When it was present in the courtroom, jail sentences were either not imposed at all or were suspended. The camera had this effect whether or not it was loaded with film and the effect continued when Kieślowski began to use a second, dummy camera, a token cinematic presence.

The anecdote is, in fact, chilling. It stands as an example of what Giorgio Agamben describes in his work on *The State of Exception* as "the original structure in which law encompasses living beings by means of its own suspension."[3] It is both a fitting image of Poland's exceptional historical times and the prism through which the effect of Kieślowski's cinematography may be grasped at all times. The presence of the camera in the courtroom at first glance counteracts the repressiveness of the regime and helps the unjustly accused remain at liberty. Although the camera seems to compensate for the immediate human costs of martial law, it, in fact, multiplies them, as it demonstrates how easy it is to place the legal system—on which individual human fates depend—in a "state of exception" that inevitably results in tragic lawlessness. According to Leland de la Durantaye in "The Exceptional Life of the State," such a state is "the legal suspension of the distinction between legality and illegality" and "the political point at which the juridical stops and a sovereign unaccountability begins."[4] For Agamben, this state of exception constitutes the terrifying essence of modern statehood. In the case of Kieślowski's unfinished martial law documentary, the camera augments the suspension of legality: The law is first undermined by the imposition of a state of emergency by the pro-Soviet regime, which created laws that were unconstitutional, and then, again, by the presence of the camera where such illegal laws were to be implemented. In the courtroom, the gaze of the (dummy) camera, bogus and blind, exposes and intensifies the crisis of the process of judgment that was at the heart of *stan wojenny* and that constitutes one of Kieślowski's abiding preoccupations in the later *Decalogue* series as well.

In this way, we are led to what is fundamental about Kieślowski's cinematography. On the one hand, he insists that good filmmaking is essentially documentary. In a TV interview about his documentary beginnings in the 1960s and 1970s, Kieślowski called the documentary genre a "marvel," for it allowed him during these difficult times "to describe a world that had not been . . . described at all" and "to say something about his relationship to what is, to what exists."[5] At the same time, Kieślowski is keenly aware that documentary films are open to certain risks and limitations. One of "the traps of documentary films" is the possibility that the filmmaker could end up disturbing the world he is trying to document at the very moment of documenting it. Surely, most filmmakers hope that their films will transform the world. But this is not the kind of impact Kieślowski is concerned about. What he fears as a "trap" is what could be called the documentary's uncertainty principle: the effect of being filmed on the film's subject. Kieślowski is emphatic that documentaries "shouldn't be used to influence the subject's life either for the better or for the worse. They shouldn't have any influence at all."[6]

But Kieślowski knows well, at least since the unfinished *stan wojenny* documentary and since *Camera Buff* (*Amator*, 1979), a fiction film, that the act of filming is never without an effect. In the film, a young married man, Filip (Jerzy Stuhr), buys an 8mm film camera to document his daughter's childhood and gradually becomes a local celebrity as the only owner of any film equipment in a small town. Eventually, Filip turns the camera on himself, but in the process he becomes so obsessed with the act of filming that his private life begins to disintegrate. So much for the camera as passive witness that does not exert "any influence at all." Yet, this is not a contradiction or double bind. Instead, Kieślowski's cinema always displays a dual artistic and ethical imperative, since the role of film is both to witness neutrally and to highlight critically the state of exception in front of the camera.

Further, the documentary form imposes even more interesting limitations. As Kieślowski explains to Danusia Stok:

> [The documentary] catches itself as if in its own trap. The closer it wants to get to somebody, the more that person shuts him or herself off from it. And that's perfectly natural. It can't be helped. If I'm making a film about love, I can't go into a bedroom if real people are making love there. If I'm making a film about death, I can't film somebody who's dying because it's such an intimate experience that the person shouldn't be disturbed. (*KK*, 86)

Kieślowski conjectures that this is why he started making fiction films. The shift to feature films is thus motivated by the continuation, rather than the discontinuation, of the documentary impulse, an impulse so strong that it begins to look for outlets in fictional setups. Let us listen to Kieślowski once again, this time in a nearly literal translation from the Polish-language version:

> I managed, on a couple of occasions, to photograph a real tear.... But now I've got glycerin. I'm afraid of these real tears—I don't know if I

have the right to photograph them. I feel like a man who's entered a realm that's really forbidden.[7]

What is at stake in the move from "real tears" to "glycerin tears"? Slavoj Žižek, whose book *The Fright of Real Tears: Krzysztof Kieślowski between Theory and Post-Theory* (2001) borrows its title from these remarks, comments that "it was precisely a fidelity to the Real that compelled Kieślowski to abandon documentary realism—at some point, one encounters something more Real than reality itself. . . . At the most critical level, one can render the Real of subjective experience only in the guise of fiction."[8] It is certainly not surprising that Žižek aims to "redeem" Kieślowski from "post-secular obscurantist readings" by means of a Lacanian approach that emphasizes how the director is caught up in the "tension between reality and the Real" (*FRT*, 7, 66). He accurately identifies what is a significant shift in Kieślowski's filmography and sheds interesting light on its dimensions, but he does not emphasize enough a key aspect of Kieślowski's framing of these remarks. It is not that real tears cannot be filmed or even grasped—they can, and Kieślowski has—but, rather, that filming real tears is a sort of transgression into "a realm that is really forbidden." Why is the filmmaker "afraid of these real tears"? First, the Polish is softer than the English translation implies: The filmmaker is merely "afraid" and not "frightened" (*KK, 86*). Second, the emphasis is on the filmmaker's affect in the presence of real tears rather than on the possibly apotropaic effect of the sight itself. Žižek argues that "we cannot ever acquire a complete, all-encompassing, sense of reality—some part of it must be affected by the 'loss of reality,' deprived of the character of 'true reality,' and this fictionalised element is precisely the traumatic Real" (*FRT*, 66). The context, however, points to a slightly different set of issues: Kieślowski's emphasis falls on the question of whether the filmmaker has "the right" to shoot "real tears" (or, in the Polish version, the pearl-like, singular "real tear"). There is an untranslatable aspect in the punctuation of the Polish syntax here, since an attempt to preserve the Polish punctuation of the sentence would give a comma splice in English: "I'm afraid of these real tears, I don't know if I have the right to photograph them." In the English translation, Danusia Stok splits this into two separate sentences, which is a standard translatorial move, but it obscures the intimate syntactical connection between the "fright" Žižek overemphasizes and the question of what the director has the right (not) to do. Žižek forecloses on the issue by folding it back into the thematic of representation and visibility: "Kieślowski seems to share the Old Testament injunction to withdraw the domain of what really matters from degrading visibility" (*FRT*, 74). In my reading of these passages, however, there is nothing degrading about visibility per se; and it is not the visibility of real tears that needs to be shielded from the light of day, but rather the "intimate experience" of a person crying, making love, or dying, a person who has the inviolable right *not* to be "disturbed" in the act. Kieślowski does not seem to think that the Real (or, simply, reality) cannot be witnessed, whether because such witnessing is impossible or because it is traumatic, but rather that it sometimes *ought not* to be witnessed, out of respect, perhaps, for the privacy of the subject's individual experience. There is something particularly arresting about the idea that a person who is dying might be engaged in an "intimate experience" that should not be interrupted. In a fairly literal translation, this passage reads: "If I'm making a film about death, I cannot film the person who is truly dying, because this is such an intimate activity that one must not disturb him" (*A*, 73). The Polish insists on the "I" of the filmmaker and on whether the filmmaker has the right to shoot what is "truly" taking place. The other person, the one dying, is engaged not in an abstract and generalizable "experience" of the English-language version, but in an intimate and personal "activity." What does it mean, anyway, not to disturb a person who is dying? (Could you wait to disturb him or her when they are done [dying]?) Kieślowski does not elaborate, but the example suggests that certain experiences are to be viewed as sacrosanct—closed off, as it were—even if it means that they are forever lost to the camera. But this is not necessarily a moment of biblical iconoclasm or Platonic distrust of mimesis: The prohibition is not against representation, but rather against intervention into another's intimacy. Kieślowski does not shy away from the suffering that real tears represent; what is troubling is, instead, the temptation real tears present to the filmmaker to commit a mortal transgression by influencing or interrupting—by means of the camera's uncertainty principle—the subject's privacy.

Still, Kieślowski wants to make psychological films in which he "attempts to scratch a few skins off of [his] characters."[9] Given his reservations about privacy in the documentary realm, he can accomplish this goal only in the world of fiction films. Certain exfoliations of character can only be staged in a fictional arena, if, that is, one wishes to protect the private realm of intimate experience. Kieślowski is rather lighthearted about it: "Of course, it may be difficult to find an actress who's willing to take off her bra, but then you just find one who is" (*KK*, 86). Fiction works not because it is more real, but because it patently is not so: The dead "get up again" (*KK*, 86). This matters to Kieślowski, I suggest, partly because the status of private experience is a topic with a particularly painful resonance in the Polish 1980s, in the context of the state of exception and its aftermath.

Žižek is right that Kieślowski's work straddles the terrains of particularity and universality, allowing for a historical reading but resisting "the historicist trap" (*FRT*, 7, 8), whereby only someone steeped in the history of that era could understand it. In fact, such historically situated universality is one of Kieślowski's intriguing directorial achievements: His particularity does not undercut his universality, and vice versa. This is apparent also in the director's own blunt description of the *Decalogue*'s situation in *Kieślowski on Kieślowski*: "I'm sick of Polish realities because everything's running its course in spite of us, above us and there's nothing we can do about it" (*KK*, 145). Even so, the films can be read, almost against themselves, in historicist terms, as an indirect, multifaceted meditation on the Polish 1980s, in which historical reflections appear on the screen like shadows in Plato's cave. Rather than filming political struggle or grim existence, Kieślowski spotlights individuals in "extreme, extraordinary situations" (*D*, xii). Refusing to film *the* State of Exception, he films states of exception instead. The director presents this choice as a stark opposition between filming politics versus filming individuals:

> During martial law, I realized that politics aren't really important. In a way, of course, they define where we are and what we are and aren't allowed to do, but they don't solve the really important human questions. They're not in a position to do anything about or to answer any of our essential, fundamental, human and humanistic questions. (*KK*, 144)

The seemingly unambiguous contrast between "individuals in difficult situations" and "anything as horrible as politics" (*KK*, 145) is itself an ideological effect, so blunt that it begs the question when rehearsed by a director otherwise keenly attentive to such nuances. In communist propaganda, the words "individual" and "individualism" acquired a pejorative cast and were often prefaced by two distancing adjectives: "rotten" and "bourgeois." Under social realism, the arts had to represent collective realities and motivations. Though these social-realist norms were no longer enforced in the 1980s (they reached their zenith between 1949 and 1956), Kieślowski's polarization of individuals and politics bears the mark of its times. Simultaneously, his unapologetic credo about the inherent value of the individual as individual, rather than leader or activist, registers as a breath of fresh air in a cinematic landscape dominated by sweeping political allegories, such as Ryszard Bugajski's *Interrogation* (1982) or Andrzej Wajda's *Man of Iron* (1981) and *Danton* (1983). Kieślowski's smaller-scale, made-for-TV films indicate an alternative prospect for critical intervention: "I believe the life of every person is worthy of scrutiny, containing its own secrets and dramas. . . . Behind each of these windows, we said to ourselves, is a living human being, whose mind, whose heart and, even better, whose stomach is worthy of investigation" (*D*, xiii). This statement is remarkable equally for its poetics and its politics. The visceral image of stomach contents being examined by the films defamiliarizes the "heart" metaphor that precedes it and more forcefully suggests the unpoetic interior depths that the director is offering to reach into. At the same time, *The Decalogue* may refuse to make an outright political statement, but its emphasis on lives as individually rather than collectively lived, its minute exploration of what goes on behind closed doors rather than in public squares, and its critical attention to contrary pulsations of individual desire make an effective—because nearly inaudible—political statement. While men and women of iron were being interned and interrogated, regular men and women were falling in and out of love; affirming or losing their religion; giving birth and dying, often of nothing more politically significant than cancer and car accidents. In the context, to represent these "unhistoric acts" on screen was to make a profound artistic and ideological shift, because the private had so long been regarded as the domain of "rotten bourgeois individualism."[10] But, as I will soon show, it is never possible to isolate the private from the historical completely, so that even Kieślowski's metonymic stomachs are never unhistorical.

In the films of *The Decalogue*, the presence of the camera has an impact similar to that which it had in the courtrooms of *stan wojenny*, deepening our awareness of the constitutive human unrest Kieślowski always valorized. In a 1979 interview, the director tells his interlocutor, Hanna Krall, that it is "unrest [*niepokój*] that makes [him] get up in the morning, and not love, hope, or whatever else you mentioned. Within unrest, there is always a question."[11] The "unrest" at stake here is not to be confused with the "moral unrest" or "anxiety" of the so-called "cinema of moral anxiety" (*kino moralnego niepokoju*), notwithstanding the use of the same term. In fact, Kieślowski liked to be defiant about it and on more than one occasion claimed that he "does not feel any moral anxiety. I do not like this name, which stuck to the cinema of the late 1970's. . . . It's a name that only pigeonholes."[12] The "unrest" Kieślowski values is that experienced by ordinary participants in everyday dramas. The ten vignettes of the films of *The Decalogue* appear as an array of fictional courtrooms in which the spectacles of judgment are played out, to be witnessed—but also to be highlighted and deepened—by the gaze of the camera. The films are set up to underscore the apparently documentary role of the camera as an arbitrary witness, an apparatus, itself without agency or deliberation, that films whatever gives itself to be filmed. The character of the "silent witness" (played by Artur Barciś) that recurs throughout the series may well be an image of the role of the film camera itself. According to the director, the opening of each episode is written to "suggest that the lead character had been chosen by the camera almost by accident" (D, xiii). Having initially entertained the idea that the camera might focus on a face selected at random from a large stadium audience or follow a chance character in the street, Kieślowski and Piesiewicz eventually selected a large apartment complex in Warsaw, "with thousands of similar windows framed within the establishing shot" (D, xiii), as the setting of the TV series. As in the courtroom, the camera was to film whatever action, whatever life, took place within its eyeshot, rather than roam in search of something worthy of documentation. In this way, the camera was set up as a witness—it happened to find itself wherever it found itself—and the key concept of the series crucially depends on this. At the same time, the camera is set up as a voyeur that commits the very transgressions that Kieślowski warned against. In a fictional form, then, *The Decalogue* explores the possibilities as well as the risks of the documentary point of view. The very premise of the series relies on the idea of the camera as a Peeping Tom that examines the entrails of the apartment block. The ten episodes of the series scrutinize the human dramas that take place within the different apartments, in a manner that appears to be documentary in its outright refusal to moralize or even interpret. The camera is there to view, and the fiction is set up in such a way as to underscore its voyeuristic dimension. Many have argued, Laura Mulvey most influentially, that film as such is a voyeuristic medium.[13] But this is not my point here. Kieślowski's *Decalogue* emphasizes and plays with this voyeurism in a self-conscious and consequential way. It begins by destroying the illusions on which classic cinema usually depends. For instance, instead of beginning an episode inside an apartment or with a classic establishing shot and then leading through a doorway into the building, allowing us to forget that we do not usually get to see what goes on in other people's lives, nearly every episode of *The Decalogue* begins with the camera dwelling, in one way or another, on the concrete walls of the apartment building before piercing them, as it were, and heightening the voyeuristic effect of the filmic medium. The director plays with the idea of an establishing shot, only to demonstrate the opposite effect: There is no natural way—no natural door or window—through which we could pass into these apartments. I argued earlier that Kieślowski valorizes the private as worthy of protecting and examining, and in this way counteracts its official devaluation. But we can now appreciate that, by the same token, Kieślowski undercuts this privacy—albeit in a fictional setup—by rendering it visible. The two motives are inseparable. The camera in *The Decalogue*, just as it did in the real courtrooms under martial law, becomes an agent that turns the uninvestigated life into the embodiment of a more profound, constitutive unrest. It creatively *induces* states of exception, which it then critically examines. In the series, the act of filming recasts the mundane here-and-now of the dwellers of a communist-era apartment block into that not-quite-local/not-quite-universal mode characteristic of Kieślowski's work. The director describes the series as "an attempt to narrate ten stories about ten or twenty individuals, who—caught in a struggle precisely because of these and not other circumstances, circumstances which are fictitious but which could occur in every life—suddenly realize that they're going round and round in circles, that they're not achieving what they want" (*KK*, 145).

The camera's dual role as witness and critic is particularly pronounced in the most metacritical of the films, *Decalogue Six*, also released in a revised feature-length version as *A Short Film about Love*, which explicitly thematizes the role of the filmic eye.[14] *Six* goes further than any other episode by doubling the voyeuristic gaze of the director's camera in the main character's telescopic obsession; in this limited sense, the main character is a figure of the author/director. In the television version, Tomek (Olaf Lubaszenko), a young postal worker, steals a telescope lens in order to spy on an attractive older woman, Magda (Grażyna Szapołowska), who lives in the apartment block opposite his. Every night he watches as she comes back home, receives visits from her lovers, and contemplates a large tapestry she is in the process of weaving. Tomek, a modern-day Peeping Tom, has been spying on Magda for a while when the film begins. He inherited the pastime from an absent friend, whose room he now occupies and whose mother is his landlady (Stefania Iwińska). Not only is he a substitute son to his landlady, he is also a substitute voyeur. But unlike his friend, who conceived of Magda solely as the object of a private sex show, Tomek falls in love with her and is pained to see her go about her life, of which he is not a part. He even confesses at one point that he no longer masturbates when watching her having sex, suggesting that he may be consumed not just by desire but also by guilt, or, alternatively, that he has begun to sublimate and idealize his feelings for the object of his daily voyeurism. In a way, Tomek's transgressions against privacy are exactly of the kind that made Kieślowski choose glycerin tears over real ones: A film camera could not record such offenses without committing an even greater, because public, transgression against the individual's inviolable right to self-possession. In addition to spying through a telescope, Tomek sends Magda forged money order notices, calls in emergency services to interrupt her lovemaking, steals and reads love letters addressed to her, and so on. Eventually, he confesses to her that he has been watching her, and, against all odds, he succeeds in manipulating her into going out on a date with him, but the night ends in humiliation so devastating to him that he attempts to commit suicide by cutting his wrists. This is when the point of view is reversed, and it is now Magda's turn to pick up a pair of old-fashioned (and ineffectual) opera glasses to look for Tomek's return from the hospital. When he does return and she goes to see him at the post office where he works, he only tells her that he does not spy on her any more. Clearly, in this film the passive act of witnessing is revealed to have a critical impact on both the witness and the witnessed; divestments of privacy are very costly to all.

The film opens with the same setting. From a contextual perspective, the post office in the film's opening sequence is a trace representation, a shadow, of the pervasive system of communist bureaucracy, in which the two actors are caught, as it were, from before the beginning of the film (Figure 8–1). The system assigns them roles that inform as well as subvert their "real-life" roles as lover and beloved. In the post office, they are clerk and client (which, in the communist context, is more appropriately termed the petitioner or the supplicant). The first shot is a medium close-up of Magda as she approaches the window where Tomek serves as a clerk. She

Figure 8–1. Magda shakes out a shoe at the post office counter in *Decalogue Six*.

steps in front of the window, and we see her from Tomek's point of view, from behind a glass partition. There is a circular opening in the glass, which is nearly transparent, except for some reflections. In a way, the circular opening heightens the presence of an obstruction, as it emphasizes that the glass is there. Magda's approach to the window is confident: She is nonchalantly fanning herself with an *awizo*, a notice, usually left in one's mailbox, that a money order can be claimed at the local post office. At this moment, she is not yet a supplicant; she expects to be able to claim the money presumably owed to her and issues only a haughty one-word command, "*Awizo!*" as she comes up to the window. Because Tomek, the clerk, is taking a while to search through a nearly empty index-card filing box on his desk, Magda coolly takes off a shoe, which we later learn to be an iconic black stiletto, in order to shake out some painful bit of detritus. The image is arresting, in that she appears to be simultaneously vulnerable (unselfconsciously removing a source of discomfort from her femme-fatale heel) and aggressive (since she makes no attempt at being inconspicuous when she taps the shoe on the counter, at the clerk's face level). When she looks up from her shoes, it is not at Tomek but at some nowhere point above. Whenever we see Tomek from Magda's point of view, her own reflection in the glass window is superimposed on the image. In one of the frames, both of Tomek's eyes are caught in the opening, as he looks Magda up and down, in a stereotypical once-over. Magda has no expectation that this will be a human encounter, and she is not cowed by her contact with the bureaucratic apparatus, either. But Tomek's gaze lingers on her for a few seconds too long, injecting sexual significance into an administrative encounter, and breaking the mold in which it is supposed to be cast. His response to her one-word demand is a foreboding "*Nie ma!*" (translated in the subtitles as "Nothing"), which, as I will later discuss, echoes through the entire film, as does this initial nonmeeting.

The significance of the post office setting in *Six* becomes more pronounced when viewed against Kieślowski's early documentary, *Urząd* (*The Office*, 1966). The six-minute film, produced when the director was still a student at the Lodz Film School, exhibits many of the features of his later, mature documentaries and shares remarkable visual and thematic similarities with the post office scenes in *Six*. According to film critic Marek Haltof, Kieślowski's documentaries were sociological in nature and much influenced by his film school teacher and important documentary filmmaker, Kazimierz Karabasz, author of such shorts as *Sunday Musicians* (1960). In these early films, Haltof writes, "Kieślowski deals with several individual cases representing a universal meaning: they are, *pars pro toto*, studies of the communist system. Unable to criticize the system openly, he focuses on its several micro-aspects in the hope of presenting its unveiled, true nature."[15] *The Office*, in particular, trains the camera on communist bureaucracy at a local branch of the PZU (a national social security agency).[16] As soon as the film's title, in stark white lettering on a simple black background, is off the screen, the viewer is assaulted by a high-pitched female voice demanding that a certificate be presented for inspection. The screen is filled with medium to extreme close-ups, shot from the back of the room, of petitioners waiting in line, shifting in place, and craning their necks toward the front of the room. The particular petitioner to whom the sharp voice directs its demand for a certificate is not visible and neither is the clerk who issues the request. In the PZU office, the clerks are young women, coiffed in the fashion of the 1960s, and obviously comfortable in their role as holders of the keys. There is nothing rebellious about their youth: They have been absorbed by the apparatus, so that even their methodical pencil-sharpening and unhurried tea-making, shown in lingering and disconcerting close-up, are unaffected by the scope and multiplicity of human tragedy on the other side of the office window. The petitioners, on the other hand, are indistinguishable from one another, forming a dense crowd of old people; their faces, unretouched by editing, are covered with lines and wizened by hard work. As though unaware of being filmed, they pathetically scratch their faces, pat their hair, and let their mouths droop. Their passivity, waiting a turn in front of the window, is staggering; they are there, it seems, to perform an act of supplication rather than to have their needs met. Though there are seemingly several windows at the PZU office, we only hear one clerk, who, emphatically, is never shown. The bureaucracy has only one voice, a voice that comes from nowhere in particular and that resembles a robot's uninflected monotone, rather than a human being's modulated speech. In fact, all the voices in the audio track are out of sync with the visual sequence: Petitioners speak, the one clerk responds, but we only ever see silent faces or mouths whose speech is drowned out by the shrill female voice at another (invisible) window. Formally, the technique of shot-reverse shot is used here in a deconstructive manner, since the removal of the accompanying auditory channel (and the continued broadcast of the jarring voiceover throughout) destroys any illusion, normally produced by shot-reverse shot, that a human dialogue is taking place. This discontinuous effect is further strengthened by the addition of a third point of view, which is that of the camera (as it shoots, for instance, from the back of the room). The documentary's achievement is to portray the voice of the bureaucratic institution, the voice of the state, as a disembodied, shrill, and merciless demand, which cannot be questioned because it issues forth from nowhere, a demand that casts the person as petitioner whose human condition registers only insofar as it is transposed into standardized bureaucratic forms. The film ends with the female voice, telling various petitioners, eight times over, to fill a "form in which you enumerate what you have done throughout your entire life." The echoing voice is heard against the panning (and Kafkaesque) image of a disordered and tattered archive, of presumably just such forms. The bureaucracy demands a standardized and total accounting of oneself, but the film shows that these accounts crumble, disused, to dust. This archive does not memorialize what it contains. To the contrary, it turns "entire lives" into crushing insignificance.

The visual echoes between the PZU office in *Urząd* and the post office in *Six* are remarkable, as is the film technique deployed in both. The post office scenes in *Six* are shot using the same shot-reverse shot technique, with the addition of a third point of view (the camera's). But what is most striking is the photographic likeness between the offices. Both scenes are defined by the presence of a window that divides the clerk from the petitioner. This partition is made of transparent glass, punctured with two openings: a circular one above, at the level of the client's face (to allow for conversation), and a semicircular one below, at the level of the counter (to facilitate the exchange of documents and money). This was, to be sure, the standard bureaucratic setup at the time, but Kieślowski's choice of the setting goes beyond the requirements of realism. In fact, *Six* is a film in which the dividing pane of glass constitutes the defining visual signifier: Tomek spies on Magda through a telescope trained at her apartment's windows, and meets with her at the post office, separated from her by a window pane. The parallels are yet stronger: The circular opening in the post office window is echoed by the mysterious circular object, most probably a wide-angle mirror, hanging in the window of Magda's apartment. Both the post office window and the apartment window are marked with circular shapes that interrupt their unity. These orifices, like bodily ones, mark the separation between the inside and the outside and constitute an opening toward communication or sexual encounter. Yet the film seems to be asking whether they are enough of an opening toward either, and thus whether dialogues and encounters can ever result. In this way, the post office setting is, I argue, integral to the artistic significance of the film, which is not so much about voyeurism as it is about divisions between viewer and viewed, client and clerk, lover and loved. Interestingly, in the screenplay, the initial post office encounter does not occur until much later; it is the sixth scene in the published script. In the TV film, the post office sequence is the opening one, and this change clearly emphasizes its significance.

Scenes at the post office trace, in fact, a sort of arc through *Six*. They stand as the first, the middle, and the last scenes of the film, demarcating its formal narrative trajectory in a perfectly Aristotelian fashion (forming the beginning, the climax, and the resolution of the plot). The opening sequence sets the tone and introduces the characters: It is only Tomek's protracted gaze that alerts viewers to a connection between him and the female client. The second post office sequence, which occurs almost exactly halfway through the film, brings the plot to a climax as it leads to Tomek's confession to Magda that he has been spying on her. Magda's awareness of being watched fundamentally changes the nature of the looking that takes place in the film, as Magda becomes, in the film's second part, first a self-conscious actor on a stage that she is beginning to control, and then herself an onlooker in search of a view of Tomek. The final post office sequence provides closure to the plot. A changed Magda comes to the post office looking for Tomek after his recovery from a suicide attempt, but he conclusively tells her that he no longer watches her, whereby the link conjoining the characters and driving the plot is untied.[17]

In what way, then, is the post office a fitting locus in a film that apparently focuses on personal and romantic, rather than administrative and bureaucratic, relationships? The image of the post office is profoundly ambivalent. On the one hand, the postal service is a textbook and nearly universal allegory for the successes and breakdowns of communication, delivering—and failing to deliver—love letters or money orders. As an image of human relationships, it demonstrates the desire to connect as much as the difficulty of connecting. On the other hand, the post office, in its resemblance to the PZU office from Kieślowski's early documentary, is the embodiment of specifically communist bureaucracy, which subtly permeates the characters' lives. All in all, the post office establishes an image both of connection and of disconnection, both of personhood and of depersonalization. It captures the complexity of human relations under communism (the historicist aspect) and gestures to their opacity at any time (the universalist aspect).

Žižek uses the post office scenes in *Six* as a quintessential example of what he calls "the function of *interface*" (*FRT*, 39). The visually arresting characteristic of these scenes—the fact that the character of Magda is doubly present, both physically "there" but also visible as a reflection on the glass partition—constitutes, from a technical point of view, nothing more complicated than "a simple condensation of shot and reverse-shot within the same shot" (*FRT*, 52). For Žižek, this has a psychoanalytic and metaphysical significance. But what if we attend to the specific context of *Six*, where the spectral reflection appears as part not of any drab reality, but the richly and specifically resonant reality of the post office? It is helpful to look at Tomek here as both the clerical subject of the post office and the amorous subject of the film's romance plot (for he is both). His intense interiority, of which his secret voyeurism is a perverse manifestation, could be seen as the not entirely unpredictable obverse of his nothingness within the bureaucratic structure of the post office, rather than an individual sexual perversion. His inwardness and awkwardness can be read not as character flaws but rather as symptoms of a social system that methodically devalues individuality and privacy. Human beings as postal clerks—we could speak, perhaps, of postal subjects—are alienated in the world-as-post-office to the point that their personal desires and individual acts assume exaggerated and perverse forms; but this perversity is a social, not an individual, condition. These forms may be an extreme manifestation of the intense interiority that communist bureaucracy, in its intent on producing sociability, paradoxically enforces.

It is entirely plausible to read the overly intense atmosphere of the apartment buildings where the series takes place—the concentration, as it were, of inner drama within the walls of these residences—as a realist portrayal of the heightened significance of the private life under communism. Communism, among many other things, was a social system in which the private itself was made perverse by the meaninglessness of the social and the system's intentional devaluation and destruction of privacy. It is a system in which an individual Peeping Tom cannot begin to compete with Big Brother, who is always watching, too. The entire episode does, in fact, make sense in these terms, though it can still be read as a universal tale about a failed romance. The characters strive to escape the post office that defines their existence, but they never escape it entirely, and they end up reenacting the meaninglessness and patterns of their official encounters in their private lives as well. Or, the other way around, the patterns of post office interaction reveal a dimension of the private that would otherwise remain hidden from view: The private world cannot provide a genuine alternative to the bureaucratized world (it either does not escape it or is itself not that different). The post office raises but does not answer the question: Is the separation and alienation of postal subjects a political effect or a universal fact?

The ghostly apparition on the glass that both connects and divides Tomek and Magda constitutes a visual manifestation of the ineluctable distance between persons or would-be lovers. The post office is the form, the structure, through which we ought to apprehend this relationship or any relationships; it is where they are constituted as a couple, where they are before they become themselves. The questions the visual stratum poses are multiple: What does Magda see when she looks at Tomek? Does she see him, or does she see her own spectral image superimposed upon him? Is the circular cutout in the glass enough of an opening for one person to reach through and touch another? Is there always a shield of glass between people, especially between lovers? While the series relies on the concept of a certain transparency—the idea that things can be seen by the film camera, lives investigated, even stomach contents analyzed—it is repeatedly revealed that privacy ought to be guarded and that human subjects are somehow fundamentally opaque to one another, and to the camera, and jealous of their opaqueness. This nontransparency is epitomized in the series by means of glass obstructions such as those that pervade *Six*: counter windows, apartment windows, glass doors, glass objects (such as bottles, cups, paperweights), and TV screens.

Similar questions are entertained in other contexts as well, through the film's settings, motifs, and dialogue. When Magda first arrives at the post office, she comes with a demand for money, and it is met not so much with a refusal as with a void: "There is nothing . . . see for yourself." The immediate reason why the money is not available is simple enough: Tomek has placed a forged money order notice in Magda's mailbox. Magda comes bearing a counterfeit, which she does not know to be one, and discovers that it cannot be cashed. When she later visits the post office with another *awizo*, she requests to see the manager, who in turn accuses her of the intention to defraud the state institution. This injustice is what prompts Tomek to run out after Magda and confess to her that the money notices were forged and that he had been watching her. In the scene that leads up to Tomek's confession, the forces are aligned in two opposed camps. On the one hand, we have the postal institution, which can, presumably, differentiate between real and forged money notices (real and glycerin tears?), and whose official stamps exist to guarantee that such distinctions are maintained. But the institution also exercises here its sovereign power to bring about a state of exception, an impasse of legality and illegality, by destroying evidence in the case. The shrill manager, who invokes the shrill voiceover from *The Office*, emphasizes the post office's standing as an organ of the state only seconds before she tears up the notices that could have been given to the police. The manager's accusation of fraud and forgery, leveled at Magda, is left hanging at the end of the scene, forever without any prospect of resolution: Neither a guilty nor a nonguilty verdict is now possible. On the other hand, we have Tomek and Magda whose attitudes evince a much more porous conception of the difference between real and forged, though in disparate ways. Tomek, to begin with, is a double agent, who misappropriates the official seal for personal reasons. Tomek passes a counterfeit money notice not for monetary gain or to dupe Magda with its face value of 24,000 zlotys but in order to make her show up at the post office—literally, to conjure her up like a visitation—and to "forge" a relationship. While Tomek issues this love summons, Magda assumes that she is in possession of a token of entitlement, and she arrives to demand the promised fulfillment, only to be told that she is holding a counterfeit. We have to wonder why she feels entitled to funds from an unknown source, but we should not overestimate the sum itself.[18] Magda cannot expect any real windfall and the actual amount is likely not significant, even to a textile artist without obvious daytime employment.

All in all, neither Tomek nor Magda share the institution's self-important interpretation that a counterfeit is always a counterfeit, or that a counterfeit is a forged or false version of the real. The counterfeit money order reveals its richest possibilities if allowed to signify as an image of human relations, like the glass partition at the post office. Read in this way, the counterfeit notices exemplify some of love's promises and pitfalls. Entering a relationship may well resemble coming to a post office bearing an *awizo* in one's hand: You assume you are holding a good check, but you may well find that you have a bad one. The *awizo* evokes all the unfounded expectations, the demands that cannot be met, the values that can be trusted but not demonstrated, and the hopes against all odds that there must be someone on the other end who will present you with a true gift and who will ask for nothing in return. That is, in short, Magda's situation. On the other hand, Tomek's approach to the *awizo* manifests the naïve and magical belief that love interests override all other interests, and that the appearance itself of the beloved will lead to a substantiation of desire in the currency of mutuality.

One of the most striking linguistic features of this dialogue, which connects it with other moments in the film, is the echoing repetition of the phrase "it's not there" (also translated in the subtitles as "nothing"). In this dialogue, the phrase is used six times and it brings the viewer back to its previous appearance during Magda's first attempt to cash the money notice in the film's opening sequence. In the Polish dialogue, the phrase is shorter and more ambivalent: "*nie ma*." For instance, in this earlier scene:

MAGDA: Awizo.

TOMEK: *Nie ma*. ("Nothing.")

MAGDA: *Ale ja mam wezwanie*. ("But I've got an *awizo*.")

TOMEK: *Nie ma*. ("There is nothing.")

"*Nie ma*" is an idiomatic and ubiquitous expression that literally means "no/not has," where "*ma*" is the third-person singular of the verb "to have" (*mieć*). The fact that the phrase has no word in the subject slot is not in itself surprising: Polish allows the subject to be omitted because the verb itself usually carries enough grammatical markers to prevent misunderstanding. But this is not the case here: The sentence equivalent "*nie ma*" does not point to a subject. There is no substitute here for the comforting "it" that English uses as a placeholder in expressions such as "it's not there." Technically, "*nie ma*" is a subjectless sentence. It could acquire a logical subject, which, if expressed, would follow the expression in the genitive (possessive) case: For instance, "*nia ma pieniędzy*" (there's no money) or "*nie ma chleba*" (there's no bread). But this logical subject—money or bread—is not the grammatical subject of the sentence, not the human subject we would expect to be the solid basis of all "having." The first thing to say, then, is that "nothing" can constitute only a very loose translation for the Polish "*nie ma*," which conveys something simultaneously less portentous and more elusive than the English noun. "It's not there" does not work, either, as it is too concrete and grammatically complete to convey the unsettling open-endedness and subjectless dispossession that inheres in the Polish phrase. "*Nie ma*" indicates a state of deprivation that is not expressible by means of a conceptual noun (such as "nothing" or "lack"), a state of being-without or having-not. In the post office scene, "*nie ma*" names the state of exception that the scene illustrates: There is no money to cover the *awizo* because the notice is forged. The state of illegality is magnified when the notice is torn up, and there is no longer evidence that a forgery has taken place: *Nie ma pieniędzy* (money), *nie ma dowodu* (evidence). The person who is accused of forgery and fraud—Magda—is the only one who committed no crime (the notice was forged by Tomek and torn up by the manager), and yet she finds herself the subject-without-grammatical-subject of a double deprivation. Tomek, too, fails to conjure up a mutuality for which he broke the rules: *Nie ma miłości* (love).

The film is, ultimately, about the state of exception described by this "*nie ma*." It raises two fundamental questions, pertaining to the logical and grammatical subjects of the phrase: What is missing? And, who or what is missing that which is missing? The questions may be unanswerable, but they can be usefully contextualized in another key sequence of the film. The film entertains the question of love—it is, after all, a "short film about love"—in the most unlikely of ways, out of what looks very much like a voyeuristic perversion (or the "adultery" of the sixth commandment) that brings together two people who should have never met, and who make the very possibility of mutuality seem impossible, risible, or sinful. But this makes the question all the more urgent. The essential dialogue of *Six* takes place when Tomek delivers milk to Magda's apartment. Does the action represent Tomek, an orphan, delivering milk to his absent mother in order to be fed? Is she a mother who failed to lactate (and who is previously seen spilling milk) and who needs milk so that she can feed her child (or herself)? Is Magda a child thirsty for the milk of Tomek's love, his semen? Is milk what is absent, what is not there—the absent subject of the film's "*nie ma*"? Tomek's symbolic delivery and the lovers' meeting occur in an unlikely space (a public corridor in the apartment building) and at an unlikely time (in the bright light of early morning). Magda, in dishabille, suddenly opens the door when she hears the clinking of a milk bottle, and the swing of the door causes Tomek to fall back, inflicting another wound on top of the black eye he had acquired the night before from Magda's lover. When Magda asks, "Why . . . why do you peep at me?" Tomek establishes the film's credo by stating, "Because I love you. . . . I really love you."

Tomek does not "really" love her, and Magda does not learn the meaning of love by the end of the film, either. There is no chance of mutuality here, but the film still engages the question of love with utter seriousness. *Six* examines love through its suspensions and absences, through its crises and states of emergency. It may simply be that Tomek is naïve or romantic, and the film goes to great lengths to underscore the mismatch of ages between the pair. But it is important that Tomek does not spy on Magda simply or only out of perverse sexual need. When he inherits his friend's voyeuristic toolbox, he fails—and this is important—to become a true voyeur himself. Though at first he watches her having sex and masturbates at his telescope, he eventually gives it up, and he even averts his gaze when sexual activity is taking place. This may well be sublimation, but the point is that his interest in Magda, at the moment when we encounter him in the film, is no longer defined solely by its sexual component. He does not respond to Magda's overt proposition: "Do you want to kiss me? . . . Perhaps you want to go

States of Exception   159

to . . . perhaps you want to make love to me?" To all these questions he replies with a simple "no." When queried, "And what . . . what do you want?" he replies that he does "not know," and when she again probes, incredulously and insistently, "What do you want?" he emphatically states that he wants "nothing": "Nothing?" "Nothing!" Nothing—not because he is too young or too shy, and not because he prefers to be aroused from behind a telescope than in the flesh. (This instance of "nothing" is correctly translated. It renders the Polish abstract noun "*nic*" rather than the previously discussed phrase "*nie ma*.") He really does not want simply to bed her, and he seems frankly taken aback by her questions. It is not that he really wants "nothing," but rather that what he desires is not simply the sexual thing. It is nothing concrete or nothing easily articulable. And though this dialogue is beginning to sound very much like a textbook example of Lacan's theory of desire and lack, it is important to my reading to dwell in the trivialities of how desire is, in fact, represented in this scene. We would do well to take Tomek at his word—this is, I would venture, the film's urgent demand on us as viewers. What does the young man want? In responding to this apparently psychoanalytic query, he wavers between "I don't know" and "nothing," and these responses, too, should be taken seriously. Tomek asks Magda: "Could I invite you to a café? . . . For ice-cream?" The frank, adolescent nature of this invitation is sexual but it also transcends the sexual. As he did by counterfeiting a money notice, Tomek again plays a conjurer: He wants to conjure up an encounter. For one, Tomek's question—he wants to invite her out—respects, in its very grammatical structure, Magda's separateness as a person. He does not presume to know her, even though he had watched her and violated her privacy in other ways as well for a year. In Polish, while Magda addresses Tomek in the familiar second-person singular ("you"), Tomek continues to address Magda, to the very end of the film, in what is the formal mode, using the third-person singular "*Pani*" (Madam): "Could I invite [Madam] to a café?" The difference in registers is partly dictated by—and it underscores—their difference in ages, but it is also the received grammar of social exchanges that are not yet intimate. Only close friends address each other in the second-person singular.

Magda's response to Tomek's invitation is not shown, lost on the editing floor or deliberately omitted—*nie ma odpowiedzi* (there is no response)—but we glean what it might have been by Tomek's ecstatic, possibly erotic reaction: In jubilation, he goes in circles, with the clinking milk wagon in tow, in front of the apartment building. This cacophony of milk bottles is set to the haunting melodies of Zbigniew Preisner's score, and the scene is bookended by extreme high-angle shots that frame it as taking place at a crossroads, where four paths meet by the side of a weeping willow. When the camera begins to track Tomek's movement in close-up, the image of the world beyond him dissolves into spinning smudges of light. This is both a triumph of Kieślowski's film art and an intimation that within the film's "*nie ma*" there inheres at least a potential for something very much like ecstasy. Without invoking the entire problematic of José Ortega y Gasset's essay on love, Tomek's emotional carousel is a fitting image of the philosopher's idea: "Love is all activity. Instead of the object coming to me, it is I who go to the object and become part of it. In the act of love, the person goes out of himself. Love is perhaps the supreme activity which nature affords anyone for going out of himself toward something else." Unlike desire, whose aim is possession, love is "centrifugal."[19]

In his autobiographical reflections, the director affirms that the most interesting aspect of the film is its "perspective": "We're always looking at the world through the eyes of the person who is loving and not through the eyes of the person who is loved" (*KK*, 166). Further, "this love is always tied up with some sort of suffering, some sort of impossibility" (*KK*, 169). The problem the film elaborates is then more the problem of love's (im)-possibility than of whether it exists or not: The question is not whether love is, but whether these characters and any characters can "have" it (it is the question of "*nie ma*": absence cast in terms of (not) having). In *Six*, the suffering love generates is intimately connected to absence ("*nie ma*"). When Tomek, dressed in a formal dark suit and white shirt, meets Magda at the café, the conversation confronts these issues head on:

MAGDA: You said that morning . . . what did you say?

TOMEK: I love you.

MAGDA: It doesn't exist.

TOMEK: It exists.

MAGDA: No.

Again, much is lost in translation. Tomek's confession of love follows the formal pattern of his speech: "I love [Madam]" (not an informal "you"). Also, Magda's "It doesn't exist" includes the film's linguistic key: "Tego *nie ma*." Magda's is a sarcastic remark about what is missing. These are performative rather than philosophical statements. Within Magda's bitter irony, there can be no love. Tomek's "It exists" is also, in Polish, a much simpler "*jest*," the Polish equivalent of "is" (third person singular of the verb to "be"). Love is, says Tomek, and his warm whisper brings about a moment of intimacy. Like the warm embrace that illustrates love in *One*, this love *is*, even as it may be missing at the same time. The rest of the conversation focuses on concrete instances of missing love: Tomek is an orphan who does not remember his parents, even though he otherwise "remembers everything from the start;" his best friend is "not here now" and is currently stationed with the UN troops in Syria; Magda's previous lover, whom she describes as a "thin boy," "left and never came back," going to Austria and then Australia, while his alliterative absence takes Magda on a longer trip through the ABC's of longing.

The lover's suffering reveals, however, a destructive and violent potential.[20] Tomek's longing leads him into the relatively benign territory of confiscating Magda's mail and reporting nonexistent gas leaks to the authorities; at the café, Magda complains that he had backed her into a corner. Magda's actions toward Tomek are, however, more profoundly traumatizing. Back at her apartment, dressed in a negligée and freshly showered, she encourages Tomek to touch the moist evidence of her desire for him. His "delicate" hands disappear under her silk slip, and he quickly climaxes, still fully dressed in the same dark suit and white shirt. From the moment their hands touch, the whole scene takes about thirty seconds; his weak moaning, more like a child's complaint than a man's release, lasts about twenty seconds and then turns into tears. Though they may well be glycerin, the brevity contributes to the scene's emotional impact. Magda's seductive warmth now changes into a cutting challenge: "Already? Was it good? That's all there is to love. Wash in the bathroom, there's a towel." Tomek's humiliation and devastation are such that he attempts suicide by cutting his wrists the same night. The question of whether love exists—of whether it *is*—is beyond the scope of such a scene. Even this much cuts uncomfortably close to the territory of "real tears."

Though the roles now switch, and Magda seems to begin to thaw internally as she takes up a pair of opera glasses earnestly to look for Tomek's return from the hospital, love continues to be "tied up with . . . some sort of impossibility." These are extreme circumstances, but Magda's ineffectual attempts register more as an ironic commentary on the changed perspectives than as a genuine intersubjective opening. When Tomek comes back from the hospital, Magda returns to the post office, making a full circle back to the paradigm that has defined the relationship, and the film's social context, from the start. Cupping her hands around her eyes to try to see better through the glare of the windows, Magda now plays the lover in search of the beloved. The glass panes, however, continue to

Figure 8–2. Magda learns that Tomek does not watch her anymore in *Decalogue Six*.

separate them. The smile gently playing on her face is wiped out, when Tomek states, in a monotone and barely lifting his head: "I do not watch [Madam] any more." Magda is reduced to a hopeful supplicant in a state bureaucracy of the postal institution (Figure 8–2). The suspension of voyeuristic activity, of watching, does suggest that genuine erotic possibility has been closed off as well. Žižek writes that *Six* shows that "there is only an immense *need* for love; every actual love encounter fails and throws us back into our solitude" (*FRT*, 115). But Žižek's "concise formula of the final lesson" of the episode omits to acknowledge what was learned on the way. Peeping, Kieślowski taught us, constituted an opening of the self to another, and it offered perhaps more than just a mirage of transcendence: The movement toward the other remained a possibility within it. Though at the end of *Six* we are left in the state of exception marked by "*nie ma*" (the dearth of love, money, milk), the film speaks to more than the necessarily frustrated "*need* for love." In the post office of human connections, the figures of Kieślowski's *Decalogue* are "going round and round in circles, . . . not achieving what they want" (*KK*, 145), but they keep going without settling into solitude. His emphasis falls on this movement, and his cinematic artistry is to bring critical urgency to the states of everyday exception he documents.

NOTES

1. Krzysztof Kieślowski and Krzysztof Piesiewicz, *Decalogue: The Ten Commandments*, trans. Phil Cavendish and Susannah Bluh (London: Faber and Faber, 1991), ix. Further references will be cited in the text using the ab-

breviation *D*. The so-called *stan wojenny* (martial law, literally "state of war") or *stan wyjątkowy* (state of exception) was introduced on December 13, 1981, by the totalitarian military government of the Polish People's Republic under General Wojciech Jaruzelski. The official reason for the declaration of the state of exception was the worsening economic situation of the country; it is now widely accepted that the actual reason for its imposition was the attempt to crush political opposition, especially burgeoning prodemocracy movements, such as the Solidarity movement under the leadership of Lech Wałęsa.

2. Especially notorious was the case of a Solidarity member, Ewa Kubasiewicz, who was sentenced to ten years in prison and five years of deprivation of citizenship rights for participating in a Solidarity strike in Gdynia and writing a leaflet declaring the state of war to be illegal and unconstitutional. See Ewa Kubasiewicz-Houée, *Bez prawa powrotu* (Wroclaw: Wydawnictwo "Wektory," 2005), especially 75–80.

3. Giorgio Agamben, *The State of Exception*, trans. Kevin Attell (Chicago: University of Chicago Press, 2005), 3.

4. Leland de la Durantaye, "The Exceptional Life of the State: Giorgio Agamben's *State of Exception*," *Genre* 38 (Spring/Summer 2005): 182.

5. "Krzysztof Kieślowski Pegaz cz. 2" (video), http://www.youtube.com/watch?v=Ig3Wswp41Vc (accessed March 3, 2012). Trans. Eva Badowska.

6. Krzysztof Kieślowski, *Kieślowski on Kieślowski*, ed. Danusia Stok (London: Faber and Faber, 1993), 68. Further references will be cited in the text using the abbreviation *KK*.

7. Krzysztof Kieślowski, *Autobiografia*, ed. Danusia Stok (Kraków: Znak, 2006), 74, trans. Eva Badowska. The English text in *KK* is on page 86. Further references will be cited in the text using the abbreviation *A*.

8. Slavoj Žižek, *The Fright of Real Tears: Krzysztof Kieślowski between Theory and Post-Theory* (London: British Film Institute, 2001), 71–72. Further references will be cited in the text using the abbreviation *FRT*.

9. "Krzysztof Kieślowski Pegaz cz. 1" (video) http://www.youtube.com/watch?v=LpyDDmOIohs (accessed March 3, 2012). Trans. Eva Badowska.

10. I borrow the phrase "unhistoric acts" from the famous last sentence of George Eliot's *Middlemarch* (1874): "For the growing good of the world is partly dependent on unhistoric acts; and that things are not so ill with you and me as they might have been, is half owing to the number who lived faithfully a hidden life, and rest in unvisited tombs." George Eliot, *Middlemarch: A Study of Provincial Life* (London: Folio Society, 1999), 759.

11. "Zrobilem i mam" ("I've done it and I've got it"), in *Kino Krzysztofa Kieślowskiego*, ed. Tadeusz Lubelski (Krakow: Universitas, 1997), 272, trans. Eva Badowska. The original interview appeared in a Polish weekly, *Polityka*.

12. "Krzysztof Kieślowski Pegaz cz. 2."

13. Laura Mulvey, "Visual Pleasure and Narrative Cinema," *Screen* 16, no. 3 (Autumn 1975): 6–18.

14. Kieślowski explains that the different ending of the feature-film version was the idea of the lead actress, Grażyna Szapołowska, who felt that the film "needed a story. Not necessarily a happy ending, but a story." In it, Magda and Tomek look through a telescope together, in a fantasy scene that holds out "a certain charm." Kieślowski, however, admits that "the television ending is far closer to the view I have of how things really are in life" (*KK*, 170). My essay will concern itself with the television version only, released in the United States as *Decalogue Six* in *The Decalogue*, DVD, directed by Krzysztof Kieślowski (Chicago: Facets Video, 2003).

15. Marek Haltof, *The Cinema of Krzysztof Kieślowski: Variations on Destiny and Chance* (London: Wallflower Press, 2004), 5.

16. *The Office*, in *The Krzysztof Kieslowski Collection: No End*, DVD, directed by Krzysztof Kieślowski (New York: Kino Video, 2004).

17. The feature-length version of the film ends differently, in a fantasy scene that takes place in one of the apartments. This further underscores the tight and intentional structuring of the TV version of the episode. See also Haltof, *The Cinema of Krzysztof Kieślowski*.

18. Poland was, at the time, in the grip of hyperinflation. Actual figures differ from source to source, but they are invariably measured in hundreds of percentage points annually, in the years between 1987 and 1990. At the time of the planned devaluation of the Polish currency in 1995, one new zloty equaled 10,000 old zlotys; in 1989, at the time the *Decalogue* series was seen on Polish state TV, the government issued a banknote with the face value of 200,000 zlotys (there were no notes below the 50-zloty denomination, and all coins were officially withdrawn from circulation). According to one brief video clip captured in a Polish bakery around 1988, a round birthday cake cost 950 zlotys. We can thus assume that the sum Magda hopes to claim at the post office could buy approximately two dozen birthday cakes.

19. José Ortega y Gasset, *On Love: Aspects of a Single Theme*, trans. Toby Talbot (New York: Meridian Books, 1969), 10 and 14.

20. Žižek argues that Tomek's feelings for Magda contain "a narcissistic attitude of idealization whose necessary obverse is a barely conceived [*sic*] lethal dimension." *Six* should thus be read as a "kind of introverted 'slasher' in which the man, instead of striking at the woman, turns his murderous rage against himself" (*FRT*, 115).

CHAPTER 9

Decalogue Seven: A Tale of Love, Failing Words, and Moving Images

Francesca Parmeggiani

According to Krzysztof Kieślowski, his task as a filmmaker is "to find out what lies behind [one's] actions," what makes one "get up in the morning" and go about one's life, and to engage the viewer in this heuristic process.[1] He also explains that only love, understood as desire ("that which moves one towards something"), grants meaning to and rules human life. As he states, "all books and films speak of love. Or the absence of it, which is the other side of love."[2] Yet, "captur[ing] what lies within" the characters, namely their feelings and emotions, the desire—a moving toward—causing and molding their actions, is no easy task; and the director admits that "there's no way of filming it. You can only get nearer to it." The consideration of the inadequacy of cinema in this regard leads Kieślowski to praise the nuance, depth, balance, and effectiveness of literature, seemingly arguing for a superiority of the descriptive written word over the "too explicit" and "too equivocal" moving image (*KK*, 194–195). The viewer of *The Decalogue* thus embarks on the complex and fateful journey each character undertakes with no apparent expectation: All stories are about love, or lack or loss of it; images will come close to representing such experience of (absent) love, but will inevitably fall short. *Seven* seems to be no exception.

Seven is the story of a mother, Ewa (Anna Polony), and her daughter, Majka (Maja Barełkowska), fighting over six-year-old Ania (Katarzyna Piwowarczyk), who is the child of both: Ewa has raised Ania as her own daughter although Majka is Ania's biological mother. After careful planning, Majka takes Ania away and tells her that she is her real mother, desperately yearning for the child's recognition and love as her mother. Kieślowski reveals the ambiguous nature of Ewa's and Majka's need for love—for loving and being loved. In his representation, the two women mirror each other in their attempt to assert their motherhood. Both are strong and tender, manipulative and affectionate, equally determined in their questionable claim for the ownership of Ania—motherly love turned into a jealous possession, vengeful and mutually hurtful.[3] Through the characters' broken dialogues, we glimpse the depth and complexity of their relationship: Ewa and Majka have become estranged over the years, exasperated by each other's exclusion from Ania's love. More important, both of them have grown to consider motherhood as defining their identities; hence their desire to be acknowledged and loved as mothers not only by Ania but also by each other.

If one considers the temporal and spatial twists and turns and gaps in the story, it comes as no surprise that Kieślowski himself once expressed uneasiness at this episode: "*À vrai dire,*" he said, "*c'est le film auquel je suis le moins attaché. Selon moi l'histoire est un peu trop compliquée, trop bavarde et mal racontée par moi-même*" (To tell you the truth, this is the film I am the least attached to. In my opinion, the story is a bit too complicated and long-winded, and I don't recount it well).[4] Most scholars have used his candid and rigorous self-criticism to point to the film's stylistic flaws, confusing plot and overly dramatic characters rather than the representational challenges it deals with. In so doing, they have also diminished the importance Kieślowski ascribes to the sound in the film's opening. I argue instead that this powerful beginning (a child's disarticulated crying) and the equally powerful end it leads to (Ania's silent gaze at a train station) magnify the disquieting psychological and emotional complexity of interpersonal relationships and human actions at the core of the film, articulate the film's distinctive perspective among the episodes of *The Decalogue* (particularly if viewed in comparison with the opening and concluding frames of *One*), and ultimately challenge the viewer's diminished expectations. Moreover, the narrative style and techniques the director employs in *Seven* demonstrate cinema's ability not only to "get nearer" to the surface of perceived reality but also to uncover what lies beyond it, and not by means of mere imagination, perhaps more persuasively and effectively than words could do. Fragmentation composed into unity, separation revealing proximity, a childlike perspective fueling adults' knowledge and understanding, and characters reflecting each other as mirrors are among Kieślowski's tools to transform representation into meaning, and to address implicitly the question of the cognitive potential of cinema and the figurative and emotional challenges it offers to viewers when it speaks of love and life. While *Seven* provides an effective test environment for the dynamic interpretive relationship the director seeks to establish with his viewer, it also draws attention to Kieślowski's effort—successful, in my view—to create a visual language of love, loss, and desire.

The Decalogue originates in Kieślowski's belief that life is a daily confrontation with one's loneliness and difficulty of relating to others. It is a struggle generated by the absence of love, a yearning for loving and being loved that, even when expressed or acknowledged, will most likely remain unfulfilled. The film series records random instances in which an individual claims her freedom, makes a choice in view of compelling circumstances, and acts upon it, only to realize that she cannot break out of the prison of her own self—filled with passions, determined by physiology and biology and ruled by conscience or a "sense of sin against yourself" (*KK*, 149–150)—nor escape the constraints of familial and societal conventions and norms. Majka's tale in *Seven* is a powerful illustration of such an attempt at breaking free, an act that also defines her initiation into adulthood. Majka, the central agent in the story, is caught between the two worlds of childhood and adulthood. She is simultaneously a child (for Ewa) and a mother (for Ania), a circumstance that intensifies her suffering and increases her responsibilities while also eliciting the viewer's empathy. Furthermore, her story is a powerful exploration of the emotional world that generates and fulfills her radical gesture, a world of unspoken love for herself and others that parenthood and family—the former understood as the establishment of a loving yet authoritative presence in a child's life (regardless of actual biological ties), the latter viewed as a microcommunity, as a place of relational functions both supportive of and normative for an individual's development—may stifle rather than nourish.[5]

Similar to other episodes of the series, *Seven* is characterized in the beginning by a fragmented narrative that the editing emphasizes, and by close-ups and shots that underscore the isolation, separation, and distance of one character from another, or their confinement within a specific space, whether real or symbolic, which in fact is always shared. In the episode's opening, the camera scrutinizes the exterior of the Warsaw apartment complex—by now all too familiar to the viewer of the series—

but appears almost indifferent to the eerie screams breaking the silence of dawn. Although it briefly zooms in when a light turns on, the camera does not stop tilting nor moves to identify the source of the cry, and the sequence ends with a distance shot of the uniformly impenetrable apartment buildings—indeed a barrier, but one that the camera and the viewers will soon break through. Kieślowski then cuts to a different setting and a different yet unspecified time, to a bespectacled, fair-looking young woman—her whiteness in stark contrast not only to the gloom of the previous frame but to the somber tone of the entire film—who is returning her student book. The viewer learns that she has been expelled from the university for reasons that remain unknown, and has decided not to appeal the decision; the last ten pages of her student *indeks* are missing.[6] A new cut returns the viewer to the sound of the unidentified crying of the opening, this time from inside a place: A man, working on a pipe organ, does not seem to hear or remains unaffected by the screams. Kieślowski's filmic language underscores the daunting tone of the episode and introduces its core motifs: The camera's first indifference foreshadows the man's apathy; the acts of ignoring, erasing and hiding, which are performed by each adult character at different moments in the film, are introduced by the young woman's resolute attitude, her unknown reasons, and the torn pages in her student book. The viewer does encounter Majka for the first time, the story's protagonist still unnamed at this point, but what can or should be said is left untold and unexplained.

Yet, as the story unfolds and time contracts, as the narrative turns from fragmented into linear, and then climaxes into the emotionally charged unity of time and space of the concluding sequence, the viewer realizes that what separates, obstructs, or confines is immaterial. All barriers, whether a bedside, a window, the leaves of a tree, a fence, or a gate, are transparent; they affect communication but do not distort nor prevent it, and at times they even provide a physical support for the characters to hold on to, and an incentive to seek further. For example, Majka puts on her glasses and looks at Ania playing with her friends and glancing at her from the distance, among the bushes fencing the school's playground; Wojtek, caught in the traditionally feminine occupation of hanging the wash to dry in the air, meets his child for the first time at the gate opening onto his property. In general, these barriers represent a threshold; they mark an emotional proximity rather than a distance, at the moment when an individual is confronted with the choice and responsibility of moving closer to or pushing away from another. The only instance of an insurmountable obstacle that cannot and will not be overcome, a distance disguised as proximity, is given in the beautifully choreographed open-air scene of the encounter—almost a duel—between Wojtek and Ewa, searching for Majka and Ania. Coming from different directions, the van of Wojtek's friend and the car of Ewa's husband stop on the opposite sides of a deserted country road. Wojtek and Ewa emerge from their vehicles and approach each other, but neither one ever steps into the physical and psychological space of the other. No touch occurs between them; no word of sympathy or concern is exchanged. An agreement is stipulated, sanctioned by Ewa's ironic fleeting reference to the circumstances that brought them together. The frame, which displays a symmetrical positioning of the two characters, reminding the viewer of a figure reflected in a mirror, is extraordinary precisely because no material object separates or hinders them, and yet they are irremediably distant. Kieślowski thus suggests that it is not physical reality that confines these characters to loneliness, but the inner walls that their pride, acquiescence or fear have built.

By contrast, and to return to the film's beginning, if fragmentation and concealment, engendering frustration as well as curiosity as Annette Insdorf explains,[7] are the dominant characteristics of the opening shots of the episode, the extreme close-ups of hands and faces of the following sequence—which presents the story's main characters, three generations of women distinguished by their age (maturity, youth, and childhood) and their reciprocal relationship—convey isolation, confinement, and authority, but also proximity and sharing, love, suffering and fear. Here the camera discloses and exposes rather than covering up or remaining indifferent, inducing the viewer's emotional involvement: The closeness suggested by the camera's eye is both that of the viewer to the story's characters and of the characters to one another. The scene plays out in the small, intimate but magnifying space next to a bed; the loud cry reveals that its source, a child, is nearby. First, the camera focuses on Majka, who tries unsuccessfully to calm down the child; the camera is at the child's level. Majka is not wearing her glasses; her sight is, one would infer, blurred, and she is unable to act decisively and effectively.[8] The camera then fixes on Ewa's hand, which brusquely pushes away Majka and vigorously pulls down the bed's bar. Ewa's gesture of eliminating the physical boundary—the bedside—between her and Ania is charged with meaning: While both women are initially confined to the same space, separated from the child, only Majka—still a child albeit being a mother—seems unable to overcome that separation and console the child. Later in the story, when Majka and Ania spend some hours at Wojtek's home, the viewer will be reminded of that initial scene; this time, however, Kieślowski shows that Majka is being assimilated to the adult world: Her stern gesture to shake Ania out of her dreams and her mention of the wolves to appease her, yet again crying in her sleep, replicate Ewa's acts and words—her language of codified, normal or expected motherhood.

The child's bedside in the beginning is the first of the only two scenes—the other being the film's final sequence at the train station—in which the three female characters are shown together, interacting in the same frame. Between Ewa's two gestures—one to reject, the other to embrace, both revealing her authority and determination—Kieślowski interjects the close-up of a child's hand, Ania's, grasping the net of the bedside. The fragmented way Kieślowski introduces Ania, deferring our viewing of her as a child among other children until a later shot, is utterly disturbing: Ania is not presented as a whole person, but only as a scream, a clasping hand, and finally a face, whose impenetrable expression is significantly captured in her wide-open, sightless eyes, her face almost filling up the screen (Figure 9–1).

Ania is the most enigmatic character of the story. She inhabits a deceptively happy world. The children's theater where Majka takes her away is a money-making enterprise; the merry-go-round, on which she learns who her biological mother is, is abandoned in the woods; and the piles of teddy bears that her biological father, Wojtek, has handmade and among which she finally falls asleep will be given away and sold.[9] These places and objects—crafted by adult hands to welcome and entertain children, but in fact fulfilling adult interests and self-centeredness—perform the conflicting functions of amusing and reassuring Ania while also bewildering her. The adult world, which she observes with her stunning blue eyes and interacts with through her piercing cries suddenly waking up from her sleep, turns her into an object of contention and revenge. By associating

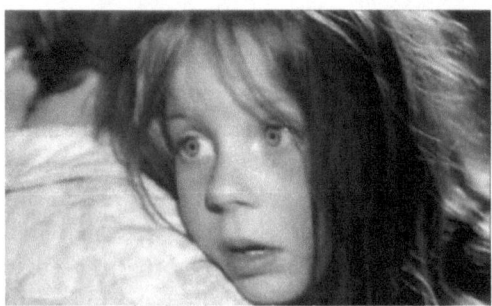

Figure 9–1. Ania awakening from a nightmare in *Decalogue Seven*.

her with the unnatural world of animal and human fairytale characters—when she dances with them on the theater stage—and the stuffed bears emitting strange sounds at the touch of their belly, Kieślowski implies that, diegetically, Ania is like a puppet, which is taught to call someone "mother" and to love and kiss upon command, or a toy, in fact a beautiful doll, and a piece of property that can be shared and eventually inherited, as Ewa proposes to Majka, or else abandoned. Paradoxically, Kieślowski himself, like his adult characters, *victimizes* Ania by reducing her to an object (initially fragmented), to being the material of his and our gaze, and worse: After all, no matter how dramatic and heartbreaking her first appearance is on screen, Ania is a plot device that makes it possible for the filmmaker to unfold Majka's story. Perhaps Kieślowski's admitted perplexity at his own storytelling in this episode originates in his misuse of this little girl. However, Ania's seeming lack of character development in the film, her being *only* a contended child, is framed between two disquieting shots, namely her sightless, inaccessible eyes in the beginning and her inquisitive gaze at the end, the latter recalling and seemingly reversing the former. Kieślowski's narrative strategy—extremely compelling, I maintain, rather than objectionable—prevents viewers from dismissing her character, and stirs them to "experience something," whether emotional or intellectual.[10] In fact, his representation ascribes the child-character a particular form of agency and viewpoint, while also engaging the viewer to articulate a response to it.

The depersonalization that marks Ania consistently throughout the film until the end, her being divested of her own will, may show her objectification and exploitation by the grownups around her and the camera alike. But, more important, it reveals how profoundly Ania affects the world she lives in. Ania is like a mirror in whose reflection Majka—but also Ewa and Wojtek—comes to terms with her past and confronts her future. In Kieślowski's skillful hands, she may indeed be a ploy, but she is also a perspective linking the gaze—the act of seeing, learning, and understanding, but also of doubling and mystifying—to the processes of identity formation and recognition both within and outside the text. I would argue that it is Ania's particular role in *Seven* that makes the presence of the witness (the mysterious character, played by Artur Barciś, who appears throughout *The Decalogue*) unnecessary, except for one moment, at the film's end, when Ania begins her own transition from childhood into youth, and Kieślowski ceases to narrate and opens the text up by drawing the viewer into it.[11] Moreover, it is the human inability to decipher what lies beyond a perceived reality or reasonable experience, in addition to the indefiniteness and innocence of childhood to adult eyes, that Kieślowski intends to express with Ania. In the episode's screenplay, Kieślowski and Piesiewicz explain that Ania's screams in her sleep originate "less from pain than from fright," and are "full of a terror which adults no longer experience."[12] Their words fail to provide an actual justification for Ania's fright. Likewise none of the adults around her understand what causes her crying, and thus project upon her their own rationalizations or personal alibi: She is afraid of the wolves in her dreams as Ewa believes, or she fears for her future as Wojtek suggests. It is the adults' blindness toward what lies beyond the surface of their known reality and belief system, their existential ineptitude, caused by reason and passions alike, that Kieślowski brings into focus with Ania—in the screenplay too—thus pressing the viewer to confront it. Rather than show the characters' regression to the irrationality of childhood in order to demonstrate the irresponsibility of their actions[13]—an interpretation of the episode that builds on the notion of human existence as a taxonomy of behaviors substituting childishness for childlikeness, and a value system stifling human agency—*Seven* articulates the idea not only of a persistence of childhood in the experiences of adults, but also of adults' need for childhood's continuance in order to maintain or reclaim their freedom, although there is no guarantee that they will be successful in their pursuit of self-determination.

Kieślowski's move is deliberate and essential to our understanding of *Seven* and the entire *Decalogue*. Ania plays a dual role in the film. On the one hand, she is a character in the story, the object of Majka's and Ewa's love, and the motivating factor for their actions; only in the film's conclusion will she become a person in her own right, initiated to the difficult and painful experience of love. On the other hand, rather than a ploy, she provides an estranging perspective that demands attention and understanding. Kieślowski further underscores the importance of this perspective when he films low-angle shots, causing the viewer to assume an upward viewing position. However, in order to preserve the cognitive and affective mystery Ania embodies as a child and her dual function in the text, Kieślowski's camera does not always identify with her eyes. In some instances, the director prevents a simplistic or unrealistic identification with the character out of empathy, and calls instead for the assumption of a childlike perspective, the sharing of a different cognitive standpoint. In so doing, he also preserves the viewer's ability to independently observe, empathize with, or object to the way all characters, Ania included, are treated, ignored, or responded to.

Kieślowski's use of this particular camera position is most noticeable in the scenes filmed in Wojtek's house, when Kieślowski raises the question of the interpersonal connection necessary for a family to exist beyond biological bonds, gender roles and societal conventions, blinding passions, or apparent reasonableness. This secluded, cozy house, immersed in nature and away from the alienating architecture of an overcrowded city, is the place where Majka takes Ania to negotiate the terms of her freedom with both Wojtek and Ewa, but it is also the space where the biological family reunites and where an opportunity for reconciliation, love, and acceptance could arise. The low-angle medium or close-up shots showing Majka's conversations with Wojtek and their interaction with Ania describe the experience of reciprocal love in the intimacy of family as an unconfessed wish or an unfulfilled possibility. In the end, Wojtek chooses the sheltering, risk-free prison of his received identity, that of being a seducer ("a really terrible, powerful sorcerer—and wicked, too" in the metaphorical, all-too-adult language of fairytales[14]), over the painful freedom that love would give him if he admitted to Ania that he is her father, thus dispelling the cloud of lies that surround her and exasperate Majka. He is a lonely scriptwriter and a toymaker, a producer of fake but compensatory realities, fearful of things to come, his parenthood ironically signified in the retrieval not of his child, but of her teddy bear at the riverbank.

Thus Kieślowski has set the stage for the concluding act of this drama, when the three female characters are reunited, for the second and last time in the film, in the same frame. The tension characterizing this final encounter is intensified by the silence of the scene; the only words uttered are Ewa's, calling Majka and perhaps, in a whisper, naming her "daughter."[15] The hopelessly dividing and distancing confrontation, which their gestures and words as well as Ania's screams reveal in the film's beginning, turns at last into a silent gaze—a moving toward—that draws them together, for they finally experience love. Each woman, including Ania, not only recognizes herself in the other but also sees the other as an intrinsic part of her self—the female lineage warrants this mirror game of sameness and difference, no longer mere proximity—at the very moment when they all either release or lose one another, and ultimately bequeath each other freedom. In the concluding sequence, the camera cuts from Ewa calling Majka to Majka looking out of the train window to Ania silently staring at the moving train. For the first time, Ewa sees Majka as her daughter and mournfully, perhaps remorsefully, looks at her two daughters, one leaving while the other is standing in front of her, both severed from her. From within the train, Majka looks back at whom she has left, her daughter and her mother both longing for her. Last, Ania stands alone between her two mothers. She is still the cause and source, but also the medium of Majka's and Ewa's actions and passions, hatred finally turned into sorrowful love; she is neither a scream nor a toy nor an object of contention, but a person who learns about love through the experience of loss. Standing alone on a station platform, she still reminds us of the teddy bear left on the riverbank; in fact, she is not abandoned, since Ewa and Stefan are with her. A close-up of her face, on which the film ends, shows her eyes as no longer lifeless and sightless, but as inquiring.

Two main, interconnected sets of questions arise from viewing the film and looking into Ania's eyes. One concerns Kieślowski's exploration of the world of interpersonal and familial relations, focusing primarily but not exclusively on motherhood presented through the lens of a mother-daughter relationship. The director engages the spectator in reflecting on what a mother does to care for her child, and indirectly suggests these questions: Can a mother's love for her child be selfish? When does this love become a form of narcissistic possession of the child, necessary for a woman's self-fulfillment and identification? Can such love ultimately be destructive of the biological and psychological bonds between mother and child? In her study of *Seven*, Italian psychoanalyst Gabriella Ripa di Meana addresses these questions and persuasively argues that Ania is to Majka the gateway allowing her to detach herself from her home and family, and thus to be a free self. According to Ripa di Meana, Majka acts upon hate for Ewa rather than love for Ania. In the episode's conclusion, however, the motivation behind Majka's behavior changes: Majka senses—we remain within the realm of emotions—that owning Ania sanctions her dependence, not her freedom. In other words, by keeping Ania, Majka would be like Ewa, for her apparent independence would come at the expense of another woman, Ania herself. The cycle of selfish love and hatred would never be broken, and the legacy of one generation of women to the other would only be that of fierce, mutual exclusion and enduring, unspoken pain. Thus, Ripa di Meana concludes, by leaving Ania, Majka both sacrifices and exalts herself as a woman and a mother.[16]

Like the characters in *Seven*, the viewer is entrapped in the same all-or-nothing logic of love as possession and also wonders: To whom does Ania belong? Who is the thief in this story? Who gets deprived of what? Who gets robbed of her or his life and love?[17] And last, are biological bonds stronger and more important than those formalized in social conventions and norms? The viewer may provide an answer almost effortlessly, only by listening to Majka's words asserting her biological right over Ania when she tells a skeptical Wojtek, "Can you steal what is yours?" (meanwhile the camera shoots a tender yet intrusive close-up of Ania asleep) or when she confronts a distraught, yet cold and aggressive Ewa on the phone: "Listen, you've stolen my child. It was meant to be different. *You've stolen my child. And the fact that I am a mother, love . . . You've both stolen yourselves from me . . . everything*" (emphasis added).[18] Kieślowski encourages his viewer to participate in the story, to analyze it and to empathize with one character or the other; primarily with Majka, but also with Ewa, and possibly with both fathers since, whether in the past or in the present, all characters experience the loss of a child (or childhood itself), and along with it, the loss of a part of their selves. Whether the viewer also condones their actions is irrelevant to the director, who is solely interested in portraying the causes and implications of the act of stealing—of taking away, depriving, or subtracting—namely pain, and the denial of the humaneness of the perpetrator and the humanity of the victim alike. The roles of the victimizer and the victim appear to be interchangeable when passions and feelings are involved, as they always are, and it becomes unclear, then, who is who (a question Kieślowski will confront in *Eight*).

Kieślowski's cinema poses questions but does not provide answers; it shows tensions, not solutions. In this story, a conclusion, not a resolution, may perhaps be drawn in compliance with the director's idea of cinema, according to which the experiences of suffering, searching, and love converge in the construction of the gaze.[19] Ewa's and Majka's blinding obsession triggers questionable actions and words, defies the very notion of motherhood in relation to them both, denies Ania's personhood, which is the source and evidence of it, and ultimately causes further unspeakable grief. Yet, their thefts also increase the value of what each of them has actually lost but eventually retrieves, when they look and finally see each other again: In the action of painfully longing and mourning, they recover the ability to love and the possibility of being loved by another. But what about the viewer, left, in the end, mirroring a child's bewildered and inquiring gaze (Figure 9–2).

The last frontal-view frame of the film is particularly effective because it brings back the memory of Ania's unsettling crying and broken imaging of the beginning, while also recalling another story of love and sorrow, Paweł's in *One*. In the film's opening, the camera and Paweł's aunt look at a ghost, namely Paweł's virtual image, enclosed in a TV screen behind a shop window. This shot accentuates a distance and engages the viewer emotionally by emphasizing the distress, the inability to make sense

Figure 9–2. Ania at Jozefow train station in *Decalogue Seven*.

of what has or will happen, and the sense of limitation and definitiveness caused, as the viewer finds out, by death. The flux of life has come to a stop, as suggested by the freeze-frame shots of Paweł, which begin and conclude the episode, the frozen waters and the winter setting. By contrast, by silently staring into the camera in the very first frames, the witness sitting near a pond challenges the viewer intellectually, prompting questions about his identity, the role that he will play in the story, and the reason for his looking at us.

Seven tells no less sad a story, but a story of fluid experience, of running trains and flowing waters rather than freezing memories of a death—in this respect, Ania's close-ups are in stark contrast to the TV broadcasts of Paweł's face, shouting with joy, that frame his tale. In *Seven*, Kieślowski still distinguishes between an emotional and an intellectual way of experiencing life as cinema represents it, but he does so through one character alone, little Ania, to demonstrate that these modes are not mutually exclusive, although a progression from one to the other is implied. Ania's unexplained screams and sight appeal to the viewer's emotions in the beginning while her inquiring gaze—like that of the witness in *One*—instigates a particular intellectual dialogue at the end.

In the concluding shots of *Seven*, the camera, positioned to face Ania, functions as a porous interface between the world the film gives life to and the world the viewer experiences. It explores a distance and a proximity by constructing the gaze as an empirical space shared by the character and her viewer. Therein, the exchange and interchange between the virtual and the real become possible. We are summoned to respond to Ania's inquisitive silence and participate in her sorrow and confusion. No answer is given; eyes look into other eyes, formulating questions to respond to other questions, which all remain unspoken. Cinema stages the failure of words and exploits it to produce meaning. Before the stories of Véronique, Julie and Valentine, among the director's mounting suspicions about the intrusive and trivializing ability of fiction cinema to turn affects into a spectacle and the virtual into the real,[20] *Seven* is a compelling and original example of Kieślowski's radical vision of the complexity of life-experience as cinema appropriates and reflects upon it. The film shows that by means of love one overcomes fright, breaches loneliness, and opens oneself up to a dialogue with others, which may well be broken, difficult, or even inconclusive, and yet is and does not end. Like Majka, Ania, and Ewa at the end of the episode, we cannot be indifferent. Whether we are left or leaving on one of the many tracks or trains of existence, we live on our own lasting and unfulfilled desires, whose objects must elude us.

NOTES

1. Krzysztof Kieślowski, *Kieślowski on Kieślowski*, ed. Danusia Stok (London: Faber and Faber, 1993), 144–145. Further references will be cited in the text using the abbreviation *KK*.

2. Serafino Murri, *Krzysztof Kieslowski* (Milan: Il Castoro, 2004), 9. The original quote reads: "Se faccio film sull'amore (nel senso più lato del termine), è perché non esiste per me una cosa più importante. L'amore, se lo si intende come ciò che spinge verso qualcosa, governa completamente il senso della nostra vita. E del resto, tutti i libri e tutti i film parlano d'amore. O dell'assenza d'amore, che è l'altra faccia dell'amore. Tutto qui" (If I make films about love—in the broader sense of the term—it is because nothing exists that is more important to me. Love, if one understands it as that which moves one toward something, rules the meaning of our lives. Ultimately, all books and films speak of love. Or the absence of it, which is the other side of love. That's all [trans. Francesca Parmeggiani]).

3. The viewer is introduced to the theme of motherly love as a form of jealous possession in *Six*, the story of peeping Tomek and beautiful Magda. Tomek's landlady acts in a maternal, yet ambiguous way. In her heart and daily life, Tomek has taken the place of her biological son, Tomek's friend. Her motherly task, then, is to take care of this newly found son while she herself feels secure: She looks after Tomek by protecting him from women like Magda, who do not know him and make him suffer, and may even take her motherly place in her child's life. The relationship with Tomek is, for this mother, a relationship of love for herself and the child, of self-fulfillment and protection, but also of jealousy and possession.

4. Krzysztof Kieślowski, "Je cherche l'explication de tout," interview by Michel Ciment and Hubert Niogret, *Positif* 346 (December 1989), reprinted in *Krzysztof Kieslowski*, ed. Vincent Amiel (Paris: Positif/Jean-Michel Place, 1997), 103. Trans. Francesca Parmeggiani.

5. Kieślowski also includes two fathers in this torn family picture: Stefan (Władysław Kowalski), who makes musical instruments in his workshop at home, is Ewa's husband and Majka's father; Wojtek (Bogusław Linda), who makes stuffed animals in his house in the country, is Majka's and, presumably, Ewa's former lover, and Ania's biological father. Critics from both sides of the Atlantic often comment on Kieślowski's attention to family in *The Decalogue*; to echo Joseph G. Kickasola, the series deconstructs the notion of home by presenting dysfunctional families and complicated domestic dynamics including selfish, careless or missing parents. *The Films of Krzysztof Kieślowski: The Liminal Image* (New York: Continuum, 2004), 220. Further references to Kickasola's study will be cited in the text.

6. *Indeks* is the Polish word to indicate the book in which professors record a student's grade.

7. Annette Insdorf, *Double Lives, Second Chances: The Cinema of Krzysztof Kieślowski* (New York: Miramax Books, 1999), 103.

8. A second instance of Majka not wearing her spectacles occurs later, when she watches and calls on a fearful Ania at the kindergarten. The two scenes present an interesting analogy. In both occurrences, mother and daughter are confined to different physical spaces by a transparent barrier—the bedside in the early sequence, and a fence in the later one—which they cannot remove although their hands clutch it for support. Majka is like little Ania, a lost and confused child awakening from a bad dream. But the noteworthy detail setting the two situations and characters apart is that in the second instance, Majka puts on her glasses. In other words, she brings into focus the object of her longing and thus acknowledges or admits to her loneliness, rage and sadness. Shortly afterward, Majka, no longer only a child, will act upon this recognition and knowledge.

9. Nothing is what it looks like in an adult-made world except, perhaps, for the carousel, which is the lonely and melancholic place where Majka tells Ania the truth—Majka is the only character to do so throughout the film—and Ania learns about her real lineage. It is a tender, intimate and peaceful moment in *Seven*, albeit one of irreversible denouement and resolution. Significantly filmed outside of the city, among the ruins of childhood (the abandoned merry-go-round)—surviving traces of a happy but irretrievable past—it hints at the nearing end of childhood for both characters.

10. Kieślowski explains: "I always want to stir people to something. It doesn't matter whether I manage to pull people into the story or inspire

them to analyse it. What is important is that I force them into something or move them in some way. That's why I do all this—to make people experience something. It doesn't matter if they experience it intellectually or emotionally. You make films to give people something, to transport them somewhere else and it doesn't matter if you transport them to a world of intuition or a world of the intellect" (*KK*, 193).

11. In the concluding frames of the film, a man with crutches gets off the train. Is he getting off "a train of broken, marred, damaged people, shuttled away" (Kickasola 224)—the same train on which an emotionally wounded and suffering Majka jumps to escape, finally acknowledging her failure—or is he joining a psychologically scarred humanity—a mother and a daughter who have been abandoned by their daughter and mother? In speaking of this character, Kieślowski explains that "he doesn't have any influence on what's happening, but he is a sort of sign or warning to those whom he watches, *if they notice him*" (*KK*, 159, emphasis added). There is no evidence to support that the characters in the story see him, but, in the sudden opening of the fictional, virtual text to the viewer's extradiegetic reality and experience, we the viewers notice him; he is a fleeting sign or warning to us, rather than the characters, that we must prepare for an extraordinary conclusion.

12. Krzysztof Kieślowski and Krzysztof Piesiewicz, *Decalogue: The Ten Commandments*, trans. Phil Cavendish and Suzannah Bluh (London: Faber and Faber, 1991), 187, 204.

13. Vincent Amiel, *Kieślowski: La coscienza dello sguardo* (Genoa: Le Mani, 1998), 97.

14. Chapter 6, *The Decalogue: Decalogue Seven*, DVD, directed by Krzysztof Kieślowski (Chicago: Facets Video, 2003).

15. In the Italian-dubbed version of the film, Ewa calls Majka *"figlia mia"* (my daughter) clearly, albeit softly (*Il Decalogue: Decalogo sette—Non rubare*, DVD, directed by Krzysztof Kieślowski [Cinisello Balsamo: Multimedia San Paolo, n.d.]). In the original Polish released in the United States, Ewa's words remain indistinct, almost inaudible.

16. Gabriella Ripa di Meana, *La morale dell'altro. Scritti sull'inconscio dal Decalogo di Kieslowski* (Florence: Liberal Libri, 1998), 165–188.

17. With gentle irony (and a slight gender bias), Kieślowski even conceives of an alter ego of the viewer in the film, that is, the lady at Jozefow train station, who reads Flaubert's *Madame Bovary* (1856)—a story centered on the themes of love and personal discontent, identity and identification, womanhood and motherhood. She takes pity on Majka, invites her to rest in the ticket office, and tries to help her out by misleading Ewa. Like the viewer of *Seven*, this woman casts her judgment and takes sides, though to no avail.

Indeed reading may lead one to blur the boundaries between reality and the imagination, between what one perceives and what one believes, and to act accordingly. As we shall see, the film's conclusion will add an interesting appendix to what this character calls to mind, namely the association of reading and seeing, the idea of representing in words or images, and the responsibility that the interpretation of any texts, verbal or visual, entails.

18. Chapters 4 and 5, *The Decalogue: Decalogue Seven*, DVD.

19. Kieślowski once stated, "If I had to formulate the message of my 'Decalogue,' I'd say, 'Live carefully, with your eyes open, and try not to cause pain.'" Insdorf, *Double Lives, Second Chances*, 124.

20. Amiel, *Kieślowski*, 72.

CHAPTER 10

Decalogue Eight: Childhood, Emotion, and the Shoah

Emma Wilson

The eighth part of Krzysztof Kieślowski's *Decalogue* begins with a brief flashback sequence where a child is led down a passageway. The scene, a liminal image of a missing child, is missing from the screenplay and not part of the initial conception of the film.

I want to begin by looking at these images more closely.[1] The shots first encountered in the film privilege movement and touch as a handheld camera passes along a passageway to the echoing sound of footsteps. The camera appears to share the viewpoint, and embodied angle of vision, of a small child. This illusion is undone, however, as two hands, a child's and an adult's, move into the frame. The camera follows in fact just behind the figures it tracks, as it keeps their clasped hands its object of attention (Figure 10-1). Color has bled out of the images; the skin of the child's hand is pallid against the gray of her gabardine sleeve. Colorless walls passed are scratched and pitted. The ground is scored with chalk. The visual quality of the images, and the somber setting, conjure the dust and decay of old photographs or film footage. The film creates a sense of fragility and intermittence, a sense of the shots as mirage, as they dissolve from time to time into the black screen that highlights the titles of the film. As the shots re-

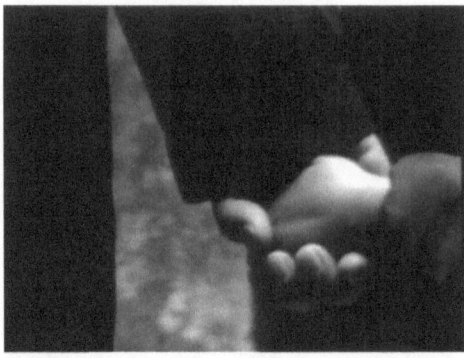

Figure 10–1. Holding hands in *Decalogue Eight*.

Figure 10–2. The fleeting image of a child in *Decalogue Eight*.

turn, we see two figures silhouetted. The small child is a dark shape against a blue-gray ground. Before the close of the sequence, there is a glimpse of her spectral face, in a backward glance. The fleeting image of the face is seen against darkness. Light highlights her cheeks, her nose, and her upper lip, but her eyes appear only as shadowed sockets, and her open mouth is shown as darkness. Her face, looking back, appears as an apparition or a ghostly death mask in the alley (Figure 10–2).

The visual composition of the shot invites comparison with certain images from Christian Boltanski's later installation, *Jewish School of Grosse Hamburgerstrasse in Berlin in 1938* (Marian Goodman Gallery, New York, 1994). Using a found image of schoolgirls, a photo of Jewish children in Berlin in 1938, Boltanski enlarged the shots of the girls' laughing or mouthing faces, reproducing them individually on separate screens. The enlarged images have the same spectral presence and imprecision found in the Kieślowski frames. The blurring of the images, their reduction to an imprint of light and shadow, heightens their immediacy and visceral appeal to the spectator. As Didier Semin writes: "Boltanski places great importance on the patina of his works. The photographs he uses are by now 'nth' generation prints, reprints of reprints or photocopies of photocopies; the loss of focus and cleanness that results from mechanical reproduction adds mystery and aura rather than taking them away."[2] From the particularity of the anecdotal school photograph, a quotidian item, Boltanski has retrieved and made visible emotive and anonymous images that look toward a future horror of child mortality. The images retain the original index of presence, showing real children, at a real Jewish school before the war, but, through photographic process and changes to scale and context, they project an intimate foreboding of the future that awaits these children. Although it is part of a feature film, and not found footage, in my invocation of Boltanski I want to suggest that the image of the child in *Decalogue Eight* looks forward to the aesthetic found in Boltanski's installations and anticipates their memory work and reflections on the future perfect and the commemoration of the dead.

Kieślowski has several times allowed the opening of his films to be absorbed with animate images of mourned children. In *Three Colors: Blue* (1993), images of Julie's (Juliette Binoche) daughter Anna, who dies in a car accident, are glimpsed in the film's opening shots.[3] The links between *Eight* and *One* are stronger still. In the opening of *One*, we see retrospective shots of the dead Paweł (Wojciech Klata), a child who drowns in the course of the film. He is glimpsed in footage playing in a shop window. As in *Eight*, and in the Boltanski installation, his face is shadowed and blurred. The footage is stilled at its close, so we see Paweł, like the child in *Eight*, as a spectral image. These points of comparison raise a question about the status of the images viewed at the start of *Eight*: Has the little girl we see here survived?

Eight is preoccupied, in various ways, with the question of the survival of the child. While the survival of children is a concern running through Kieślowski's filmmaking, in *Eight* the concern is explored in interrelation with questions about the Shoah. This question is bound up with issues about whose story is told in this film and how the Shoah is approached. The representation of children, in film and photography, will be seen to open onto questions about the emotions and about remembered infant selves.

Eight is rare in Kieślowski's corpus in treating the Shoah and in reflecting on this era in Polish history. Annette Insdorf cites the director:

He explained that the wartime context of *8* was indeed factual: "By chance, one of my friends told me the story of a [Jewish woman] to whom someone had promised help and who finally didn't give it. I understood that the subject was close to me, and that it wasn't bad to speak very naturally about Polish-Jewish relations in daily life without giving Polish or Jewish identity preponderant roles."[4]

Like the other films of *The Decalogue*, *Eight* is set in the present in Warsaw and apparently meditates on one of the Ten Commandments, in this instance: "You shall not bear false witness against your neighbor" (Exod. 20:16 RSV). Departing quickly from its opening shots of a child in the past, the film unfolds in the leafy surrounds of the housing estate that is the setting for the whole series. It follows Zofia (Maria Kościałkowska), a philosophy professor, as she exercises in the morning and prepares for her day. There is a sense of calm, order, and levity as the film observes Zofia's solitary routines. Her serenity is carried into the classroom, a privileged space in this film, and arguably for *The Decalogue* as a whole.

Like the courtroom in Kieślowski's trilogy, the classroom in *Eight*, like that in *One*, forms a type of metatextual space in which the narratives of the series may be opened up for debate. Zofia's classes create a forum for the discussion of ethical questions. We witness a class about "ethical hell" in which Kieślowski approaches questions about the Shoah. The class is visited by Elżbieta Loranz (Teresa Marczewska), a Polish-born American who works for an institute that researches the fate of Jewish war survivors.

The first example that is presented in class is effectively the narrative of *Two*. A young woman narrates the story of the wife of a dying man:

> It turns out the woman [his wife] is pregnant. The father is another man and her husband doesn't know about it. Furthermore, she has never been able to conceive before. The woman loves her developing child but she also loves her husband. If he is going to live, she must have an abortion. If he will die, she may have the baby. The doctor realizes, like it or not, he must decide on the baby's life.

After the narrative and before discussion, Zofia adds: "To complicate your task, I can tell you that the child lives and probably this is what really counts in the story." This meaning is offered with some trouble or disturbance as Elżbieta interrupts the class, getting up, as if to leave. But we see instead that she moves forward, to a place in the lecture theater from which she can record the teacher's words. She causes Zofia to repeat herself and to state again: "It lives and I consider that the most important factor." While, in this repeated interpretation, Zofia may offer tools for the understanding of *Two*, a more interesting connection is forged with the narrative that unfolds in *Eight*. The statement that the child lives affords a story that Elżbieta will seek permission to relate to the class.

Elżbieta's story, which she relates dispassionately, is about a six-year-old Jewish girl. It is the winter of 1943. She has been temporarily sheltered in a Polish family's cellar. She is found another hiding place, but her future guardians lay down the condition that she must have formal documentation proving she has been baptized. The girl's protectors seek a couple to become the girl's fictional godparents, and thus to claim she has been baptized. Everything is arranged for her, and she is taken to the place where her fictional godparents live. While Elżbieta has previously interrupted Zofia, at this point in her narrative she herself is interrupted by the arrival of an intruder in the classroom. His sudden eruptive presence breaks the attention of the class and intimates the disruptive emotion that Elżbieta has brought into this space. The containment and calm of the class are discomposed. Zofia regains order through questioning Elżbieta before encouraging her to continue. Elżbieta goes on:

> Finally, the woman says what he finds so difficult to say. They must go back on their promise. After careful consideration, they cannot bring themselves to lie to Him they believe in who orders them to be charitable, but forbids false witness. The false witness they were about to commit consciously was incompatible with their principles.

As she is speaking, the camera, as if animate, pans sideways down the rows in the lecture hall. It has done this before, moving among the students, but now it moves in search of the figure of the angel (Artur Barciś), the silent witness who appears in all but one of the *Decalogue* films. Here he is a student in Zofia's class. He looks out at his teacher as Elżbieta reaches her words about false witness. Zofia's face, which we look on to, is framed as the object of his attention. By the end of Elżbieta's account, the camera has slid back along the rows to rest again on her.

Elżbieta's narrative invites discussion of the commandment at the center of the film. One student says: "The motivation seems impossible, if they were true Catholics. Such witnessing wouldn't have been dishonest." Another student suggests a different motivation: "Fear, if an hour earlier a Jewish child had been found in the house, its brains bashed out and the family which hid it shot in the courtyard." While the camera is on Zofia, Elżbieta returns: "Do you think fear justifies it?" The student replies: "A motive, not a judgment." Zofia curtails discussion, saying: "We are going too far." She continues: "The ethical problems posed will be worked out by all of you individually. Please try to present us with the woman's point of view. Try to understand her." *Eight* challenges us to understand this woman. And the short film moves further to explore implications of its embedded narrative of the Jewish child.

Elżbieta sits alone as the class empties out, and we hear the same music that played over the sequence with the child at the start. In telling her story in Zofia's class, Elżbieta has chosen to confront another woman with a truth from their shared past. The editing of the shots in the classroom sequence and Zofia's bodily reactions have made her connection to the story clear. The scene closes with the blurred shapes of students passing Elżbieta. The film cuts to similarly indistinct images, now net curtains in near darkness. The camera again pans to the left until it finds Zofia in lone reflection. As she later paces the corridors of the university, in shots that might only reflect her inner life, she finds Elżbieta waiting for her. "It's you," Zofia says. "You are alive. I've wondered all my life." The shadow of the corridor here and the light glimpsed at its end offer an aura of unreality to the scene and the encounter it stages.

The rest of the film charts the awkward fascination between the two women as they confront the apparent fact of Elżbieta's survival after Zofia's refusal to act as her godparent. Zofia tells Elżbieta the truth which is hidden behind her lie about false witnessing: Her husband was in the counter-espionage section of Poland's Home Army and they received information that the people who were due to hide the child were agents of the Gestapo. She acted to protect her husband's resistance work. Her political choice brought affective consequences, as Zofia states: "I didn't know you were alive. I left you alone. I sent you to an almost certain death." She repeats again: "No ideal, nothing, is more important than the life of a child."

Discussing this episode, Slavoj Žižek writes of the irony of the woman's actions during the Second World War in contrast to her current beliefs; he suggests: "One can speculate that she became a professor of ethics, dedicating her life to philosophy, in order to clarify her mistake, i.e. to account for why and how, at a crucial moment, she made the wrong choice."[5] The film itself suggests that Zofia acted with courage at other times. Elżbieta remarks: "Your activities, even after me, are well known. Thanks to you, several people of my world are still alive." But the film offers little sense that Zofia's later actions have offered clarity or recompense. As the statement about the life of a child is repeated several times by Zofia, so the film finds different ways to show her conviction endorsed. While the survival of a child is made the matter of prime importance through the film, *Eight* draws on the summoning and survival of the emotions of childhood to do justice to its subject.

In *Upheavals of Thought: The Intelligence of the Emotions*, Martha Nussbaum argues that we should consider emotions as a deep-rooted part of the system of ethical reasoning. She ties one strand of her argument specifically to questions about childhood, suggesting that the upheavals of thought that "constitute the adult experience of emotion involve foundations laid down much earlier in life, experiences of attachment, need, delight, and anger."[6] For Nussbaum, "early memories shadow later perceptions of objects, adult attachment relations bear the traces of infantile love and hate" (6). She elaborates: "In a deep sense all human emotions are in part about the past, and bear the traces of a history that is at once commonly human, socially constructed, and idiosyncratic" (177). She argues particularly that emotions reveal us as vulnerable, and vulnerable to events and encounters that we do not control. Her thinking works to treat childhood emotion and attachment with due seriousness, and to refuse their detachment from the realm of the composed adult. In moments of vulnerability, the adult may be exposed to the discomfiting rush of emotion, bringing or responding to a loss of control over feelings and events. What is important for Nussbaum, the extremity of emotion does not remove it from the realm of thought. Rather, "the peculiar depth and the potentially terrifying character of the human emotions derives from the especially complicated thoughts that humans are likely to form about their own need for objects, and about their imperfect control over them" (16).

It is through its examination of childhood and the emotions that *Eight* draws out its possible meanings. Kieślowski uses two particular filmic tropes to conjure emotion and make it part of the system of thought of the film: movement and touch, both privileged already in the sequence at the start of the film. It is through returning to the features of these liminal images that Kieślowski draws childhood emotions forward into the present. This happens significantly in a scene that follows the initial encounter between Elżbieta and Zofia.

Having invited Elżbieta home for supper, Zofia drives her instead to the location where they met previously. Zofia invites this traversal of the past, yet quickly loses control of the returning scene. Elżbieta leaves the car and, echoing her childhood footsteps, walks through an external arch into a complex of tenements. The film shows her departing, watched from Zofia's perspective. As Elżbieta moves on through the recognizable confines of the alley, her emotions are not revealed. No attempt is made to tie the child experience we see at the start of the film to the adult perceptions we watch here. This act of association is withheld until Elżbieta herself withdraws, hiding near the entrance to the complex. Leaving the car to locate her missing guest, Zofia in turn now enters the building, witnessed by Elżbieta from the shadows. Zofia's stature is slighter than Elżbieta's and her movement through this dark space more timorous. It is Zofia, rather than Elżbieta, who retraces the footsteps and summons the emotions of the missing child. She goes further than Elżbieta, entering the tenements as she searches for the missing adult. She goes inside, and asks for her friend, but is met with hostility and mocked as a madwoman. A man she encounters tells her that there is no other exit, and that maybe her friend never entered the building. Zofia cries out Elżbieta's name and finds her voice echoed by the returning taunts of a neighbor. Zofia's bearings are lost, and her gravitas is diminished. She exits the space to find Elżbieta outside, sitting in her car. Zofia says: "I was afraid you were lost. You weren't there." Perhaps she speaks here both to the woman she has found and to the child she abandoned previously. Her loss of control over her environs, revealed through her violent emotion at the loss of Elżbieta, endorses the avowal that there is no cause or ideal more important than the life of a child. As Zofia is reminded of the speechless anguish of the child she had abandoned in this locale, as she traces the child's path and momentarily shares her lack of control over her life, the film attaches emotional understanding, the shock of sensation, to ethical statements. Emotion is brought out through motion. As the film echoes its own opening, childhood sensations of loss and fear are brought from the past to govern the recognition and reparations the narrative will entertain.

Annette Insdorf argues that "Elżbieta's vengeful hide-and-seek game has forced Zofia once again into the role of fearful protector" (112). This reading overlooks the different effect of Zofia's infantilization. As the film continues, however, we do see Zofia seeking to play some protective role to Elżbieta. Before exploring this, its links to touch and the pursuit of the film's engagement with the emotions and ethics, I want to raise here a further question about the memories of the Shoah the film conjures.

The sequence at the start, which appears the only literal figuration of the endangered Jewish child, and her fearful emotions, is never specifically placed or anchored. As Mroz writes of the opening shots: "There is not much to indicate that this scene is a flashback, it is just something that does not yet fit into the narrative" (175). Although it bears a relation to Elżbieta's narrative—we see a child led along by her guardian—we do not learn whether the scene figures the approach to Zofia's house or the departure of the child and her guardian after the baptism has failed to take place. Elżbieta speaks of the place later as the witness, in bricks and mortar, to her humiliation. The returning music, after Elżbieta's narration, may link the early shots to a memory now in her mind. But there is no further evidence to confirm this. Her seeming lack of emotion as she revisits the location creates a wedge between what might be remembered and what is relived now. Zofia's more visceral reaction to the locale hints instead that these early shots may be her imagining of the scene, of the child's arrival at her home or forlorn departure. Perhaps the shots are (as Gilles Deleuze has put it) a "memory for two" that the two women construct between them in their remembering.[7] Or perhaps they are anchored in the subjective perception of neither protagonist, but merely hover like a screen memory for the film, implying, but yet concealing, the full horror of the event that has taken place.

Indeed the film is rife with concealment or doubt. Initially the opening shots appear to have no connection to the equanimity of the morning shots in the present. Zofia's routine does not belie her emotional trouble (though a picture falls insistently aslant in her apartment). Her encounter with Elżbieta Loranz at the university is seemingly tranquil. It is only in the classroom, in the thick of her ethical statements about the life of a child, that connections between the opening and the ensuing narrative are felt. While the narrative of the woman deciding whether her unborn child will live or die summons the narrative Elżbieta offers, we may also wonder whether Elżbieta's identity as (or confusion with) the child Zofia failed to save is a reparative fantasy fostered forth by the initial story.

The film offers no obvious indications that the drama we view is one of wish-fulfillment rather than one of supposed actuality. But some hesitation about this may add to a sense of the complexity, and ethical interest, of the story that unfolds. Consider the scene where Zofia enters the housing block where she has lived formerly. None of the other residents sees or hears Elżbieta. This may be entirely inconsequential. But the inexplicable absence of Elżbieta takes hold of the film for a few moments, compounded by comments that she may never have been there. At a loss, Zofia may imitate or recall the emotions of the missing child. Yet she also faces further the possibility that the child's survival, and adult presence, is only a reparative fantasy. In the delusion of her moves through this enclosed space in search of Elżbieta, she may face the truth of her fears. Even though we have seen her hiding, the achievement of the scene is to make us wonder, for a few minutes, if Elżbieta was really there.

Zofia finds her again in her car and quickly takes her home to her apartment. Still, the scene seems marked by the wish to revisit a past event and play it differently, even with the mature adult the missing child has become. Zofia serves Elżbieta hot tea in an ornate cup. In the earlier narrative, Elżbieta has mentioned that the child was chilled and that hot tea was served, but she had no time to drink it. The encounter between the two women in Zofia's apartment has the aura of a wish-fulfilling moment, a lapse in time when Zofia can show tenderness to Elżbieta. As they talk of the past, Zofia goes to stand behind Elżbieta. Elżbieta's image is blurred in the foreground; Zofia, standing behind her, cannot look into her face. What she does instead is put her hands on Elżbieta's shoulders, touching her, holding her, and feeling her presence. Elżbieta's head is bowed and her eyes are closed, as they will be later when she prays. This moment of contact—conjuring the trope of touch mentioned above—comes as Zofia confesses that she sent the child to almost certain death. Elżbieta's mouth quivers as Zofia states again the importance of the life of a child. She reaches up to touch Zofia's hand. A train or siren is heard in the background, an occurrence that will become significant later.

In following scenes, in an uneasy composition where both actresses are shot within the same frame, Elżbieta questions Zofia about her teaching, about her works, and about how to lead a life. What is strange in the whole exchange, indeed in the film more broadly, is that Elżbieta's emotions or thoughts are barely addressed. Her gesture, touching her, has brought comfort to Zofia. Zofia may have been conjured by Elżbieta as her accuser and confessor in the classroom, but in the privacy of the apartment, in this reparative fantasy of containment and tenderness, Elżbieta brings composure and absolution, facilitating the smooth continuation of Zofia's orderly life. Elżbieta offers no account of her own past, of the loss of her parents, or of the status of her present work. She begins to seem like a surviving adult whom Zofia's imagination has fostered forth for comfort.

Here, thinking about the primacy of touch in the film, in the shots at the start and in the contact between Zofia and Elżbieta, it may be useful to refer to Emmanuel Levinas on the caress. While Levinas apparently refers to the caress in an amorous context, he concedes: "The loving intention goes unto the Other, unto the friend, the child, the brother, the beloved, the parents."[8] One of his insights into love comes in the recognition: "To love is to fear for another, to come to the assistance of his frailty" (256). Extreme fragility and vulnerability are part of the tenderness of this encounter and part of its hesitance and difficulty. For Levinas:

> The caress consists in seizing upon nothing, in soliciting what ceaselessly escapes its form toward a future never future enough, in soliciting what slips away as though it *were not yet*. It *searches*, it forages. It is not an intentionality of disclosure but of search: a movement unto the invisible. In a certain sense it *expresses* love, but suffers from an inability to tell it. (257–258)

The caress is not about capture, contact, or revelation. It is a feeling search in invisibility or darkness. In the touch between Zofia and Elżbieta, attendant doubts about Elżbieta's presence or absence allow the film to intimate something of the impossible encounter with the other.

Zofia invites Elżbieta to stay in her apartment. Where the film has been interrupted previously by acts of intrusion, here it is marked by her hospitality. Elżbieta asks her if the room was her son's, and Zofia replies that her son did not want to stay with her. Through this synoptic account of her affective relations, the film seems to hint at a possible failure in love, or failure in maternity, on Zofia's part. Her refusal to shelter the child, to play the role of her godparent, is aligned with a possible failure to act as actual parent.

Eight approaches questions about the Shoah through a narrative of a missing child. The opening shots—the child's small hand, the glimpse of her spectral face—are the visual tokens the film uses to signal threat and horror. That this sentient child should be endangered, and that an adult can, through error or lapse of judgment, fail to protect her from almost certain death, displays in magnified form the senseless horror and ethical hell of the Shoah. This is its point of contact with the later work by Boltanski. The narrative of Zofia and Elżbieta that Kieślowski develops in *Eight* is one that pertains to the specificity of the Shoah and its atrocities (more so, I think, than he himself acknowledges in the lines quoted above). It is also aligned in his work with other narratives about the protection, or endangering, of children. As Insdorf notes: "The credit sequence of *8* . . . is continuous with *7*: as they are walking, an adult takes a child's hand in close-up" (107). *Seven*, a narrative about contested maternity, segues into *Eight* about a woman who fails to save a Jewish child. Meanings seep from sequence to sequence.

Boltanski likewise appears in his artistic practice, and in his statements about his art and himself, to endorse connections between regular life experiences and losses, and those unnatural tragedies of genocide. His art encompasses images of children who died in the Shoah, images of children in Dijon who "seem to have died from unnatural (if unspecifiable) causes" (Semin 99), and images of himself and other children. Marianne Hirsch, suggesting that images with no indexical relation to the Shoah may yet carry its meanings, says of *The Children of Dijon*:

> Although the actual children depicted may well still be alive, their images form altarpieces, reminiscent of Byzantine icons, commemorating the dead. Through iconic and symbolic but not directly indexical implication, Boltanski connects these images of children to the mass murders of the Holocaust: the pictures themselves evoke and represent the actual victims, but neither we nor the artist has a way of knowing whether the individuals in the photos are Holocaust victims or enlarged faces of random schoolchildren.[9]

Boltanski also suggests no strict demarcation between images of the dead and images of now missing past selves; he has said, "I began to work as an artist when I began to be an adult, when I understood that my childhood was finished, and was dead. I think we all have somebody who is dead inside of us. A dead child. I remember the Little Christian that is dead inside me."[10] It seems disturbing to align past selves with literally dead others, children who have died before they have reached adulthood and indeed children who have died through genocide. Yet it is peculiarly the case that photographs—objects with which Boltanski works extensively in his installations—necessarily make no category distinction between a past self and missing others. As Jacek (Mirosław Baka), preoccupied by a photograph of his dead sister, asks in *Five*: "Can you tell from a photograph whether a person's dead or alive?" Retrospective knowledge that a child imaged has died in infancy, childhood, or adolescence invests any image of him or her with the emotions attached to the future anterior (in Roland Barthes's terms), the horrified knowledge that he or she is now dead, that the death was impending even as he or she was imaged alive. But this patina of emotion is laid over an image that might otherwise exist as any family relic. This lack of distinction raises questions of whether emotions that usually attach to family photography and to images of children have bearing in the exorbitant context of the Shoah.

Hirsch argues that "the Holocaust photograph is uniquely able to bring out this particular capacity of photographs to hover between life and death, to capture only that which no longer exists, to suggest both the desire and the necessity and, at the same time, the difficulty, the impossibility, of mourning" (20). She explains: "Holocaust photographs, as much as their

Decalogue Eight

subjects, are themselves stubborn survivors of the intended destruction of an entire culture, its people as well as all their records, documents, and cultural artifacts" (23). She includes in her discussion "pictures which are connected for us to total death and to public mourning—pictures of horror and also ordinary snapshots and portraits, family pictures connected to the Holocaust by their context and not by their content" (20). Starting from a different place from Boltanski, and retaining an indexical link to the Shoah, she nevertheless correlates pictures of horror and family snapshots, implying contact between the affect of each. In writing about Boltanski, Hirsch refers in passing to "the transcendently painful figure of the dead child" (263), yet she does not otherwise separate images of children from other photographs.

In his memorial volume, *French Children of the Holocaust*, Serge Klarsfeld writes:

> The eyes of 2,500 children gaze at us from across the years in these pages. They are among the more than 11,400 children whose lives are chronicled here[:] innocent children who were taken from their homes all over France to be deported and put to death in the Nazi camps. . . . More than 50 years have passed since the murders of these beautiful children . . . perhaps it is time to share this with others so they may know how these terrible events happened and come to know some of the young victims, arrested in the streets you will find if you visit France.[11]

Klarsfeld states that the work was born out of his obsession that these children should not be forgotten. He describes the book as their collective gravestone. The volume holds images that offer a sign, an index, of the anterior presence of these several thousand children. While their images—family snapshots, studio portraits, occasional identification photos and even images from gravestones—are not distorted visually, like Boltanski's, they are likewise overlaid with knowledge that their subjects have been murdered. So many of the images are tender, intimate, and disarming. A bid to resurrect the past lives here—"to come to know some of the young victims," in Klarsfeld's words—requires some desperate attempt to link the domestic or studio setting to a future situation of genocide, to separations, to physical suffering, and to almost certain death. Emotion here is bound with knowledge, as memories of our own attachments and losses, infinitely minor in this context, are hesitantly present in attempts to look at these children.

The images in Klarsfeld's volume surely also resist such an appropriative gaze. Hesitation derives from the privacy of the images—these are images for the family—yet also from the future vulnerability by which they are shadowed. We may long to protect these children, but they remain also untouchable, remote. With difficulty, one may imagine the moment in the studio or in the drawing room when the picture was taken. I imagine a child taking up the pose that has been captured immemorially in the image. In such imagining, I attempt to find animate and haptic images of the anterior presence of these missing children. But such virtual images, powered by the wish to see or know a child alive, are all too fleeting. Such hesitant imagining is what I think Kieślowski tries to capture in the emotive shots at the start of *Eight*. Emerging out of darkness are shots conjured by an imagination attempting to feel and trace a child's emotion.

Examining the Klarsfeld images may afford a further insight into the reparative and imaginative acts of *Eight*. A film such as Thomas Gilou's *Paroles d'étoiles* (2002) shows interviews with adults who survived the Shoah and who speak about their childhood. As each adult reveals his or her age in 1942, he or she seems strangely aligned with the photographs of children murdered. The distance between the children in Klarsfeld's volume and the present seems momentarily covered. We see and hear witnesses who conjure images of the adults the dead children might have become. Klarsfeld's volume itself is seen at one point in *Paroles d'étoiles*, and its pages are turned as a woman speaks of her memories of children clinging to their mothers. The uncanny presence and youthfulness of the adults in the film, found too in the faces of the witnesses who speak in a documentary such as *Into the Arms of Strangers: Stories of the Kindertransport* (2000), makes the images of the murdered children and the horror of their missing destinies more immediate, more the matter of living memory and revived emotion, yet also incommensurable.[12]

It is this possibility of viewing the adult the child might have become that is found in *Eight*. At stake in the emotions conjured is the wish to see the live adult avatar of the abandoned child. When the living adult seems to be found, or convincingly imagined, Zofia will seek some means of assuaging her guilt and grief through reparative acts of tenderness. Delicately evoked, the mother/child relation seems to be involved in the reparative moments, or fictions, of the film. This is particularly apparent in later sequences.

We see Zofia glimpse Elżbieta as she prays in the guest bedroom of the apartment and, like a parent checking on a child at night, she gently closes the door upon her. The room is closed in darkness, the tones and textures of the shot recalling the sequence of images at the start of the film. The train or siren heard as the women touched earlier is heard again here. The

Decalogue Eight

scene has taken on the shade of memory rather than actuality. As before, Kieślowski cuts to external shots of the morning woodland and of Zofia running. Elżbieta is only found again when Zofia is back in the apartment. The guest has made breakfast and brought white peonies. Zofia holds the flowers carefully, touched by Elżbieta's gesture. Here, together, they attend to each other. When Zofia later takes Elżbieta to meet the tailor who was due to hide her, she waits outside. Where Elżbieta was missing before, Zofia is now present. The two women talk in the street and their image is glimpsed from inside the building, and through a barred window. The film ends with a distanced image, through glass, of the renewed tenderness between the two women, of Zofia reaching again to touch, and protect Elżbieta.

Eight begins with shots that may be a memory, or an imagined image, of a child who may not have survived. While the surface narrative offers affirmation that this child has survived, there are moments where this seems less certain. This doubt, this returning uncertainty, plays a part in the meanings of the film. If we remain uncertain of Elżbieta's status—as survivor or as specter—we can never fully reach her or grasp her experience. She remains at once vulnerable and untouchable, as, in the Levinasian image evoked above, touch itself is infested with failure. Where, in the film's tenderness, Elżbieta is never finally fixed and held, also the film's survivor memories, or the memories of the dead, are left untouched. The film approaches instead the pathos of another woman's fascination with a specter from her past, a wish-fulfilling fantasy of the apparition, in her classroom, of a grown child she would have wished once to save.

The film offers insight into the emotions that insist in this relation to a child from the past, emotions that have their roots in past childhood experiences of loss and separation, of helplessness and lack of control. Speaking of child experience, Martha Nussbaum writes, "So the child is always inhabiting a world that is both safe and dangerous, aware of herself as both hard and terribly soft, both able and unable to rely on receiving nourishment and security from her caretakers. This intermittence of care, and the intermittence of safety that results, is an essential part of becoming able to live" (209).

The context of the Shoah offers a horrifically magnified vision of danger, insecurity, and the intermittence of care. In *The Decalogue*, Kieślowski explores connections between this exorbitant vision and other instances of love, abandonment, and grief between parents and children. The unspeakable emotions conjured have some relation, for protagonists and viewers alike, to childhood attachments. As Nussbaum insists, intimacy, sensations of love and loss, are, and should be, bound into our ethical decisions. Emotions, summoned in *Eight* through a moving image of a missing child, summoned elsewhere in testimonies and visual culture through images of children who have died, here rarefy these memorial works.

NOTES

1. A beautiful account of the film and of this scene in particular is offered in Matilda Mroz, *Temporality and Film Analysis* (Edinburgh: Edinburgh University Press, 2012), 175–176. I want to signal the importance of Mroz's approach to *The Decalogue* in its analysis of the films' affective and emotional force. Her reading of the relations between objects and memory in *Eight* (158–159) is extraordinarily precise and revelatory. Further reference to Mroz's analysis will be cited in the text.

2. Didier Semin, Tamar Garb, and Donald Kuspit, *Christian Boltanski* (London: Phaidon, 1997), 88. Further references will be cited in the text.

3. See Emma Wilson, *Cinema's Missing Children* (London: Wallflower, 2003), 18.

4. Annette Insdorf, *Double Lives, Second Chances: The Cinema of Krzysztof Kieślowski* (New York: Miramax Books, 1999), 112–113. Further references will be cited in the text.

5. Slavoj Žižek, *The Fright of Real Tears: Krzysztof Kieślowski between Theory and Post-Theory* (London: British Film Institute, 2001), 116.

6. Martha C. Nussbaum, *Upheavals of Thought: The Intelligence of Emotions* (New York: Cambridge University Press, 2001), 6. Further references will be cited in the text.

7. Gilles Deleuze, *Cinema 2: The Time-Image*, trans. Hugh Tomlinson and Barbara Habberjam (London: Athlone Press, 1989), 118.

8. Emmanuel Levinas, *Totality and Infinity: An Essay on Exteriority*, trans. Alphonso Lingis (Pittsburgh: Duquesne University Press, 1969), 254. Further references will be cited in the text.

9. Marianne Hirsch, *Family Frames: Photography, Narrative and Postmemory* (Cambridge, Mass.: Harvard University Press, 1997), 258. Further references will be cited in the text.

10. Christian Boltanski, "Studio: Christian Boltanski" (December 1, 2002), http://www.tate.org.uk/context-comment/articles/studio-christian-boltanski (accessed April 3, 2015).

11. *French Children of the Holocaust: A Memorial*, ed. Serge Klarsfeld (New York: New York University Press, 1996), xi.

12. Mark Jonathan Harris and Deborah Oppenheimer, *Into the Arms of Strangers: Stories from the Kindertransport* (London: Bloomsbury, 2000).

CHAPTER 11

Divine Possession: Metaphysical Covetousness in *Decalogue Nine*

Philip Sicker

Recalling his underlying assumptions and method in the *Decalogue* films, Krzysztof Kieślowski casts himself as a psychological and ethical detective: "I believe everybody's life is worthy of scrutiny, has its secrets and dramas. People don't talk about their lives because they're embarrassed. They don't want to open old wounds, or are afraid of appearing old-fashioned and sentimental. So we wanted to begin each film in a way which suggested that the main character had been picked by the camera as if at random."[1] In setting the primary action of all ten films in and around an anonymous-looking Warsaw housing estate, Kieślowski provides a locus for the hidden lives of various characters whose paths briefly intersect, but whose "secrets" are known only to the filmmaker and his audience. Devoting himself to revealing "what's going on inside" these characters' lives, the director notes that he used the apartment complex's "thousands of similar windows" as an establishing shot in each film, sometimes letting the camera slowly pan across these indistinguishable glass barriers (as at the start of *Seven*) before moving into a particular interior and penetrating one or more private lives (*KK*, 146). In framing the *Decalogue* films this way, Kieślowski draws intriguing connections between his cinematic enterprise, which monitors individual lives "caught in a struggle" with circumstance, and various forms of surveillance.

Kieślowski's underlying idea that "the camera should pick somebody out from a crowded street and then follow him or her throughout the rest of the film" (*KK*, 146) recalls Edgar Allan Poe's story of "The Man in the Crowd," which held such fascination for Charles Baudelaire and Walter Benjamin. However, the filmmaker's roving camera is not confined to scrutinizing the outward behavior of individuals in the passing parade, the perceptual praxis of the *flâneur* with his hermeneutic gaze from the pavement. Kieślowski regards such external urban spectatorship not as the province of a specialized observer but as a collective habit, a symptom of communist Poland's spiritual malaise in the mid-1980s: "You're always watched by others ... neighbours, family, loved ones, friends, acquaintances or even by strangers in the street" (*KK*, 149). In an atomized culture where "people are terribly afraid of loneliness," each individual is the object of manifold scrutiny, yet these gazes—refractory, furtive, superficial—do nothing to alleviate the prevailing sense of "egotistic" estrangement and "hopelessness" (160). Kieślowski describes a paradoxical epistemology in which those who desperately seek knowledge and connection through the gaze retreat from the eyes of others, fashioning an "outside" face "appropriate for strangers" and hurrying home to "lock the door on the inside and remain alone with themselves" (146, 160). In stressing both the omnipresence of observation and the oppressiveness of being observed, Kieślowski inevitably alludes to the censorious eye of the state, under which he labored in creating *The Decalogue*, and to a monitory agency it controlled: "the newspapers" (149). Given Kieślowski's capacity for self-mockery and ironic self-awareness, one might be tempted to suppose that he regards his cinema camera as akin to the post-Enlightenment technologies of political surveillance and social control that Michel Foucault laments in *Discipline and Punish*. Indeed, Kieślowski's description of his cinematic method—infiltrating various lives sealed behind mortar and glass for presentation on Polish television screens—might suggest a more refined version of Bentham's disciplinary *panopticon*, which brought the "captive shadows" of enclosed cells into "full lighting" and the "trap" of visibility.[2] In his urgent observation of covert human conduct, Kieślowski's confining lens seems to trap agonized protagonists in moments of ontological crisis, but it does so in the absence of any regulatory system of judgment or punishment. More important, in exploring the private experience of his characters, Kieślowski is ultimately less concerned with their traceable actions than with the psychological tensions that produce them. Throughout the *Decalogue* films, he uses close-ups to suggest complex processes of thought, conflicted feelings, unfulfilled desires for which there is no adequate human register within the world of the film. Ultimately, the comprehensive awareness behind these rich illuminations of interior life finds its appropriate analogue not in the gaze of the urban sociologist nor in the watchful perspective of the state, but, as Joseph G. Kickasola has suggested, in the omniscient eye of God.[3]

In his reflections on the *Decalogue* project, Kieślowski specifically associates this divine optics with the God of Abraham and Moses, "the God of the Old Testament" who "leaves us a lot of freedom and responsibility, observes how we use it and then rewards or punishes" (*KK*, 149). While the director maintains that such a supernatural "authority does exist" and that His commandments provide an "absolute" ethical "point of reference," the *Decalogue* films themselves persistently question the harsh judgment (and, at times, the existence) of this all-seeing, unforgiving God and probe the ambiguity of His moral imperatives (*KK*, 149, 150). Nowhere is this critique more urgent than in *Decalogue Nine*, a film that self-consciously utilizes cinema's capacity for omniscient surveillance both to examine the immorality of the protagonist's attempt to appropriate this invasive power and to question the justice of a God who monitors humankind's inner life. Notwithstanding Kieślowski's observation that the *Decalogue* films bear no simple or sequential correspondence to specific commandments and that one could exchange the sixth and ninth commandments,[4] the aims and methods of the penultimate film in the series reveal a searching response to the unique and ambiguous injunction presented in Exodus 20 and repeated in Deuteronomy 5: "You shalt not covet your neighbor's wife" (Exod. 20:17 RSV). Whereas the previous commandments all regulate forms of conduct or action, the ninth (as numbered in Catholic and Lutheran Poland) imposes an ethical restriction on thought and motive.[5] While the sixth commandment forbids the commission of adultery, the ninth identifies the mere desire for unlawful possession as a transgression in the eyes of an all-perceiving deity who "ruthlessly demands obedience to his principles" (*KK*, 149). Far from constituting a redundancy or an admonitory afterthought, the ninth commandment is a stern, purposeful reminder that God's inescapable vision detects even the briefest and most clandestine motions of the mind and heart.

If Kieślowski can aptly characterize the Old Testament Jehovah as "cruel" (*KK*, 149), the ninth commandment's alignment of covetous desire with sin establishes the divine eye as an explicit instrument of investigative terror, punishment and control. At the same time, the commandment poses the kind of ambiguity that fascinates the filmmaker: Whereas the tenth explicitly warns against coveting others' material possessions (ox, donkey, "or any thing that is thy neighbor's"), the ninth raises the question of what it means to covet another human being and fails to specify whether the unlawful desire for acquisition is sexual, legal or domestic. Jealous avarice for another's goods is sinful because it may logically lead to theft, a violation of the seventh commandment, but in the ninth commandment the relationship between coveting another's wife and the sin of adultery (sexual intercourse in violation of marriage bonds) remains sufficiently fluid and uncertain that Kieślowski has Roman (Piotr Machalica) covet not his neighbor's wife but his own. Thus, in exploring the commandment, the film's stress falls upon the psychology of covetous desire for another person and the immaterial forms that this urge to possession can take. Interrogating the unique demands and implications of this most troubling Mosaic injunction, Kieślowski offers in *Nine* a sustained meditation on the entwined concepts of divine omniscience and possessive desire that inhere in the ninth commandment. In an inspired act of cinematic compression, Kieślowski gives his male protagonist a double function within this ethical inquiry: Roman sins against the spirit of the commandment by coveting his wife Hanka (Ewa Błaszczyk), not as a sexual object but with a metaphysical longing to invade and possess her every thought and feeling, a drive for totalizing knowledge of her inner experience that mimics not only the filmmaker's exposure of secret lives but God's relentless omniscience. Thus, in Kieślowski's elegant formulation, Roman embodies, at once, man's putative sin against God and God's inquisitory cruelty toward man.

Kieślowski establishes the film's concern with the hidden details of his characters' lives through an intercutting of intimate moments at the start. The opening shot is a brief close-up of Hanka as she sleeps and then suddenly wakes in a state of alarm. Already the camera has infiltrated the bedroom, the most private of domestic spaces, and it seems poised to enter the world of Hanka's dreams. Cutting abruptly away, Kieślowski shifts from the Warsaw apartment to Cracow, where Roman is engaged in a painfully confidential conversation with his friend, a urologist who impassively informs him that he is permanently impotent. Unlike most of the *Decalogue* films, which confine themselves to Warsaw and, in some cases, claustrophobically, to the area around the apartment complex, the ninth film immediately demonstrates the cinema camera's godlike capacity to move freely across space and time in pursuing its disclosures. In his first words to his friend, Roman demands "the truth," foreshadowing both his insistence that Hanka and he discuss their private lives "to the limit" and his desire to align his visual perspective with that of the penetrating camera. When he returns home, the agonized Roman stands outside the apartment building exposing himself to the rain, as if to delay the humiliating disclosure to Hanka that truthfulness demands. In the intercutting of shots leading up to this conversation, Kieślowski and his cinematographer, Piotr Sobociński, repeatedly frame images of husband and wife and of their visual perspectives through blurred, dirty or refractory glass: As Hanka, anxious for Roman's return, enters their apartment, we see her image distorted through a translucent vase, Roman appears through the car windshield as he drives back to Warsaw, and as he pulls into the dark parking lot we see the car from Hanka's perspective through the rain-streaked kitchen windowpane. Upon arriving, Roman gazes at a lamp blurred by the wet car window and is himself glimpsed through the darkened glass entrance to the apartment building. A moment later, Hanka's image appears in this angled door, converting a medium of supposed transparency into one of self-reflection and linking this homecoming to a host of other mirror shots of both characters that occur early in the film.

Cumulatively, this trope of visual distortion and indirection suggests the emotional barriers and lies that have separated Roman and Hanka and that the couple must overcome through open and honest conversation. At the same time, however, Kieślowski's early inscription of window-framed views introduces the central theme of surveillance and the epistemic methods that Roman will employ in his surreptitious pursuit of Hanka's secrets. Knowledge of another, Kieślowski suggests, finds its proper ethical place somewhere between Hanka's evasive claim that "some things shouldn't be discussed to the limit" and Roman's obsessive need to appropriate her inner life. As the couple take the elevator up to their apartment, the director subtly reinforces the disturbing visual superintendence inherent in both divine omniscience and the filmic perspective: We catch intimate images of Hanka stroking Roman's face and Roman touching her shoulder as the lift moves between floors, but the alternation of light and darkness has the disquieting effect of a zoetrope or of a film projector moving so slowly that we see the interstices between the frames. In this cinematic self-reference, Kieślowski suggests what Laura Mulvey and Christian Metz have long maintained: The experience of sharing a film's revelatory perspective as we sit watchfully in the dark (as Roman later will) binds the viewer in complicit voyeurism.[6] However, by appearing to slow down the moving frames in the elevator ride, Kieślowski deliberately fragments the diegesis to produce an unpleasurable visual sequence that forces the viewer to reflect upon the inherent perversity of such detection. At the same time, the filmmaker reflects upon the intrusive power of the cinema camera and invites his viewer to share in this meditation. Kieślowski offers intimate and probing disclosures of multiple lives, rather than the fetishistic surveillance of a single individual, but by frequently aligning his camera angles with Roman's voyeuristic detection, he acknowledges how easily this ethical distinction can be blurred.

Roman's conversation with the urologist lays the groundwork for what becomes his compulsive drive to penetrate the secret domain of Hanka's thought and feeling. The twin motors of this covetous obsession are his long-standing habit of desire and the added spur of jealousy. Asked how many women he has slept with, Roman replies "nine, ten . . . maybe fifteen" and implies that some of these affairs have occurred during the ten years of his marriage. Very likely, he has been guilty of coveting the wives of other men. As a successful surgeon, invited to Zagreb to give lectures and assist at difficult operations, Roman commands power and prestige, and his history of sexual conquests seems to parallel his professional development. Later, as he tells a beautiful young heart patient of his early desire to become a doctor, his lingering gaze of sexual interest and futility suggests that his subsequent life has been ruled by a succession of physical desires and fulfillments. Sexual dysfunction renders the act of phallic possession impossible and, in curtailing the pattern of desire and gratification that has shaped and sustained Roman's life, it forces him to question whether life without sexual desire and possession is worth living. The urologist's impertinent question, "Is your wife attractive?" crystallizes this existential dilemma, distilling Roman's sense of powerlessness and loss, but providing a peculiar (and unintended) impetus to the renewal of desire. When Roman answers, "Very," his friend offers a word of cynical advice: "Divorce." Convinced that other men will inevitably crave Hanka—and that she will naturally seek sexual satisfaction outside marriage—the urologist suggests a pragmatic alternative to the humiliation of cuckoldry. Ironically, in doing so he not only plants the seeds of jealousy by insinuating the presence of rivals, but also makes Hanka more desirable in Roman's eyes by stressing her appeal to others. Roland Barthes, in *A Lover's Discourse*, refers to this familiar figure in the representation of desire as "induction": "The loved one is desired because another or others have shown the subject that such a being is desirable."[7] It is this state of longing, predicated upon his wife's transfigured desirability through the competitive interest of other men, that Roman needs to preserve even before he determines what new form his ardor will take. Thus, when he discloses his impotence to Hanka, he does not advise her to divorce him but urges her to take a lover, "if you haven't taken one already." What appears to be generous concern for his wife's sexual needs is, in fact, a gesture intended, perhaps unconsciously, to generate a rival (the more established the better) whose physical possession—or threat of possession—can arouse in Roman the drive for a more totalizing metaphysical possession. This new species of desire that Roman seeks to call into being through jealousy has no prior existence in his marriage: It is an appropriative compulsion for an all-pervasive command of Hanka's hidden life that will serve as substitute for the missing sexual possession.

For all of the cruelty, perversity and egotism inherent in Roman's visual and auditory prying, Kieślowski makes it clear that these acts are driven not by the sadism that Mulvey finds underlying male voyeurism, but by ontological necessity. In this respect, Roman's behavior throughout *Nine* irresistibly suggests Freud's eros/thanatos paradigm: Throughout his life, he has been torn between the promised and remembered gratifications of sexual desire and the more powerful "urge inherent in organic life to restore an earlier state of things" through death.[8] In the face of this elemental urge to nonbeing, Roman has sustained life primarily through projections of desire, identifying and filling specific sources of lack. When impotence threatens to deprive Roman of this mode of being, the impulse to suicide becomes overwhelming. As he drives at high speed back to Warsaw from Cracow, he veers off the road and loses control of the spinning car. When the car stops, facing the wrong direction but still on the highway, he pounds the steering wheel in a gesture of rage and despair not simply at the loss of his manhood but at his failure to end his life. The glove compartment, which later plays a crucial part in his compulsive detection, uncannily opens at this moment, and Roman's furious attempts to close it only underscore his feeling of helplessness. By the time he arrives home, he is so thoroughly unmanned and exhibits so little inclination to live that his wife coaxes him inside out of the rain, helps him unbutton his wet shirt, and begins to dry his hair as if he were a child.

Anticipating and fearing what Roman will tell her, Hanka asks him to delay the news until after dinner. She meets his disclosure first with tacit disbelief and then with kind but facile reassurances, which, though meant to comfort, provide Roman with no new foundation for a life built on desire. "The things we have are more important than the things we don't have," Hanka insists, but in view of their mutual infidelities, separate careers, and joint decision not to have children it is not readily apparent what they do share. Attempting to separate marital commitment from sex, she claims that "love is in one's heart, not between one's legs," adding that it is not reducible to "biology" and involves much more than "panting in bed five minutes a week." As a basis for marriage, she proposes a reciprocal, nonphysical devotion, but one that neither acknowledges the exigent pressures of physical desire, nor anticipates the rise of its metaphysical counterpart. Ironically, Hanka's characterization of sex as a brief, physiological release seems drawn from her ongoing but unacknowledged affair with the young physics student, Mariusz (Jan Jankowski). Roman's refusal to answer her repeated question, "Do you love me?" suggests that he regards her affirmation of love as friendship, affection, and spousal support as insufficient grounds for continuing to exist and that he dreads committing himself to such a life. Paradoxically, what begins to renew Roman's tenuous interest in life is not Hanka's solemn declaration of enduring love but rather her intriguing contradictions. A moment after quickly assuring Roman that she has not taken a lover, she adds that they should not look into such questions very closely. Then, as if to demonstrate the sustaining power of their sexless emotional bond, she asks Roman for "a cuddle." The scene quickly becomes a moment of failed intimacy and frustrated longing that undermines Hanka's dismissal of intercourse as a nonessential component in their marriage: As Roman holds her, Hanka curls her leg around him more tightly and writhes against him with desperate sexual hunger. During this sequence, Roman's face reflects helpless desolation. Robbed of the capacity for phallic performance, he seems to hold himself back from the pain of unconsummated desire. However, his expression also suggests a strange surmise at his wife's impassioned behavior, one that recalls the urologist's lubricious innuendos about Hanka and that will lead Roman to initiate his detection the next morning.

During a sleepless night, Roman suggests that a child might make their life together "easier," but the abrupt cut from the quiet, dimly lit bedroom to the harsh morning light and cacophony of traffic indicates that he will reconfigure his relationship with Hanka in a less conventional way. As a milky glass window opens, we share Hanka's overhead view of Roman as she watches him prepare to drive to the hospital—and, we momentarily discover, as she scans the street for her lover's imminent arrival. If this opening shot sequence establishes Hanka's anxiety about her secret life, it also introduces the position of commanding surveillance that Roman will increasingly adopt in infiltrating it. The shift from turbid glass to transparency anticipates the revelations that he comes to associate with this lofty perspective. Roman's first act of detection, however, is from below: He cranes his head at an awkward angle and looks up through the car's passenger side to see if Hanka is standing at the apartment window. Although she has retreated to the margin of its frame, he waves at her before she closes the pane. As the day begins, husband and wife observe one another with mutual suspicion. Turning his head forward, Roman sees a blond young man (Mariusz) walking toward the apartment building and registers a look of acute suspicion even before the object of his gaze spots him, stops and moves clumsily in a different direction. By lowering the visor, the first of several literal and figurative covers, Roman seeks the invisibility that characterizes the visual perspectives of voyeurs, detectives, and divinities.

Roman is not only prepared for the appearance of his wife's lover, but he also actually requires and welcomes this rival as the needed stimulus for the regeneration of his own desire to possess Hanka. Indeed, his behavior conforms closely to René Girard's classic formulation of "triangular desire" wherein the *vaniteux* (desiring male subject) exaggerates the glamour, potency, and emotional claims of a challenger in order to make the coveted object "more infinitely desirable in his eyes."[9] Young, virile and sexually potent, Mariusz is the ideal "mediator" for Roman, "a veritable artificial sun [from whom] descends a mysterious ray which makes the object shine with a false brilliance" (Girard 18). So necessary is this figure, Girard suggests, that a disillusioned subject who desires to desire will even bring a rival into existence in order to heighten his own longing by imitating another man's. All such lovers, according to this paradigm, become further complicit in their fevered unhappiness by acting in ways that preserve the mediator's presence and the covetous jealousy that it generates. Roman's behavior finds close corollaries in the self-tormented protagonists of Stendhal and Proust. After finding abundant evidence of Hanka's poorly disguised affair, he violates his code of truth-telling by not directly confronting her with this knowledge, for to do so would bring both the liaison and his surveillance to an immediate end. Instead, Kieślowski provides a symbolic illustration of the extent to which Roman will indirectly assist in Hanka's infidelity when he offers to help a colleague fill his gas tank in the hospital parking lot. Annette Insdorf has noted that the "blatantly phallic" shape of the funnel that Roman holds seems a rather unsubtle reminder of his lost manhood (117), but this short, transitional scene is richer in implication. Coming just after Roman's first sighting of Mariusz has aroused suspicions, his act of holding the funnel to assist another man prefigures his facilitation of a sexually potent rival's affair with Hanka.

Girard notes that the desiring subject unconsciously seeks interest and intensity in his life through a competitive relationship with an obstacle that is, at once, a source of fearful envy and intense hatred (7). In order for Mariusz to fulfill this doubly exalted mediatorial function, Roman must regard him as more than a naïve university student who satisfies Hanka's biological needs. He needs to imagine (incorrectly) that his rival commands

Hanka's love and thus has special access to aspects of her private life that she hides from Roman. Only such a Mariusz can pose a vivifying threat and stimulus to the emotional and psychological forms of possession to which Roman dedicates himself; and only through this artificial magnification of Mariusz's "prestige" (13) in Hanka's life can Roman summon the requisite jealousy to eavesdrop on her phone conversations, sift the contents of her purse as she sleeps, search her mother's apartment for clues to the affair, and watch the couple's final assignation from inside a closet. At the same time, however, Roman's bitter hatred for his rival prompts him to denigrate the young man as his material antithesis, one whose leonine mane seems to mock his own receding hairline. Roman derisively refers to him as "that physicist," as if to contradistinguish the young man's study of mechanical laws from his own noncorporeal investigations. Finding Mariusz's incriminating physics notebook in the glove compartment, Roman hurls it into a trash bin, where it is covered with decaying garbage. After a moment's hesitation, he retrieves the soiled notebook, not as evidence with which to confront Hanka but as a fetish to spur and perpetuate his own anguished desiring. The gross materiality of this item reflects the rival's physical possession of his wife and feeds Roman's contempt, but it also aids in sharpening his own desire for metaphysical possession, the only ground on which he can wage a struggle. Kieślowski's camera frequently lingers on the golden plentitude of Hanka's curly hair, but with the birth of metaphysical desire her erotic womanhood no longer conjures Roman's fascination or longing. As Girard notes, a woman's "physical qualities . . . can neither rouse metaphysical desire nor prolong it," and her beauty "diminishes in importance" for the *vaniteux* as his drive for penetration and control of her inner being increases (88, 85). While a totalizing command of another's thoughts and feelings is humanly impossible, this difficulty not only sustains Roman's enterprise but increases its urgency.

Even after his first sighting of Mariusz, Roman's suspicions might never have become a monstrous obsession were it not for an ill-timed phone call that he takes while his wife is out. Looming in the foreground, the magnified image of the ringing telephone provokes Roman's jealousy, while also inaugurating his preoccupation with the phone as an instrument of auditory omniscience. At the same moment, Kieślowski establishes the aerial subject position that comes to characterize Roman's visual surveillance: Looking down unseen through window blinds, he sees Hanka walking toward the apartment building entrance. When she presents Roman with a new sports jacket, he models it awkwardly and self-consciously, seeming to view the garment as an absurd compensation for what she is giving to her lover. As if to crown his humiliation, the foregrounded phone rings again, and, as Hanka hastily answers it and speaks to Mariusz, Roman strains to listen in the background. However, the next shot sequence reverses these relative positions and implies a correlative shift in the control of knowledge within their relationship: We now see Roman, in medium close-up, using a soldering iron to install a listening device inside the living room phone and then eavesdropping as Hanka talks to her mother on another phone in the bedroom.

In this moment, Roman commits himself to invisibility and psychic infiltration as nothing less than an all-consuming way of life, and Kieślowski marks this existential turning point by framing the three telephone calls in the apartment between a pair of revealing conversations at the hospital. In both, Roman advises Ola (Jolanta Piętek-Górecka), a talented young singer with a heart condition that threatens her professional career. She seeks Roman's counsel on a risky operation that could repair the damage, allowing her to pursue the concert career for which she has long trained, but that could just as easily kill her. Her dilemma mirrors Roman's own and raises the central questions of being that torment him: What does one need in order to live? Is a life without passionate desire and conquest worth living? Pressed by her mother to have the operation, Ola hesitates. Although she has embraced challenges in the past, including the music of Van Den Budenmayer ("He's difficult but I sing him"), she tells Roman that she will settle for a life of contentment: "I want to live. That's enough for me. I don't have to sing." Holding her fingers an inch apart, she measures the small quantity of experience that will suffice: "That much." Far from contradicting her, Roman supports her reluctance, noting that the surgery in question is normally used only when there are "no other possibilities." As the young woman retreats down the hospital corridor in a provocatively short gown, he gazes after her, as if measuring how much he needs to live in the absence of sexual pursuit and satisfaction. Roman continues this self-evaluation in relation to Ola as he sits at home listening to a recording of the haunting vocal music of Van Den Budenmayer (the fictional name of Kieślowski's musical collaborator, Zbigniew Preisner). The ringing telephone and Hanka's disquieting arrival interrupt this moment of meditation, as if demonstrating to Roman the impossibility of a life of domestic contentment and neutralized desire. In his next meeting with Ola, he listens to her rendition of the composer's work and pronounces it "beautiful"—but now chides, "It's a pity you don't want to sing." In implicitly urging a dangerous operation, Roman tempts Ola to a choice that could intensify her life or cause her death (as it does in the screenplay), but he also reveals his collateral commitment to a perilous course of action that is meant to prolong his life but that nearly destroys him. Both as a consulting surgeon and as investigating husband, Roman assumes a god-like power over a woman's life as a counterresponse to his powerful urge to extinction.[10]

Girard traces "the metaphysical roots of desire" to "a more or less conscious attempt at an apotheosis of the self," which he regards as an underlying psychological component in the structure of romantic love in Western narrative (63). Roman's pursuit of omniscient possession is, by contrast, a compensatory response to impotence. Yet, even as a survival strategy, his desire partakes of the exalted egotism that Girard describes, for it seeks the complete mastery of Hanka's mind and soul through the simulation of transhuman visual and auditory perspectives. In this respect, Roman's ultimate mediator is not Mariusz but the God of the ninth commandment, whose disembodied comprehension is the true model that he strives, but fails, to emulate. Kieślowski offers a comic distillation of this point when Roman goes to his mother-in-law's apartment on the pretext of retrieving her scarf and umbrella, but really to search the unmade bed, coffee table, and mail for evidence that Hanka is conducting her affair there. His investigation turns up a love note that Mariusz had recently mailed: a postcard showing God's representative on earth, the Polish pope John Paul II, playfully curling his fingers around his eyes, as if spying through binoculars. This papal parody of divine detection reveals the absurdity of Roman's crude snooping—calling a number he finds in his wife's purse, secretly purchasing a duplicate key—and the hopeless metaphysical compulsion that underlies it. As Roman pursues increasingly elaborate methods of surveillance, Kieślowski juxtaposes shots from his subject position with images of Hanka's experience that he cannot see. When he follows her to an assignation at her mother's apartment, for example, the camera cuts from a close-up of Hanka during sex, her face racked with anguish and guilt, to a shot of Roman sitting on a flight of stairs above the apartment door, hidden by shadows. We share his downward view as the buoyant Mariusz leaves, but we also recognize the insufficiency of his perspective: He does not know that his wife took no pleasure in the encounter inside. A moment later, Kieślowski reiterates Roman's pursuit of an airborne perspective traditionally associated with a God's-eye view. He watches from a balcony as Hanka walks to the parking lot, gets in the car, and slumps over the steering wheel as the vehicle's alarm goes off. The headlights flashing in the darkness recall the elevator ride, again reminding viewers of their inscription in the voyeuristic economy of both the protagonist and the filmmaker. However, the shot selection here re-emphasizes the epistemic limits of Roman's fixed point of view: Kieślowski cuts from the protagonist's balcony angle to a closer view of Hanka directly through the windshield. Her body posture and face reveal a state of paralyzing remorse that Roman, obstructed by the car's frame, cannot fully comprehend.

Roman is not only increasingly aware of the doomed nature of his hermeneutic enterprise but consumed with unbearable shame and self-disgust as he undertakes it. These feelings are so acute that the exercise of covetous desire meant to fend off the death wish sometimes increases its urgency. Shortly after beginning his surveillance, he rides his bicycle along an elevated highway that is still under construction in a rehearsal of the suicide he will later attempt. Stopping where the roadside slopes sharply down to a river, he seems to consider crashing into a concrete bridge pillar before steering the bicycle into the water and wetting his face with his hands. If, as Freud suggests in *Beyond the Pleasure Principle*, "each organism wishes to die only in its own fashion" (39), Roman craves death as a passive surrender to gravity that will relieve him of the arduous labor of metaphysical desire, as a plunge from some height in which the quest for transcendental knowledge is replaced by the physical laws of mass and momentum that Mariusz studies. His self-generated longing for possession fails as a stay against suicide, in part because spying brings him none of the conventional satisfactions of male voyeurism, which, according to Laura Mulvey, include not only scopophilia but the viewer's imagined control of a female object upon whom he can project personal fantasies. Inherent in this "determining" aspect of the male gaze is the sadistic pleasure of "forcing a change in another person" (33, 35). Tomek's voyeurism in the early stages of *Six* conforms to this erotic model: He views Magda as a source of masturbatory pleasure and enjoys controlling her movements with silent phone calls. While Kickasola is right in noting that both Roman and Tomek seek "unlimited observational power" (234), they are moved by very different epistemic aims. Tomek seeks, initially, to objectify Magda as a purely physical spectacle in order to shape his fantasies freely around her, but for Roman such objectification is antithetical to his craving to possess those immaterial qualities in Hanka that are most intimately and uniquely human. His sin is not, as Slavoj Žižek ingeniously proposes in his theory of Kieślowski's "displaced" commandments, a covetous conversion of his wife into mere "goods," but rather a desire for abstract appropriation beyond man's ethical scope and cognitive powers.[11] Roman seeks a nonsexual, immaterial mode of possession that eschews visual pleasure and controlling fantasy in the pursuit of psychological and moral penetration. Just as his espionage brings him no sadistic satisfaction, so too Roman finds no masochistic enjoyment in the degradation of half-obstructed peeping on Hanka and her lover from a closet, and he suffers only unbearable shame when she uncovers him after breaking off her affair with Mariusz. Speaking gently at first and then forcefully, Hanka summons her husband out of the darkness as she had earlier drawn him in from the rain; but when the rejected Mariusz briefly returns, Roman retreats into the bathroom, overcome with weakness and nausea. Nor does this ordeal conform to Freud's moral masochism: Despite Roman's philandering, his suffering brings him no self-punishing relief for past sexual betrayals of his wife. Instead, spying becomes an intolerable addiction that yields no satisfactions, and the self-generated jealousy that drives it becomes a psychopathology from which he cannot free himself. Like several other characters in the *Decalogue* films, he is "imprisoned by [his] passions and feelings" (*KK*, 150).

The agonizing mutual exposure outside the closet marks a decisive turning point in *Nine* because Roman and Hanka, rather than casting blame, recognize the pain that their lies have inflicted on one another. Roman's admission, "I've no right to be jealous," finds its complement in Hanka's compassionate apology, "I didn't think you'd be so hurt." This scene of shared suffering and forgiveness produces a reconciliation in which the couple commit themselves to a future of complete transparency and, after a short period of separation, plan to adopt a child. Yet Kieślowski reveals the fragile and tentative nature of this accord through several details. Roman's insistence that Hanka be the one to go away suggests that he can overcome the compulsion to jealous spying only by removing the desired object from his sight. There is also a hint of anxious control in his purchase of skis for her weekend trip to Zakopane, as if he wishes to insure that she act out her plans for an innocent vacation. More notably, as he stands by the window of the departing train, Roman pointedly does not answer Hanka's fervent appeal, "Do you trust me?" While fear had kept him from responding to Hanka's earlier request that he acknowledge his love for her, honesty now accounts for Roman's silence. During Hanka's absence, we see Roman looking down from the apartment window at a little girl (Ania from *Seven*) playing with her doll. While the context of this image is the couple's plan for a family, the familiar elevated perspective dramatizes Roman's destabilizing struggle with the habit of surveillance. Ironically, it is not careful detection but a chance spotting of Mariusz loading skis onto his car that plunges Roman into suicidal despair. When the young man's mother confirms that he has gone to Zakopane, Roman is consumed by uncontrollable jealousy and a sense that he can neither trust Hanka nor ever know her

Figure 11–1. Hanka tries to telephone Roman from Zakopane in *Decalogue Nine*.

mind. Leaving a suicide note by the telephone, he sets off to die while it is still ringing. His refusal to answer this frantic call from Hanka is, at once, a denial of their future together, a renunciation of spousal trust, and a final rejection of metaphysical desire as a mode of life-sustaining interest (Figure 11–1).

The Hitchcockian intercutting of Roman, pedaling toward suicide, and Hanka desperately riding the bus back to Warsaw to reassure him, visually stresses the fracturing of their relationship, as do several images: the broken white lines, the abrupt end of the unfinished highway, and a bicycle wheel turning randomly after the fall (Figure 11–2). Kieślowski presents Roman's collision with the earth from below and in slow motion, but then, in an extraordinary gesture, he moves to a long, hovering overhead shot of the twitching body and battered bicycle, as if viewed from the divine perspective that Roman had sought. In rising upward from this shattered scene, the camera also initiates an unexpected movement toward visual and emotional integration that crowns the film: From the highway's edge the camera accelerates backward along the road Roman has traveled until it blends seamlessly with one where Hanka's bus is moving, linking the couple's lives and destinies in a moment of acute crisis. Given the film's previous association of aerial perspectives with the invasiveness of human egotism and divine cruelty, this introduction to Roman's nearly miraculous survival and final words of reconciliation with Hanka may seem mystifying.

The key to Kieślowski's intentions at the end of *Nine* may lie in a distinction he draws between "a God of the Old Testament and a God of the New" (*KK*, 150). While the filmmaker frames Roman's hypervigilance as

Figure 11-2. Roman's suicide attempt in *Decalogue Nine*.

a version (or perversion) of the demanding, unforgiving vigilance of the God of the ninth commandment, he displaces this deity in the film's final moments and tentatively suggests as an alternative a God who oversees human conduct not to judge and punish but to save and forgive. While this New Testament divinity has full access to individual consciousness, His true dwelling place is not above man but within him, for He is manifest in all forms of human love. We glimpse the potential presence of this God only fleetingly and ambiguously throughout the ten films, rather than in clear or consistent dialectical opposition to the God of Abraham and Moses. In *One*, Paweł's Aunt Irena tells the boy that God resides in their love for one another, and in *Eight*, Zofia speaks of a God who dwells inside us. Such a deity, working through human feeling and action, may be manifest in Dorota's painful devotion to her dying husband in *Two*, an unarticulated but saving love that only a compassionate God could knowingly reward.

Prior to Roman's equally miraculous survival at the conclusion of *Nine*, Kieślowski insinuates the possibility of such a merciful God by encrypting two alternative forms of subliminal knowledge within the film's visual texture. The first is suggested by the gaze of Kieślowski's perpetual witness, the nameless young man (Artur Barciś) "who comes and watches" characters in crisis throughout *The Decalogue* (*KK*, 159), but whose appearances in the ninth film seem sufficiently rich in spiritual implication to justify Insdorf's characterization of him as protective "angel" (74), an emissary or extension of a generous God, and to support Kickasola's suggestion that in "his secret knowledge" he "bears the traits of God" (165). We first glimpse him passing on a bicycle when Roman drives off the road after learning his impotence is incurable; later he appears in a long tracking shot as he rides parallel to Roman and watches with grave, prescient concern as he nears the edge of the road. Finding the fallen Roman beneath the overpass, the young man, shot through the foregrounded bicycle spokes, surveys the situation before riding off—quite possibly to call the ambulance that saves Roman's life.

Kieślowski offers a still more intriguing and vital form of "secret knowledge" in Hanka's seemingly telepathic comprehension of Roman in his moments of most acute pain. She wakes in sudden fear at the start of the film as he receives his medical diagnosis, wakes again in alarm at the instant when Roman rides his bicycle into the river, and reacts with panic on the slopes at Zakopane when Mariusz arrives, as if sensing that her husband must somehow know of his presence. These divinations, for all of their numinous implications, appear to be rooted in the loving concern that Hanka earlier told Roman is in her "heart"—a love in which the New Testament God makes His home and through which He bestows His grace.

Curiously, the couple's most complete moment of unity comes through the more mundane circuitry of Roman's telephone call from the emergency room. In the film's final shot sequence, we see Hanka, having read Roman's suicide note, reclining with her head near the phone as her blond hair fills the foreground like an aureole. A moment later, she answers the call from the bandaged Roman who has learned that she had tried to tell him of her immediate return. Their brief exchange converts a device heretofore used for adulterous appointments and eavesdropping into a cord of healing connection, and it also provides a kind of benediction: "You're there, God, you're there," Hanka says, and Roman answers, "I am." In this curious moment of inadvertent identification, Roman resembles something quite different from the punitive God of Mosaic Law whose investigatory cruelties he had tried to practice. Although Kieślowski may think most often of a God who offers "no appeal or forgiveness" (*KK*, 149), his cinematic gaze is sufficiently ambivalent and far-reaching to register, if only briefly, the immanence of a different deity in the secret lives of men and women. Such a God, if He is truly present within the *Decalogue* films, dwells in innuendo, ambiguity, and contradiction. Thus, despite the pagan associations of his name, Roman incongruously wears a cross around his neck throughout the film; and if the name recalls the power and privilege that the fallen man once enjoyed, it may also allude to the first of Paul's epistles in which he urges his Roman readers to emulate God's forgiveness and to "Let love be without dissimulation" (12:9).[12] If Kieślowski is identifying his protagonist with divinity in the film's final frames, it is not with the harsh monitor of the ninth commandment but, poignantly and improbably, with the broken yet regenerate Christ.

NOTES

1. Krzysztof Kieślowski, *Kieślowski on Kieślowski*, ed. Danusia Stok (London: Faber and Faber, 1993), 146. Further references to this work will be cited in the text using the abbreviation *KK*.

2. Michel Foucault, *Discipline and Punish: The Birth of the Prison*, trans. Alan Sheridan (New York: Pantheon, 1977), 200.

3. Joseph G. Kickasola, *The Films of Krzysztof Kieślowski: The Liminal Image* (New York: Continuum, 2004), 165. Further references will be cited in the text.

4. Annette Insdorf, *Double Lives, Second Chances: The Cinema of Krzysztof Kieślowski* (New York: Miramax Books, 1999), 71. Further references will be cited in the text.

5. The commandments are divided and numbered differently in Jewish and Protestant denominations, excluding Lutheranism. In particular, these religious traditions combine the coveting of a neighbor's wife and goods as a single commandment—the tenth. In all faiths, however, the injunction against coveting marks a departure from emphasis on outward behavior in the earlier (eighth or ninth) commandments: Six of these forbid certain forms of conduct (false worship, blasphemy, murder, theft, adultery, false witness) and two mandate virtuous actions (honoring the Sabbath and one's parents).

6. Laura Mulvey, "Visual Pleasure and Narrative Cinema," *Issues in Feminist Film Criticism*, ed. Patricia Erens (Bloomington: Indiana University Press, 1990), 28–40. Further references will be cited in the text. Christian Metz, *Psychoanalysis and Cinema: The Imaginary Signifier*, trans. Celia Britton et al. (Bloomington: Indiana University Press, 1982).

7. Roland Barthes, *A Lover's Discourse: Fragments*, trans. Richard Howard (New York: Hill and Wang, 1978), 136.

8. Sigmund Freud, *Beyond the Pleasure Principle*, trans. James Strachey, in *The Standard Edition of the Complete Psychological Works of Sigmund Freud*, Vol. XVIII (London: Hogarth Press, 1955), 36. Further references will be cited in the text.

9. René Girard, *Deceit, Desire and the Novel: Self and Other in Literary Structure*, trans. Yvonne Freccero (Baltimore: Johns Hopkins University Press, 1965), 7. Further references will be cited in the text.

10. Roman's behavior bears comparison with that of two other figures in the *Decalogue* films. Like the suicidal Ewa of the third film, who seeks out a former lover to keep her alive on Christmas Eve, Roman generates and sustains desire in resistance to death. In his exercise of godlike authority over

the life of his patient, he willingly embraces the role that the consulting doctor in *Two* initially refuses to enact for Dorota and accepts only to save the life of her unborn child. Kieślowski illuminates Roman's egocentric response to Ola when he notes that this "fine," intriguing singer appears only briefly in the film because she functions as "a sort of window, as a contingency for the main character" (*KK*, 177).

11. Slavoj Žižek, *The Fright of Real Tears: Krzysztof Kieślowski between Theory and Post-Theory* (London: British Film Institute, 2001), 114.

12. If Roman undergoes a moral transformation following his suicide attempt, it is worth noting that Paul's letters emerge from a conversion experience that also featured a violent fall: A sudden, blinding vision of Christ knocked him off his horse as he rode to persecute Christians in Damascus.

CHAPTER 12

Laughter Makes Good Neighbors: Sociability and the Comic in *Decalogue Ten*

Regina Small

In Krzysztof Kieślowski's *Decalogue* series, a cloistered apartment building in an alienated and shattered communist-ruled Poland serves as the backdrop for a sober examination of the significance of each of the commandments. The actions and attitudes of the characters (all tenants within these isolated, lonely quarters) drive each installment, as Kieślowski examines the weighty moral and ethical decisions each faces. The series is characterized by a grave treatment of the subject matter with precious few moments of levity, impressing upon the viewer the critical nature of choice. Although in the tenth and final film of *The Decalogue* the exploration of these everyday choices is no less earnest, Kieślowski treats the material in a distinctively different manner. Unlike the films that have preceded it, *Ten* contains several darkly comic elements.[1]

This departure from the characteristically somber tone of *The Decalogue* for the final film suggests that there is something essential about comic perspective. In spite of Kieślowski's claim that *The Decalogue* is a collection of ten individual films and not a series, that the final film revolves around the completion of a series seems undeniably self-referential and can be regarded as a reflection on *The Decalogue* as a whole.[2] In fact, the laughter shared by the film's protagonists, brothers Artur (Zbigniew Zamachowski) and Jerzy (Jerzy Stuhr), in the final scene is the key to not only the film itself but also the entire *Decalogue* series. It is the moment when they realize the absurdity of their fanatical and selfish obsession and laugh, along with the viewer, at their foolishness. In this way, laughter comes to aid individuals in moving beyond their private consciousness; the viewer, by laughing together with the characters, realizes her significance to the larger social context of which she is a part, an important motif that underlies *The Decalogue*. By examining the operation of comedy in *Ten*, the audience gains greater clarity about the issue of individual responsibility within a social context, which is at the center of the entire *Decalogue* series.

The series begins in *One* by introducing us to the apartment complex through a low-angle establishing shot that tilts up the side of the building. As we follow a pigeon's flight to a nearby windowsill, we are left with the peculiar sense that it is by pure chance that we stumble upon Krzysztof and Paweł's story. Indeed, Kieślowski affirmed that he wanted to "begin each film in a way that suggested that the main character had been chosen by the camera as if at random," emphasizing that "everybody's life is worthy of scrutiny" (*KK*, 146). In this manner, Kieślowski expresses the importance of each life, not only individually but also as a part of a social context. Using the apartment building with its connected yet isolated cells as a metaphor for the hermetic, self-focused, and often obsessive existence led by each of his characters, Kieślowski constructs *The Decalogue* as a series of films that examines the interconnectedness of human life and the necessity of recognizing the world beyond our own private consciousness.

In *Ten*, Kieślowski examines the nature of covetousness (the central injunction of the tenth commandment in the Roman Catholic and Lutheran traditions) by tracing specifically the effects wrought by the persistent and avaricious desire for acquisition. The central characters are consumed by the need to possess and to safeguard that which they have obtained. Interestingly, while such a theme could easily lend itself to the severe approach and grave tone that has characterized *The Decalogue* thus far, it is precisely this single-mindedness that makes the content and characters comedic fare. As Artur and Jerzy learn more about the value of their deceased father's stamp collection and become increasingly single-minded, the world of their responsibilities and obligations recedes, giving rise to humorous situations (Figure 12–1).

This humorous single-mindedness takes the form of a fixation, a central element of Henri Bergson's model of comedy, outlined in "Laughter" (1901). In *Ten*, we see what Bergson would term a "mechanical arrangement," in

Figure 12–1. Jerzy and Artur after their father's death in *Decalogue Ten*.

the way in which events unfold and characters behave.³ This mechanical arrangement in comedy takes the form of absent-mindedness on the part of the characters that results from their obsession with a fixed idea and distracts them from their obligations and responsibilities as social beings. Consequently, the normal progress of life is impeded. As Bergson points out, "life presents itself to us as evolution in time and complexity in space. Regarded in time, it is the continuous evolution of a being ever growing older; it never goes backwards and it never repeats itself" (118). At the level of individual consciousness, life is a continuous flux in perception, thoughts, and responses. But the introduction of an overwhelming and fixed idea—in the case of Artur and Jerzy, the incipient desire for the acquisition of something of material value—makes events and the characters involved less "mindful of their own course," thus leading life, as portrayed in comedy, to be filled with situations that repeat themselves (118). Life, in this fictive and comedic formulation, does not progress but instead finds itself subject to an almost mechanistic repetition of events.

Though theorists of the comedic mode frequently cite the Bergsonian model, it has had its share of detractors as well. In *The Idea of Comedy*, Jan Hokenson claims that "critics and theorists tend to dismiss 'Laughter' as a rather Victorian document," one that "suffers in critical esteem primarily because it is read as moralistic, subordinating the comic to 'social morality.'"⁴ Hokenson insists that this is a misinterpretation of "Laughter," and she asserts that we "tend to view such dicta as 'the purpose of laughter is to correct,' through our own post-Auschwitz, post-1960s lenses, reading Bergson as a stern moralist although he says little about morality, and detecting didacticism and political conservatism where there is nothing of the sort" (57). Clarifying Bergson's thesis, Hokenson writes that "it does not incorporate the mean or norm of social behavior as a yardstick of value. There is no norm. There is only sociability and its temporary deficiency" (57). If one applies Hokenson's reading of Bergson to the end of *Ten*, when Artur and Jerzy laugh at the absurdity of their behavior, it becomes clear that they are not, to use Hokenson's words, "laughed back to a norm of conventional behavior" but are "laughed back to self-consciousness as ... social being[s]" (57). Viewers can conclude that Artur and Jerzy's reaction is not motivated by the imposition of a strict set of moral values but instead powered by the recognition of their vain, self-focused foolishness and a developing self-awareness. It is this self-consciousness that leads to a better understanding not only of one's own nature but also of one's place in relation to others and to one's obligations.

Viewing *Ten* from this perspective, we can see that Kieślowski uses Artur and Jerzy's absurd behavior to illustrate how laughter allows the individual to step outside of self-obsession, recognizing the harm his single-mindedness has caused. In allowing themselves to become consumed by the value of their father's stamp collection, both Artur and Jerzy forget their duties as part of a larger society. Artur essentially abandons his bandmates while Jerzy ignores his family, and both fail to recognize their duty to each other as brothers. Bergson's model seems particularly applicable in light of Kieślowski's admission that *The Decalogue* is about people who "suddenly realize that they're going round and round in circles, that they're not achieving what they want." He presses this point further: "We've become too egoistic, too much in love with ourselves and our needs, and it's as if everybody else has disappeared into the background" (*KK*, 145). Familial and social duties are pushed aside in favor of egocentric, antisocial and ultimately meaningless conquest and possession.

The applicability of Bergson's model to *Ten* becomes more readily apparent when Bergson distinguishes between the mechanistic process in comedy and life. He believes that "each living being is a closed system of phenomena" and further explains that "a continual change of aspect, the irreversibility of the order of phenomena, the perfect individuality of a perfectly self-contained series: such then are the outward characteristics—whether real or apparent is of little moment—which distinguish the living from the merely mechanical" (118). The mechanical counterparts and hence the "methods of light comedy" are defined by Bergson as "repetition, inversion, and reciprocal interference of series" (118). The absent-mindedness that results from the characters' single-minded obsession not only stimulates this mechanization of life but also "expresses an individual or collective imperfection which calls for an immediate corrective. This corrective is laughter" (117). For Bergson, this corrective has an essentially social character: The laughter occasioned by witnessing absent-mindedness functions as a corrective insofar as the viewer, through her laughter, implicitly renders a negative judgment of the character's foolish behavior, disassociating herself from the character's actions. This disassociation is a fundamentally social response for it keeps the viewer from engaging in similar behavior or, at the very least, produces an awareness of the need to resist such conduct, recognizing that the character's behavior is fueled by a self-involved obsession.

The mechanization arising from this absent-minded conduct and its subsequent corrective of laughter are particularly evident in *Ten*. In the aftermath of their father's death, Artur and Jerzy initially mock the old man's paranoid need to protect his impressive stamp collection. Neither brother can understand the mad lengths to which their father has gone, from installing countless locks on his front door to nailing his windows shut, all for the sake of preserving a simple collection of stamps. However, only days later, they realize the monetary value of the stamps, and they repeat their father's covetous actions. As soon as a local expert reveals that their father's collection is worth tens of millions of zlotys, they no longer roll their eyes at their father's eccentric behavior. Instead, Jerzy suggests placing bars on the window as a more effective way of guarding against intruders, without any sense of the Bergsonian irony that he is repeating his father's obsessive and paranoid behavior.

This desire to protect the collection and the drive for new acquisition becomes so powerful that the exact object of their pursuit becomes unclear. While they are awed when the veteran stamp collector translates the stamp collection's worth in terms of what can be bought if the stamps were sold, the brothers seem struck, not by the specific possessions they can acquire, but rather, perhaps even more perversely, by the abstract worth of the collection. At one point, Artur is asked very pointedly, "Do you want the stamps or the money?" to which he responds, "the stamps." Although Artur ostensibly means that he wishes to acquire the stamps for their monetary value, both the question and his answer are very telling. They reflect the extent to which the desire to possess has taken root, indicating that the object itself (whether it is money or the stamp itself) is essentially irrelevant; its relevance lies partly in how much others desire it and, consequently, the extent to which it represents the abstract notion of fabulous wealth. This drive toward ownership becomes the sole aim of their quest.

Whether they decide to maintain their father's collection or complete it only to sell it becomes a moot point; as they both agree that it is a "comfort" to possess things and that "if you don't want [something], it ceases to exist," the viewer learns that it is always covetousness that informs the brothers' actions and insinuates itself into their lives. It also seems to imply that they have an understanding that value is a function of desire, and is also suggestive of a belief system that posits there is no objective value; it is only desire that is able to confer value, and this desire drives their avarice.

Thus, this single-minded obsession distracts both Artur and Jerzy from life. Jerzy neglects his family, forgetting about his son's dentist appointment and spending a great deal of time away from both his wife and son. They are pushed to the margins of his life and, consequently, to the margins of the film. This is particularly evident when Jerzy admits that he "quite forgot" about his problems and is happy for this escape from his commitments. Much like Jerzy's prior suggestion that they bar the windows to their father's apartment, Jerzy's neglect perfectly exemplifies Bergsonian repetition. Jerzy, in his drive to obtain something of material value, perhaps even in a misguided attempt to prevent his son from living the impoverished life he was forced to live as a result of his father's obsession, ends up re-enacting the very negligence that was visited upon him. As Joseph G. Kickasola notes, Jerzy's father "supplanted his own children as a material surrogate" with his stamp collection.[5] The same can now be said of Jerzy, who, like his father, has begun to privilege something with greater material value over the value of family. While the situation, when laid out so plainly, may not strike one as humorous, it becomes comedic insofar as the viewer observes not only the repetition itself, but also the dark irony of Jerzy's failure to recognize how he is becoming his father.

Similarly, Artur, also consumed by this foolish desire to possess something of worth, trades something that previously held some value for him (namely, his career) for the abstract idea of extravagant wealth. This sacrifice becomes even more poignant when a fellow band member asks if he is dropping out of the band's tour schedule for "a bit of skirt," since a romantic interest would at least lend some deeper meaning to his abandonment of music. There is an almost pathetic sadness to his assent to this question, since both he and the audience know that his sacrifice does not even possess that level of emotional or social significance, but is instead a crass, pecuniary trade-off for something that is only valuable to him in its abstractness. Much like Jerzy, Artur fails to realize how he is reinscribing the emotional deprivation experienced and enacted by his father in forfeiting something that can possess profound personal meaning and social value (that is, his music) for merely the idea of tremendous value embodied in the stamp collection and in the acquisition of the Rose Mercury stamp.

Kieślowski emphasizes this notion of repetition in the trope of stamp collecting itself. Each series of stamps involves a repetition of images in order for the series to be complete. It is thus beautifully and poetically appropriate that the drive to collect stamps in order to complete a series is simultaneously a drive for and of repetition. Jerzy and Artur narrowly seek the repetition of images (stamps) that will complete their collection and in so doing, practice a kind of absent-minded, mechanical behavior that is almost fanatical in its narrowness; they are completely distracted by their obsession with the collection's value.

We again find the repetition essential to Bergson's notion of comedy, to a lesser extent, in Jerzy's and Artur's separate interactions with the police investigator. Here, Kieślowski mirrors the repetitive behavior of the characters in the plotting of the film. Both Jerzy and Artur are, in the wake of the robbery, suspicious of the other and proceed to set up a meeting with the investigator, engaging him in identical conversations, wherein each suggests that the other might have planned the robbery. This instance also illustrates the way Artur and Jerzy's single-mindedness has led them to transgress against the familial bond that they share as brothers.

On a greater scale, the climactic robbery of the stamp collection is actually a repetition of the earlier swindling of Jerzy's son. Further, the principal repetition is essentially all about different characters (Jerzy, Artur, the suspicious stamp trader, the teenage hooligan) put in the same situation: They are all, at different times, being deceived or swindled in some manner. We sense that, perhaps because Jerzy and Artur's father owed the first villain a large amount of money, their father has swindled the man. But the man seems suspicious and crafty, and viewers are left with the impression that he is attempting to dupe Artur and Jerzy. This is repeated throughout the film as the teenage hoodlum cheats Jerzy's son out of the prized Zeppelin stamp; the stamp trader nearly swindles Jerzy; and Artur blackmails the stamp trader into returning the stamp. Of course, the pivotal deception centers around the trickery involved in getting both Artur and Jerzy out of their father's apartment under the guise of a necessary operation so that another necessary operation, that of breaking into the apartment, can occur. It is necessary in an ironic sense, since Jerzy does not need to give up his kidney for the Rose Mercury stamp—he does so only out of avarice—and necessary in a nonironic way, insofar as the operation will allegedly save a life. There is perhaps a more profound irony that the ostensibly selfless act of giving a kidney to a stranger is motivated only by selfishness and greed, not by a sense of social duty or obligation. In this juxtaposition, Kieślowski also plays with the notion of cutting, as he intersperses the surgical incisions into Jerzy with the cutting of the bars on the window, thus drawing a crucial ironic association between that which is truly, physically vital (Jerzy's kidney) and that which only seems vital (the stamp collection and its abstract worth), in a cinematic conceit that Annette Insdorf has termed "visual rhyming."[6] The same situation, of contrivance built upon contrivance and lie built upon lie, is repeated throughout the film.

Bergson describes this repetition as "a series of imaginary events which affords a tolerably fair illusion of life, and within this ever-moving series . . . one and the same scene [is] reproduced either by the same characters or by different ones." This repetition "contrasts with the changing *stream* of life," illustrating how the fixation with one idea (in this instance, covetousness) causes a repetition of the same incident (that is, someone being tricked and defrauded), bringing the normal progression and evolution of life to a standstill (119). This is the central device of the film, where the humor arises from watching the characters trapped in this repetitive cycle. According to Bergson, the circumstances of the repetition "become more laughable in proportion as the scene repeated is more complex and more naturally introduced" (119). Similarly, in *Ten*, as the accumulation of recurrent deception and defrauding culminates in the juxtaposition of Jerzy's operation (his sacrifice) with the robbery (the destruction of that for which he is making the sacrifice), the situation becomes more and more humorous, albeit in a darkly comic manner.

But it is not entirely this repetition of trickery that renders the situation laughable. In many of the repetitions of deception, the roles are constantly reversed, or as Bergson would term it, "inverted." Inversion, the second method of mechanization in comedy, emerges when "you reverse the situation and invert the roles" in a kind of perfect symmetry (Bergson 121). Often in this film, the roles are reversed; the person who thought he was deceiving someone or getting the better end of a certain agreement ends up realizing that he was the one who was deceived. As Bergson notes, "not infrequently comedy sets before us a character who lays a trap in which he is the first to be caught. The plot of the villain who is the victim of his own villainy, or the cheat cheated, forms the stock-trade of a good many plays" (122). In this film, the relative strength of the characters' positions in relation to others is consistently inverted or reversed. For example, the teenager cons Jerzy's son out of the valuable Zeppelin stamp, leaving both Jerzy and Artur in a less powerful and more desperately avaricious position.

There is a brief reversal and darkly comical element when Jerzy confronts the teenage hoodlum who has deceived his son, twisting the hoodlum's nose until it bleeds. However, both Jerzy and Artur ultimately remain in a vulnerable spot when Jerzy meets with the balding stamp trader. It is only when Artur returns to the scene, armed with a tape recorder, that he places himself in the position of power, once again inverting the roles by blackmailing the trader, who believes that he has the upper hand. The humor arises from the unexpectedness of the inversion that pleases and amuses the viewer. Interestingly, the tape recorder itself functions as a symbol of Bergsonian repetition, in its capacity to move backward and forward with mechanical exactitude.

It is also interesting to note that, in another instance of inversion, the only thing of significant monetary value that is not subject to commodification is the signed City Death album that Artur gives to Jerzy as a gift for Jerzy's son. Obviously, since City Death appears to be a fairly popular, if subpar, band (at least popular enough for Artur to be recognized and to receive sexual favors because of it), such a possession would have a certain, no doubt significant, amount of economic worth. However, it is given freely, as a gift, and none of the characters (neither Artur, nor Jerzy, nor Jerzy's son) ever think of selling the album for financial gain. Rather, for Jerzy's son, this object holds significance most likely beyond monetary value as well as forms an emotional connection with an uncle he has not seen in years. Not only is this a subtle inversion of the avariciousness that permeates the film, but also, from an optimistic perspective, it can function as a foreshadowing of the eventual realization that both Jerzy and Artur experience—namely that worth is relative and that the abstract concept of wealth is perhaps less important than human interconnection.

Finally, after the shock of robbery has abated and both Jerzy and Artur witness a meeting between the three suspicious figures (the man to whom their father owned money, the teenage hoodlum, and the stamp trader) on the street, accompanied by two large dogs that greatly resemble the ultimately ineffectual guard dog Artur bought, the viewer realizes that this scene is the greatest inversion of all. Jerzy and Artur began the film in possession of a tremendously valuable collection of stamps without any interest or knowledge of its worth, resentful of the impact that it had on their childhood. Now, they possess more than a fair amount of knowledge about stamp collecting and a significant interest in their father's stamp collection, but the collection has been stolen, having wreaked havoc on their lives just as much in its absence as in its presence. All of the inversions and reversals of power that have occurred thus far are possibly part of a greater stratagem, one that leads up to an inversion ending with the three villains benefiting.

It is this twist to the narrative, the notion that these three characters are not only acquainted, but also that they may have planned this scheme from the moment they heard of the old man's death, that conforms to the third method of comic effect, which Bergson defines as the "reciprocal interference of series" (123). As Bergson states of this method, "a situation is invariably comic when it belongs simultaneously to two altogether independent series of events and is capable of being interpreted in two entirely different meanings at the same time" (123). The meeting of the three figures is inescapably comic because, as Bergson states, "we waver between the possible meaning and the real" (123). When the viewer sees these three figures meet with a friendly greeting, she is left to wonder: Is it possible that these three have planned this from the beginning? Could they have really anticipated how both Artur and Jerzy would behave in this situation? It is certainly possible since both Artur and Jerzy have a look of wonder on their faces that suggests that this is their conclusion—an interesting deduction since we have never seen Artur and the teenager on screen together. Did they have some off-screen acquaintance? It is not hard to imagine the teenager as a fan of City Death or as some sycophantic hanger-on. Could he have possibly been the friend who helpfully advised Artur to buy the exact same type of dog owned by the other two villains, thus allowing the robbery to run smoothly? This is speculative, but not without basis, since he is the only character with whom Artur is not (ostensibly) acquainted and yet Artur is still dumbstruck by the presence of all three characters. The possible meaning is that this has been an elaborate scheme, while the real meaning is ambiguous. We are tempted to believe that this has been planned, but we are only left to conjecture, since neither Jerzy nor Artur—nor Kieślowski himself—resolves the ambiguity of this scene. It is this coincidence (if it is indeed a coincidence) of the two independent series that produces the comic effect.

After all of the repetition, inversion, and finally this last interference of independent series, the viewer might wonder: Toward what is this comedic mode directed? What is the point? For both Bergson and Kieślowski, these situations produce laughter, not merely for its own sake, but to function as a necessary corrective of human behavior. As Jerzy and Artur's absent-mindedness stimulates the mechanization so often involved in comedy, they grow less mindful of life. Consumed by the thought of owning (exemplified by the City Death lyric at the beginning of the film, "everything is yours," which Artur himself enacts in his abandonment of his music for the possibility of coarse, material gain) Artur and Jerzy invest all of their energy in this single pursuit. Life, in turn, stops its linear progress, and merely begins to unfold in repetitive ways. Inversion is simply a variation on this theme; the situation is the same, only the relative positions of the characters change. The interference of two independent series contains a sense of mechanism, almost as if certain events, like this possibly coincidental meeting of the three villains, are "due to the working of strings or springs" (Bergson 117). In this case, it is Kieślowski who purposely arranges this coincidence to produce the comic effect—the consequence of the mechanistic repetition occasioned by Jerzy and Artur's absent-mindedness.

Comedy, by pointing out how life's progress toward change and flux is hindered by such absent-mindedness, plays out what the viewer thinks of as absurd situations, but, in doing so, essentially provides its own corrective. Bergson believes that "actual life is comedy just so far as it produces, in a natural fashion, actions of the same kind," and "the ludicrous in an individual character always results from some fundamental absent-mindedness in the person" (126–127). So the type of absent-mindedness that occurs in comedy could occur in life and could lead to the type of monomaniacal behavior that both Jerzy and Artur exhibit in this film. The viewer's ability to laugh at their folly, their absent-mindedness and its effects, functions as a preemptive corrective to such behavior for the viewer in question. She is forced into a state of self-reflection, recognizing the imprudence and inhuman, mechanical nature of Artur and Jerzy's behavior, implicitly agreeing that she would never engage in such behavior. This laughter is distinctly different from the laughter Artur and Jerzy enjoy at the beginning of the film, as they mock their father's obsession. According to Hokenson, since "comedy mocks the unthinking and the unbecoming," it is "intelligent, reflective laughter" that Bergson envisions as the optimal response to comedy. She then explains that, in Bergson's view, "[laughter's] bringing to consciousness is the *only* way comedy corrects manners" (57).

Kieślowski takes this Bergsonian corrective a step further, by actually allowing his characters to laugh at their own folly in a gesture of self-correction. They, along with the audience, benefit from this corrective and now, as they gaze over their identical randomly assembled series of stamps (random in that neither Jerzy nor Artur realized that the other bought the same stamps, though hardly random for Kieślowski), they realize how foolish they have been for prizing material worth over the greater social values of family and connection. As they laugh, their joined foreheads signify a new sense of emotional and psychic connection, which they perhaps

Figure 12–2. Jerzy and Artur finally connect in *Decalogue Ten*.

have never had. Their laughter brings them back into self-consciousness as social beings, and they grasp that they have a duty greater than the pursuit of their own obsessions. They have not just literally completed a series by serendipitously buying the same stamps but also they themselves, as brothers, joined now by this touching and comic revelation, complete a series, having reversed their father's perverse legacy of covetousness (Figure 12–2).

As the City Death song closes the film with "you are the only hope, the only light in your tunnel. Because all around you is in you. Everything is in you," we discover that the corrective has worked—the song might remain the same, but the perspective of the characters has altered. A lyric such as "all around you is in you" suggests a deeper connection to the larger world, as we are not only a part of the world but the world is part of us. The song is no longer prescribing avaricious seizure of all desirable things or unapologetic hedonism; rather, it tells the viewer and the characters that a phrase such as "everything is yours" may be less about possession and more about connectedness between individuals. Artur and Jerzy laugh themselves back into self-consciousness, forging a new connection between them as they relinquish their foolish quest, clearing the path for each of them to connect more deeply with others.

It is this conclusion, the priority of human interconnectedness, present in *Ten*, which makes it a fitting end to *The Decalogue*, which is, like the stamps in the film and Jerzy and Artur themselves, a series. Accordingly, it is only fair to Kieślowski to attempt to understand his implementation of the Bergsonian corrective of laughter as a corrective not only for the characters in *Ten* (as well as the audience) but also for the characters featured in the entire *Decalogue*.

The characters in the entire *Decalogue* are, as a whole, isolated from one another, closed off in their cell-like apartments, unaware of each other's private dramas (the only possible exception being Zofia's apparent knowledge, in *Eight*, of Dorota's situation in *Two*). They are all ultimately distracted by a particular, fixed idea that prevents them from recognizing their roles in a larger context; for Krzysztof in *One* and Dorota in *Two*, it is the need for certainty that can only be provided by certain authorities (either empirical reasoning or a godlike figure); for Janusz in *Three* and Anka in *Four*, it is the weight of familial responsibility counterbalanced by the ambiguities of their own desires; for Jacek in *Five*, it is the chaotic violence of a cruel and random universe; for Tomek and Magda in *Six*, it is the voyeuristic and exhibitionistic avoidance of a real relationship; for Zofia and Elżbieta in *Eight*, it is the specter of a past that neither can continue to ignore; for Majka and Ewa in *Seven*, as well as Roman in *Nine* and both Jerzy and Artur in *Ten*, it is the possession of what is or what they feel should be theirs. All become so fixated on this one particular idea that, while only *Ten* explicitly enacts the theme of repetition, the entire *Decalogue* itself is an act of repetition as these narrow attitudes, these self-obsessions persist in each film, leaving the problem unresolved. It is only when *Ten* directly and self-referentially tackles the question of absent-minded behaviors that there can be a conclusion, an end to the series.

Ten, with its implicit critique of the negative (albeit humorous) effects of absent-minded behavior of its characters, thus also critiques the absent-minded (or single-minded) behavior of all of characters in *The Decalogue*. Just as Jerzy and Artur find themselves repeatedly experiencing the same situation, so too does the audience find that each film brings the same underlying conflict: An individual (or group of individuals) is sealed in his or her own subjectivity, isolated from others (illustrated beautifully by the sequestered nature of each individual apartment) and focused on one, single idea that drives their actions. *Ten* addresses this issue and offers a corrective—that of laughing at the folly of one's behavior and the subsequent recognition of one's foolishness. But in this metacommentary, not only are the characters (Jerzy and Artur) able to attain a level of connection and intersubjectivity, but additionally the audience, in laughing with Jerzy and Artur, also establishes a vital connection with them. The message of human connectedness transcends the text of *The Decalogue*, as the viewer laughs herself into self-consciousness, and, one can hope, builds a richer and more expansive engagement with those around her.

NOTES

1. Annette Insdorf identifies the "ironically upbeat tone" of the episode from the opening credits; see *Double Lives, Second Chances: The Cinema of Krzysztof Kieślowski* (New York: Miramax Books, 1999), 121. Marek Haltof defines *Ten* as "a black comedy, a satire on human obsession, greed and egoism"; see *The Cinema of Krzysztof Kieślowski: Variations on Destiny and Chance* (London: Wallflower Press, 2004), 106.

2. Krzysztof Kieślowski, *Kieślowski on Kieślowski*, ed. Danusia Stok (London: Faber and Faber, 1993), 155. Further references to this work will be cited in the text using the abbreviation *KK*.

3. Henri Bergson, "Laughter," in *Comedy*, ed. Wylie Sypher, trans. Cloudesley Brereton and Fred Rothwell (Baltimore: Johns Hopkins University Press, 1980), 116. Further references will be cited in the text.

4. Jan Hokenson, *The Idea of Comedy: History, Theory, Critique* (Madison, N.J.: Fairleigh Dickinson University Press, 2006), 55. Further references will be cited in the text.

5. Joseph G. Kickasola, *The Films of Krzysztof Kieślowski: The Liminal Image* (London: Continuum, 2004), 238.

6. Annette Insdorf, commentary to *The Double Life of Veronique*, DVD, directed by Krzysztof Kieślowski (Irvington, N.Y.: Criterion Collection, 2006).

ACKNOWLEDGMENTS

We conceived of the idea for a collection of essays on *The Decalogue* during a faculty seminar organized by Philip Sicker and sponsored by the program in Literary Studies (now Comparative Literature) in 2004–2005 at Fordham University. These engaged discussions between faculty and students encouraged us to delve deeper into Krzysztof Kieślowski's work and to seek further dialogue with scholars from diverse disciplines. Phil has been the greatest advocate of this endeavor and has been not only the most supportive colleague but also the toughest one, when our work seemed to slow down, by reminding us of how important this research was and how close we were to completing it. We deeply appreciate his friendship, support, and guidance. We are also extremely grateful to all of the authors who contributed original readings of Kieślowski's series to this volume, and we thank them for their promptness and patience throughout the process of composing and revising it. We are particularly grateful to the referees of this collection for their insightful comments. Their careful readings and constructive suggestions enabled us to make far-reaching changes, and offered us an opportunity to consider and review our work with a fresh eye. Tom Lay has guided us wisely through the challenges of the review and publication process, succeeding Helen Tartar at Fordham University Press. Helen, whose great intellectual curiosity and sensitivity drove her editorial vision, believed in us and in our collaborative project from the very beginning. So did our fellow comparatist Chris GoGwilt, who advised us on our relationship with the Press on several occasions. We also want to acknowledge our colleague and mentor Eva Stadler, whose essay on *Decalogue Two* and *Decalogue Eight* is included in this collection. We miss Helen and Eva, who are no longer with us, tremendously. No words can adequately express the gratitude that we feel to each of them for their critical acumen and unwavering encouragement.

The publication of this volume has been made possible through a Faculty Research Grant awarded by Fordham University. Additional funds were provided by the Department of Modern Languages and Literatures at Fordham through the Faculty Research Expense Program, and by the Polish Cultural Institute New York. We are particularly grateful to Bartek Remisko of the latter for his support of the project.

CONTRIBUTORS

Eva Badowska is Associate Professor of English and Comparative Literature at Fordham University. Her publications include articles on Victorian fiction (in *PMLA* and *Victorian Literature and Culture*), feminist theory (in *Tulsa Studies in Women's Literature*), psychoanalytic theory (in *The Psychoanalytic Review*) and Polish poetry (in *Parnassus: Poetry in Review*). She is now working on a book entitled *Kieślowski in Theory and History*.

Michael Baur is Associate Professor of Philosophy at Fordham University, and Adjunct Professor of Law at Fordham Law School. He is translator of J. G. Fichte's *Foundations of Natural Right* (Cambridge University Press, 2000), editor of the "Cambridge Hegel Translations" series (Cambridge University Press) and Director of Fordham's Natural Law Colloquium. He has published articles and book-essays on topics including the philosophy of law, the philosophy of popular culture, epistemology, metaphysics, and ethics, and on thinkers such as Kant, Fichte, Hegel, Aristotle, Aquinas, Heidegger, Lonergan, Adorno, Rawls, and Gadamer.

Moshe Gold is Associate Professor of English and the Director of the Rose Hill Writing Program at Fordham University, where he teaches courses in literary and critical theory, pedagogy theory and practice, and horror films. He is co-editor of *Joyce Studies Annual*, and his publications on Joyce, Plato, Levinas, Derrida, and the Talmud have appeared in *Representations, Joyce Studies Annual, Criticism, James Joyce Quarterly, Levinas and Medieval Literature*, and *ELH*.

William Jaworski is Associate Professor of Philosophy at Fordham University. His research is mainly in the areas of philosophy of mind, metaphysics, and the philosophy of religion. He is the author of *Philosophy of Mind: A Comprehensive Introduction* (Wiley-Blackwell, 2011). Other work of his has appeared in *Philosophical Studies, Mind, Erkenntnis, European Journal for Philosophy of Religion*, and *Synthese*. He has also written on the philosophy of film in *More Matrix and Philosophy* (Open Court, 2005).

JOSEPH G. KICKASOLA is Professor of Film and Digital Media and the Director of the Baylor Communication in New York program, Baylor University. He has also served as Visiting Professor of Religion and Film at Princeton Theological Seminary and is the author of *The Films of Krzysztof Kieślowski: The Liminal Image* (Continuum, 2004). Other publications include essays in *Film Quarterly*, *The Routledge Companion to Philosophy and Film*, *The Quarterly Review of Film and Video*, *The Journal of Religion and Film*, and numerous academic anthologies.

REV. JOSEPH W. KOTERSKI, S.J., is Associate Professor of Philosophy at Fordham University, where he has taught since shortly after his priestly ordination in 1992. He serves as the editor-in-chief of *International Philosophical Quarterly*. He regularly teaches courses in natural law ethics and in medieval philosophy. Among his recent publications are many articles, the monograph *Introduction to Medieval Philosophy: Basic Concepts* (Wiley-Blackwell, 2009), and such co-edited volumes as *Medieval Education* (Fordham University Press, 2005), *The Two Wings of Catholic Thoughts: Essays on Fides et Ratio* (The Catholic University of America Press, 2003), and *Karl Jaspers on Philosophy of History and History of Philosophy* (Humanity Books, 2003).

FRANCESCA PARMEGGIANI is Associate Professor of Italian and Comparative Literature at Fordham University. Her research focuses on contemporary Italy, women's writing, and cinema. She is the author of *Lo spessore della letteratura* (Longo, 2007), a study of the fictional adaptations of scripture by Italian writers in the 1960s and 1970s, and the co-editor of *Forme, volti e linguaggi della violenza nella cultura italiana* (Edibom, 2012), an essay collection on the representation of violence in Italian culture. Her articles have appeared in *Annali d'Italianistica*, *Cahiers d'études italiennes*, *Italica*, *Italianistica*, and *Romance Languages*, among other venues.

GABRIELLA RIPA DI MEANA, a native of Rome, is a psychoanalyst. For more than three decades, she has been holding psychoanalytic seminars in several Italian cities and universities. Her book publications include *Figure della leggerezza* (Astrolabio, 1995; *Figures of Lightness*, Jessica Kingsley, 1998), *La morale dell'altro* (Liberal libri, 1998; http://www.lacan-con-freud.it, 2016), *Modernità dell'inconscio* (Astrolabio, 2001), *Frammenti per una teoria dell'inconscio* (Biblink, 2006), *Il sogno e l'errore* (Astrolabio, 2008), *Foollear* (Bulzoni, 2009), *Dialogo immaginario con Jacques Lacan* (Nottetempo, 2010), *Lacune* (Nottetempo, 2012), and *Onore al sintomo* (Astrolabio, 2015). Her articles have appeared in Italian and international journals.

PHILIP SICKER, Professor of English at Fordham University, specializes in late nineteenth- and twentieth-century British and European fiction. He is the author of a critical study of Henry James and numerous articles on such modernist writers as Eliot, Lawrence, Mann, Nabokov, and Joyce. He has recently published a series of essays exploring Joyce's relationship to cinema, and he is currently completing a monograph on visual representation in *Ulysses*. He is the co-editor of *Joyce Studies Annual*.

REGINA SMALL, a Fordham University graduate in English and philosophy, is currently executive editor at *RT Book Reviews*, a Brooklyn-based magazine dedicated to covering women's genre fiction. Her writing has appeared at online media outlets such as *The Awl* and *Full Stop*.

EVA M. STADLER was Associate Professor Emerita of English and Communication at Fordham University and published on literature and cinema in *Studies in Twentieth and Twenty-First Century Literature*, *Quarterly Review of Film & Video*, *Antemnae Review*, and *Francographies*, among other venues.

EMMA WILSON is Professor of French Literature and the Visual Arts at the University of Cambridge and a Fellow of Corpus Christi College. Her publications include *Sexuality and the Reading Encounter: Identity and Desire in Proust, Duras, Tournier and Cixous* (Oxford University Press, 1996), *French Cinema since 1950: Personal Histories* (Gerald Duckworth & Co. Ltd., 1999), *Memory and Survival: The French Cinema of Krzysztof Kieślowski* (Legenda, 2000), *Cinema's Missing Children* (Wallflower Press, 2003), *Alain Resnais* (Manchester University Press, 2009), *Atom Egoyan* (University of Illinois Press, 2009), and *Love, Mortality and the Moving Image* (Palgrave Macmillan, 2012).

INDEX

abandonment 106, 170–171, 174, 178–179, 188, 194–195, 219, 221, 225
absence 2, 9, 79, 111, 117–118, 158, 160–161, 165, 167, 177, 189, 191, 198, 207, 210, 224
absolution 190
actuality 189, 195
Adamek, Witold 12
adultery 2, 95, 106, 115, 158, 199–200, 214
affect 8, 30, 34, 64, 143, 172, 177, 186, 191, 193, 196
Agamben, Giorgio 141, 163
Akiva, Rabbi 61–64, 77
Alexander, Peter 29
Alighieri, Dante 133, 139
Amiel, Vincent 93, 178, 179, 180
amodal 32
animal 20, 37, 43, 56–57, 60, 76, 77, 126, 128–130, 171, 178
Anscombe, G. E. M. 20, 29
anti-Semitism 45
apparatus 147, 150–151
arbitrariness 9, 114, 116, 147
Aristotle 20, 29, 54, 153
Arnheim, Rudolf 35, 48
atheism 63, 77
Attell, Kevin 163
awizo 150, 155–157

Baka, Mirosław 24, 122, 192
Bakhtin, Mikhail 85, 89, 94
Baranowski, Henryk 54
Barciś, Artur 77, 81, 89, 135, 147, 171, 185, 212
Bardini, Aleksander 27, 81
Barełkowska, Maja 166
barrier 119, 150, 152–153, 155–156, 168, 178, 197, 201

Barthes, Roland 192, 202, 214
Benecchi, Valdo 121
Bentham, Jeremy 198
Berenson, Bernard 43
Bergson, Henri 11, 34, 217–226, 228, 229
Biedrzyńska, Adrianna 27, 109
Binoche, Juliette 183
Biró, Yvette 87, 93
Błaszczyk, Ewa 200
Bławut, Jacek 12
Bluh, Susannah 12, 47, 75, 120, 162, 179
body 8, 30–31, 33–34, 36, 41–47, 50, 71, 209, 211
Boltanski, Christian 182–183, 191–193, 196
bondage 53, 65, 71–72, 78, 98
Brand, Ulrika 13
Brereton, Cloudesley 229
Britton, Celia 214
Bruno, Giuliana 48
Buber, Martin 44, 50
Bugajski, Ryszard 145
bureaucracy 149, 151–154, 162

camera: as critic 53, 63–64, 82, 88, 90, 92, 141–142, 146–148, 151–152, 160, 169, 171–173, 176, 211; as voyeur 40, 82–83, 144, 147–149, 155, 175, 197–198, 200–202, 206, 208; as witness 41, 55, 58, 71, 84–86, 89–90, 104, 147–148, 151–152, 167–168, 175, 181, 185–186, 197–198, 200, 217
Campan, Véronique 13
Carr, Jay 11
Cartesian. *See* Descartes, René
causal(ity). *See* causation
causation 54–57, 131, 133
Cavendish, Phil 12, 47, 75, 120, 162, 179
chaos theory 42

childhood 39, 142, 167, 169, 171–172, 175, 178, 187–188, 192, 194–196, 224
Ciment, Michel 93, 178
"cinema of moral anxiety" 4, 146
Clement of Alexandria 43
Coates, Paul 13, 14, 49, 71, 73, 78, 79, 123, 139
comedy 217–219, 222–223, 225–226, 229
comic. *See* humor
Commandments, the 1–6, 8, 15–17, 19–20, 23, 31–32, 36–37, 39, 41–47, 50, 52, 54–55, 57, 60, 66, 69, 93, 95–97, 99, 106–107, 114–115, 120, 184, 199, 214, 216
communism 3, 49, 63, 77, 140, 145, 148–149, 151, 153–154, 198, 216
community 3, 7, 9–10, 76, 87, 122, 124–125, 127, 132–133, 135, 138, 167
compassion 9, 45, 66, 98, 102–103, 105–107, 210, 212
connectedness 2–3, 6, 9, 11, 26, 29, 80, 92, 99, 114–115, 127, 133, 143, 153, 162, 173, 185–186, 189, 191, 195, 197–198, 213, 217, 224, 226–228
Corliss, Richard 11
court 122, 140–141, 146–148, 184
courtroom. *See* court
covetousness 10, 97, 199–200, 202, 205, 209, 217, 220–221, 223, 227
Crespi, Alberto 5, 13
cut 109, 116, 118–119
cycle 1–3, 5–6, 12, 120, 134, 174, 223
Cytowic, Richard 47, 50

D'Amasio, Antonio 48
daughter(hood) 9, 27, 39, 108–113, 116–119, 166, 173–174, 178, 179
De Balzac, Honoré 81
De la Durantaye, Leland 141, 163
(de)legitimation 110, 112, 116
Deleuze, Gilles 34, 189, 196
DeMille, Cecile B. 3
Descartes, René 44, 48, 50
desire 3, 6, 9–10, 18, 20, 23, 25, 28, 42, 45, 68, 71, 97, 101, 108, 110–111, 113–118, 120, 135, 138, 140, 146, 148, 153–154, 156, 159–161, 165–167, 177, 192, 199–200, 202–211, 214, 217–218, 220–221, 228
Deuteronomy 69, 96, 199

dialogue 4–6, 8, 11, 37, 41, 80, 83, 88, 151–152, 155–159, 166, 176–177
(dis)connection. *See* connectedness
(dis)honor 9, 59, 97, 98–99, 110–116, 119–120, 214
(dis)possession 10, 26–27, 113, 149, 156–157, 160, 166, 174, 177, 199–200, 202–203, 206, 208–209, 219–220, 224, 227–228
disquiet(ing) 4, 6, 113, 118, 166, 171, 201, 207
division 29, 32, 44, 58, 60, 62, 74, 133, 152, 154, 167, 169, 193, 195, 210
documentary 1, 6, 9–10, 30, 81, 87, 140–144, 147, 150–151, 153, 194

ecstasy 50, 160
effect 5–8, 22, 29, 37, 41, 56, 88, 118, 130, 141–143, 145, 147, 151, 154, 188, 201, 217, 225–226, 228
elephant 6–7, 11, 14, 56
Eliot, George 163
Eliot, T. S. 45, 54
Ellington, James W. 29
Elokim. *See* God
embodiment 6, 10, 31, 33–34, 36, 40–41, 46–47, 49, 50, 70, 136, 148, 151, 153, 181, 208, 222
Emerson, Caryl 94
emotion 3–4, 6, 9–10, 15–16, 19–26, 30–31, 33, 34–46, 48, 51–52, 65, 68–69, 72, 81, 84, 87, 110, 148, 160–161, 164, 165–169, 171, 174–176, 179, 183, 185, 187–196, 199–206, 209–212, 221, 224, 226
enigma 99, 116–120, 170
envy 113, 205
Epstein, Joseph 75
Erens, Patricia 214
eros 110, 203
Estève, Michel 93
ethics 2–4, 6, 8, 9–11, 15–20, 22–23, 29, 43, 45, 52–53, 59–65, 67, 70–72, 74, 81, 87, 89, 91–92, 115–116, 122, 142, 184–189, 191, 196, 197, 199–202, 209, 216
exegesis 52–54, 61, 65, 69, 72, 115
existence 6, 19–20, 36, 42, 52, 55–57, 59, 62, 66–68, 71–72, 76, 91, 114, 123, 127–128, 132, 135, 145, 154, 172, 177, 199, 202–203, 205, 207, 217

Exodus 2, 23, 50, 53–58, 60–61, 63, 65, 67–69, 71–73, 77, 78, 96–98, 184, 199
experience 6, 8–9, 11, 25, 29, 31–39, 42–47, 48, 50, 54, 63, 65, 87, 92, 96, 118, 142–145, 165, 171–177, 179, 187–188, 191, 195, 198, 200–201, 207–208, 215
Ezra, Ibn 65, 78

fairytale 9, 171, 173
faith 4, 46, 53, 58–60, 66, 126, 214
family 3, 26, 34, 46, 71, 81, 83, 98–106, 108, 167, 173–174, 178, 185, 192–194, 198, 210, 219, 221, 226
fantasy 92, 104, 118, 133, 164, 189–190, 195, 209
father(hood) 9, 25, 27, 39–40, 53, 59, 67, 69–71, 73, 77, 78, 83, 98, 106, 108–119, 132, 170, 173, 221
fear 3, 30, 42, 85, 103, 105, 133–134, 138, 169, 173, 178, 185, 188–189, 205, 210, 213
feeling. *See* emotion
Findlay, J. N. 48
Flaubert, Gustave 179
Foucault, Michel 198, 214
fragmentation 167, 169
frailty 16, 26–28, 190
Freccero, Yvonne 214
Freedberg, David 43, 49
freedom 16, 18, 20, 22, 28, 71–73, 78, 96, 128–131, 134, 167, 172–174, 199
Freud, Sigmund 203, 209–210, 214
Frost, Robert 136, 139
Fulford, Robert 1, 11
Furdal, Małgorzata 12, 13, 120

Gajos, Janusz 27, 109
game 9, 22, 25, 110, 115–116, 173, 188
Garb, Tamar 196
Garbowski, Christopher 5, 13, 73, 79, 107, 137, 139
Garton Ash, Timothy 49
gaze 10, 81, 99, 107, 141, 147–148, 150, 153, 158, 166, 171, 173, 175–176, 193, 198–199, 202, 205, 209, 212–213
Genack, Menachem D. 75
Genesis 50, 55–56, 72, 74, 76
genocide 191–193
ghost(ly). *See* specter
Gibson, W. R. Boyce 48

Gilou, Thomas 194
Girard, René 205–206, 208, 214
glass 84, 86, 109, 150, 152–153, 155–156, 161, 195, 197–198, 201, 204
Globisz, Krzysztof 25, 122
God 4, 6, 8, 10, 37, 41, 43, 45–46, 50, 53–59, 61–73, 76, 77, 78, 84, 89, 91, 95–98, 101, 106, 134, 136–138, 199–200, 208, 211–213
Gorringe, T. J. 46, 50
greed 6, 9, 26, 112, 133, 223, 229
grief 73–74, 102, 175, 194–195
guilt 115, 148, 156, 194, 202, 208

Habberjam, Barbara 196
Halevi, Yehudah 65, 78
Haltof, Marek 14, 73, 76, 107, 150, 164, 229
Hamlet 25, 29
haptic 33–34, 36–40, 45–46, 48, 194
Harris, Mark Jonathan 196
Hasecke, Jan Ulrich 13
Heidegger, Martin 138, 139
hermeneutics 52, 61, 198, 209
Hirsch, Marianne 192–193, 196
Hirsch, Rabbi Samson Raphel 71–72, 79
history 10, 26, 33, 43, 58–59, 72, 96, 99, 137, 145, 183, 187, 202
Hitchcock, Alfred 211
Holquist, Michael 94
Horatio 25
hospitality 191
Howard, Richard 214
humor 11, 20, 38, 43, 56, 91, 208, 216–218, 221, 223–228
Husserl, Edmund 33, 35, 48

ideal 31–32, 36–37, 41, 45, 47, 68, 75, 186, 188, 205
idolatry 77, 134
Idziak, Sławomir 12, 29
imagination 33, 92, 166, 180, 190, 194
(im)material(ity). *See* matter
immediacy 30–31, 47, 183
(im)morality 19, 23, 28, 36, 43, 45–46, 58–60, 63–64, 106, 199, 218
Imparato, Emanuela 13
imperative 2, 7, 11, 142, 199
impulse 7, 36, 124–125, 140, 142, 203
incarnation 32, 47
incest 108, 110, 118, 120

index 36–37, 44–45, 183, 192–193
individualism 145–146
individuation 114
infantilization 188
injunction 67, 77, 109, 143, 199–200, 214, 217
(in)justice 26, 56, 59, 63–64, 66, 127, 155, 187, 199
Insdorf, Annette 13, 14, 76, 77, 81, 92, 93, 169, 178, 180, 183, 188, 191, 196, 205, 212, 214, 223, 229
intention 33, 35, 46, 108, 111, 154–155, 164, 190–191, 211
intentional(ity). *See* intention
interconnectedness. *See* connectedness
interdiction. *See* prohibition
interface 42, 45, 153, 176
interiority 10, 146, 154, 199
intimacy 10, 26, 37, 39–40, 144, 161, 173, 196, 204
intuition 31, 33, 35, 46, 179
inversion 219, 223–226
(in)visibility 7, 82, 143–144, 148, 151, 153, 183, 191, 198, 205, 207
irony 160, 179, 186, 220–222
(ir)responsibility 6, 27, 53, 58, 66, 70–72, 74, 78, 83, 87, 122, 167–168, 172, 180, 199, 217–218, 228
Irwin, Terence 29
Iwińska, Stefania 148

Janda, Krystyna 27, 81, 83
Jankowski, Jan 204
Jaroszewicz, Andrzej 12
Jaruzelski, Wojciech 163
jealousy 10, 110, 177, 202–203, 205–206, 210
Johnson, Mark 35, 48

Kant, Immanuel 15, 17, 29
Karabasz, Kazimierz 150
Kaufmann, Walter 50
Kickasola, Joseph G. 2, 12, 14, 24–25, 28, 29, 47, 48, 50, 70–71, 73–74, 76, 79, 93, 107, 178, 179, 199, 209, 212, 214, 221, 229
Kieślowski, Krzysztof: *Camera Buff* 142; *The Double Life of Veronique* 30, 229; *The Office* 150–152, 164; *The Three Colors Trilogy* 30, 80: *Blue* 183
Klarsfeld, Serge 193–194, 196
Klata, Wojciech 53, 183

Kłosiński, Edward 12
knowledge 20, 31, 33–36, 41–42, 45, 47, 89, 110–111, 113, 116, 128, 167, 178, 192–193, 198, 200–201, 205, 207, 209, 212–213, 224, 228
Komorowska, Maja 58
Kościałkowska, Maria 22, 87, 184
Kowalski, Władysław 178
Krall, Hanna 13, 146
Kubasiewicz-Houée, Ewa 163
Kubrick, Stanley 5, 13
Kuc, Dariusz 12
Kuspit, Donald 196

Lacan, Jacques 143, 159
lack 117–119, 157, 159, 203
Lagorio, Gina 13
Lathem, Edward Connery 139
laughter 11, 216–220, 225–228
law 2–3, 5, 39, 55–57, 60–62, 67, 69–70, 72, 74, 75, 76, 78, 95–96, 98, 120, 125, 127, 131–133, 140–141, 145, 148, 163, 206, 209, 213; Oedipal law 113; symbolic law 115
legality 141, 155, 157
Lemon, Lee T. 49
Lesch, Walter 13
Levinas, Emmanuel 190, 195, 196
Leviticus 69
Lichtenstein, Rabbi Aharon 75
limitation 28, 41, 53, 68–71, 73, 113, 142, 176
Linda, Bogusław 178
Lingis, Alphonso 196
Lis, Marek 13
Łomnicki, Tadeusz 27, 91
Loretan, Matthias 13
loss 16–17, 27–28, 83, 117, 143, 165, 167, 174–175, 183, 187–191, 193, 195–196, 202–203
Lotman, Yury M. 83, 93
love 2, 4, 6, 9–10, 12, 16, 18, 20, 22, 25, 28, 30, 39, 43, 66, 74, 78, 95, 101, 103, 106, 110, 113, 116, 120, 126, 132, 134, 136–137, 142, 144, 146, 148–149, 153, 156–162, 165–167, 169, 172–175, 177, 179, 187, 190–191, 195–196, 203–204, 206, 208, 210, 212–213, 219
Lubaszenko, Olaf 148
Lubelski, Tadeusz 13, 163
Łukaszewicz, Olgierd 27, 81
Lustiger, Arnold 75

Index

Machalica, Piotr 200
MacIntyre, Alasdair 20, 29, 126, 139
Madonna 53, 60, 63, 67, 72–73, 79
Mandelbaum, Allen 139
Manichaean 44–46
Marczewska, Teresa 27, 184
Marks, Laura U. 34, 38, 48
Marxism 59–60, 63
mastery 44–45, 50, 82, 117, 208
maternity. *See* mother(hood)
matter 6, 9, 20, 27–28, 39, 42–47, 50, 66, 82, 114, 127–130, 168–169, 200, 206, 209, 218, 221, 226
McCabe, Herbert 126, 133–134, 137, 139
memory 7, 10, 32–36, 38, 45, 60, 77, 97, 100, 106, 175, 183, 189, 194–195, 196
Meredith, M. Alex 32, 47
Merleau-Ponty, Maurice 32–33, 47
metaphysics 10, 18, 30, 37, 41–44, 55–56, 60, 73, 76, 114, 138, 154, 200, 203–204, 206, 208–209, 211
Metz, Christian 201, 214
Mill, John Stuart 29
mind/body dialectic. *See* body
mirror(ing) 6–7, 83, 152, 166–167, 169, 171, 173, 175, 201, 207, 222
(mis)judgment 22, 59, 76, 125, 141, 146, 179, 185, 191, 198–199, 220
mother(hood) 9, 25, 59, 63, 76, 77, 79, 109–120, 158, 166–167, 169–171, 174–175, 177, 179, 191, 194
Mroz, Matilda 11, 14, 188, 196
Mulvey, Laura 147, 164, 201, 203, 209, 214
The Muppets: Kermit 56; Miss Piggy 56
Murri, Serafino 177
mutual(ity) 8, 32, 57, 62, 117, 126, 156–158, 166, 174, 176, 203, 205, 210

Nachmanides. *See* Ramban
nature 18–19, 30, 36, 46, 54–58, 60, 63–65, 68, 76, 78, 114, 124, 126, 131, 134, 147, 160, 171, 173, 191–192, 199, 226
Niogret, Hubert 93, 178
(non)transparency 150, 152, 155, 168, 178, 201, 204, 210
(non)verbal 32, 34–35, 37–38, 87, 180
Nordlicht, Rabbi Milton 75
Noveck, Simon 75
Nussbaum, Martha C. 187, 195–196

obstruction. *See* barrier
Oedipal 110, 112, 113
Olbrychski, Daniel 100
omniscience 10, 199–201, 206, 208
opaqueness 155
Oppenheimer, Deborah 196
origin 52, 98, 104, 110–112, 114, 117–118, 120
original sin 125–127, 129–130, 133
Ortega y Gasset, José 160, 164
Otto, Rudolf 46, 50

pain 6–7, 30, 36, 39, 44, 72–73, 104, 172, 174–175, 180, 204, 210, 213
Pakulnis, Maria 100
Pakulski, Krzysztof 12
parent(hood) 69, 105, 112–113, 115, 161, 167, 173, 178, 190–191, 194–195, 214
particularity 145, 183
partition. *See* barrier
Peck, Agnès 93
Peeping Tom 147–148, 154, 177
perception 8, 31–35, 37, 44, 66, 69, 78, 187–189, 218
personhood 44, 153, 175
perversity 154, 201, 203
phantasm. *See* specter
phenomenology 36
Piesiewicz, Krzysztof 1, 3, 5, 12, 13, 44, 47, 52, 75, 114, 120, 147, 162, 172, 179
Piętek-Górecka, Jolanta 207
Piwowarczyk, Katarzyna 166
Plato 20, 43, 144–145
Poe, Edgar Allan 198
politics 3, 6, 11, 30, 49, 55, 57, 59, 70, 72, 125, 140–141, 145–146, 154, 163, 186, 198, 218
Polony, Anna 166
postsecular. *See* secular
Prédal, René 92, 93
Preisner, Zbigniew 159, 207
presence 34, 46, 50, 52, 66, 73, 111, 116–117, 120, 133, 136, 141, 143, 146, 150, 152, 167, 171, 182–183, 185, 189–191, 193–194, 198, 202, 205, 212–213, 224–225
Prinz, Jesse J. 48
privacy 7, 10, 59, 72, 86, 142, 144–146, 148–149, 154–155, 159, 190, 193, 197–198, 200, 206, 217, 228
prohibition 97, 116, 144

punishment 54–56, 66, 125, 131, 198–199

Rakeffet-Rothkof, Aaron 75
Ramban (acronym of Rabbi Moshe ben Nahman) 69, 72, 78
Rashi 54–55, 57, 59, 61–62, 65, 67, 72, 78
rationality. *See* reason
realism 82, 143, 145, 152
reality 7, 28, 30, 39, 41–44, 54, 82, 85, 117, 143–144, 154, 166, 169, 171–172, 179, 180, 186
reason 7, 33–34, 41, 48, 58, 62–64, 130, 172
reciprocal 44, 169, 173, 219, 225
redemption 46, 72, 90
Reis, Marion J. 49
religion 4, 6, 42, 51, 54, 63, 74, 77, 81, 87, 106, 125, 134–135, 146
reparation 188–190, 194
repetition 82, 156, 218–219, 221–226, 228
repression 116, 141
resonance 36, 77, 92, 145
response 6, 8, 10, 20, 22, 34–36, 38, 45, 51–53, 56, 58, 60–74, 77, 102, 132, 137, 150, 159, 171, 199, 208, 215, 218, 220, 226
revelation 67–70, 108–110, 113, 117, 137, 191, 204, 227
Ripa di Meana, Gabriella 13, 120, 174, 179
Robinson, Jenefer 34, 48
Rothwell, Fred 229

salvation 46, 138
Santilli, Paul C. 75, 77
Schjeldahl, Peter 49
Schreiber, B. David 75
science 35, 58, 64, 125
scripture 50, 51–52, 78
secular 42, 58–60, 62, 143
seduction 99, 106, 110–111, 113
Semin, Didier 183, 192, 196
semiosis 33
sensation 33, 35, 37–38, 48, 188, 196
senses 32, 34, 42–43, 45–46; sight 32, 34, 69, 143, 169–171, 174, 176, 210; taste 49, 50; touch 4, 10, 31–32, 34, 36–41, 43, 45–46, 48, 52, 155, 161, 169, 171, 181, 187–188, 190–191, 194–195, 201, 227
separation. *See* division
series 2–3, 5, 8, 11, 12, 13, 28, 29, 30–31, 36–37, 41, 46, 49, 52, 64, 85, 90, 92, 95–96, 122–123, 125, 136, 141, 147–148, 154–155, 164, 167, 178, 184, 199, 216–217, 219, 222–223, 225–228
Shakespeare, William 29
Shapiro, David 74, 75, 76, 78
Sheridan, Alan 214
Shklovsky, Viktor 41, 49
Shoah 10, 183–184, 188, 191–195
Sibony, Daniel 115, 121
signifier 116, 119–120, 152
Simonigh, Chiara 13
Smith, Colin 47
Smith, Murray 75
Sobchack, Vivian 33–34, 36, 42, 44–46, 48, 49
Sobociński, Piotr 12, 201
Sobolewski, Tadeusz 12, 14
sociability 10, 154, 219
solidarity 25; Solidarity movement 163
Soloveitchik, Rabbi Joseph B. 51, 52–53, 55–57, 59–72, 74, 75, 76, 77, 78
specter 112, 117, 154–155, 175, 182–183, 191, 195, 228
spirit(ual) 4, 8, 18–20, 25, 30, 43–47, 49, 57, 60, 64, 76, 77, 92, 98, 114, 198, 212
"state of exception" 140–142, 145, 155, 157–158, 162, 163
"state of war" 140, 163
Stehlik, Milos 49
Stein, Barry E. 32, 47
Stok, Danusia 12, 49, 78, 139, 142–143, 163, 177, 214, 229
stomach 30, 35, 44, 146, 155
Strachey, James 214
Stuhr, Jerzy 27, 142, 217
subject 9, 33, 65, 113–117, 142, 144, 154–155, 157–158, 193, 202, 205–206, 208
surveillance 10, 198–199, 201–202, 204–206, 208–210
survival 183, 186–187, 189, 208, 211–212
sympathy 42, 45, 102, 123, 169
synesthesia 31–47, 49, 50, 69

Sypher, Wylie 229
system 4, 10, 19, 42, 50, 59–60, 63–64, 68, 75, 77, 93, 108, 113, 116, 125–127, 130–133, 135, 137, 140–141, 149, 151, 154, 172, 187, 198, 219, 221
Szapołowska, Grażyna 148, 164
Szczepkowska, Joanna 100

Talbot, Toby 164
Talmud(ic) 54, 64, 78
temptation 44–45, 102, 106, 118, 144
tension 3, 9, 22, 31, 39–41, 63, 91, 117, 143, 173, 175, 198
Tesarz, Jan 24, 122
tetragrammaton 55, 65, 68, 76, 78
theology 5–6, 11, 31, 36–37, 41–44, 46, 50, 51, 58, 60, 65, 78, 115, 125, 135–136, 138
Tomlinson, Hugh 196
toothache 6–7, 11
Torah 54, 61, 67
tradition 2, 29, 50, 51–52, 71, 73–74, 76, 96, 98–99, 125, 129, 133, 138, 140, 214, 217
transcendence 4, 42, 53, 58, 60–61, 68, 74, 76, 162
transgression 143–144, 147–149, 199
translation 54, 56, 60, 64, 66, 68, 96–97, 99, 142–144, 157, 160
transmodal 32, 34, 36–37, 39, 41–42, 45
truth 20, 44, 82, 87, 98, 103–105, 109–113, 115, 117–119, 166, 178, 186, 189, 200, 205
Turigliatto, Roberto 12, 13, 120

uncertainty principle 142, 144
unconscious 9, 113, 116, 119, 202, 205

universal(ity) 5–6, 15, 17, 32, 36, 39, 49, 65, 67, 115, 126, 139, 145, 148, 150, 153–154
unrepresentable 74
unrest 4, 11, 82, 146, 148
utilitarianism 15, 17

Vaillancourt, Yves 13
vision 32, 34, 50, 58, 72, 96, 109, 118, 177, 181, 195, 199, 215
void 117–118, 155
voyeur(ism) 40, 147–148, 152, 154, 158, 162, 201–203, 205, 208–209, 228

Wajda, Andrzej 145
Waldstein, Michael 50
Wałęsa, Lech 163
Wartenberg, Thomas E. 75
Wenders, Wim 81
Wierzbicki, Krzysztof 14
Wilson, Emma 93, 196
witness(ing) 25, 28, 34, 53, 56, 58, 69, 81, 84–85, 89, 96, 115, 123, 136, 140–142, 144, 146–149, 171, 176, 184–186, 188–189, 194, 212, 214, 220, 224
Wojtyła, Karol (Pope John Paul II) 43–44, 49, 50, 67, 208
Woodward, Steven 14

Yishmael, Rabbi 61–62, 76

Zamachowski, Zbigniew 27, 217
Zapasiewicz, Zbigniew 25
Zdort, Wiesław 12
Zeki, Semir 48
Žižek, Slavoj 2–3, 12, 14, 85, 93, 143, 145, 153–154, 162, 163, 164, 186, 196, 209, 215

www.ingramcontent.com/pod-product-compliance
Lightning Source LLC
Chambersburg PA
CBHW030439300426
44112CB00009B/1067